WAGING PEACE
IN SUDAN

"People say there is peace,
but there are still two sides of the river."

To the Agar woman who said this and to all Sudanese
on the other side of the river:
May you once be able to cross over.

Any income generated from the sale of this book will go to UNICEF's education programme in Southern Sudan and other marginalized areas of the country. It is the young Sudanese that will live with the consequences of our collective decisions. Sudan's future is in our – and their – hands.

WAGING PEACE IN SUDAN

The Inside Story of the Negotiations That
Ended Africa's Longest Civil War

HILDE F. JOHNSON

sussex
ACADEMIC
PRESS

Brighton • Portland • Toronto

2 4 6 8 10 9 7 5 3

First published in 2011, reprinted with corrections 2011, in Great Britain by
SUSSEX ACADEMIC PRESS
PO Box 139
Eastbourne BN24 9BP

and in the United States of America by
SUSSEX ACADEMIC PRESS
920 NE 58th Ave   Suite 300
Portland, Oregon 97213–3786

and in Canada by
SUSSEX ACADEMIC PRESS (CANADA)
90 Arnold Avenue, Thornhill, Ontario L4J 1B5

British Library Cataloguing in Publication Data
A CIP catalogue record for this book is available from the British Library.

Library of Congress Cataloging-in-Publication Data
Johnson, Hilde F.
Waging peace in Sudan : the inside story of the negotiations that ended
   Africa's longest civil war / Hilde F. Johnson.
p. cm.
Includes bibliographical references and index.
ISBN 978-1-84519-453-6 (h/c : alk. paper)
ISBN 978-1-84519-458-1 (p/b : alk. paper)
   1. Sudan—History—Civil War, 1983–2005—Peace. I. Title.
DT157.672J64 2011
962.404'3—dc22

                                        2010041528

Typeset and designed by Sussex Academic Press, Brighton & Eastbourne.
Printed by TJ International, Padstow, Cornwall.
This book is printed on acid-free paper.

Contents

Foreword by Kofi Annan

It is a sad truth that waging peace is always much harder than waging war. Fortunately, it is infinitely more rewarding. The Comprehensive Peace Agreement (CPA) that ended Sudan's second civil war in 2005 took almost three years to mature and would never have been signed had it not been for the dedication of a small number of individuals from Sudan and the broader international community. Amongst the latter, Hilde F. Johnson, at the time Norway's Minister for International Development and now Deputy Executive Director of UNICEF, stands out for her tireless efforts to help bring the protagonists together.

This book is Hilde's inside account of how the two parties to Africa's longest running civil war, the Sudan People's Liberation Movement/Army (SPLM/A) and the ruling National Congress Party (NCP), negotiated an end to over 20 years of bloodshed. Profiting from her unique access to both the SPLM/A's late leader John Garang as well as Ali Osman Taha, Sudan's First Vice President, she takes us on a fascinating journey from the beginning of the talks in Nairobi to the signing of the 260-page agreement in Naivasha over 16 months later. This journey is as full of deep insight into the political dynamics of Northern and Southern Sudan as of compelling conclusions on the mechanics of mediation and the need for forceful engagement by the international community.

For almost two decades Sudan's North–South conflict was one of those complex, intractable problems that seemed beyond solution unless the larger policy environment were to change dramatically. As Hilde points out, the tragic events of September 11, 2001 resulted in just such a change and provided the impetus for the CPA. Without the sense of urgency that the images of crashing planes and falling towers created, it is highly unlikely that the governing elite in Khartoum would have agreed to the necessary compromises. But as helpful as the external dynamics were to the negotiations, their very indispensability also serves to highlight the scale of internal deadlock within Sudan. The sluggish and problem-fraught implementation of the CPA over the last five years has shown that this problem remains and may even grow as the critical referendum on the future of Southern Sudan gets under way. The need to wage peace in Sudan is thus as great as ever and this book is indispensable reading for anyone involved in, or wanting to know more about, how this is done.

KOFI A. ANNAN, *Secretary-General of the United Nations, 1997–2006*

List of Illustrations

Acknowledgements

This book is a result of my own journey. But it would not have been possible without the advice and assistance of many colleagues and friends in Sudan and elsewhere.

First, sincere thanks go to Senior Advisor Kjell Hødnebø whose knowledge and dedication to Sudan were essential from the beginning. Without him, I may not have started my engagement for peace in the country. It was Sudanese, however, who made me stay the course. The way they embraced my contribution to the peace process made me want to see it through to completion. I had the company of many people along the way, when working with colleagues on the American and British side and with the chief mediator, General Sumbeiywo and political leaders in the region, my thanks to them all, as well as my own Sudan team, whose support was critical for me. In this respect, late Halvor Aschjem played a major role. He was the first representative for Norway both to Khartoum and to the SPLM/A, and managed to build excellent relations to both, providing me with invaluable guidance. Norway's two Special Envoys during the period of negotiations, Vegard Ellefsen and Tom Vraalsen also deserve my most sincere thanks.

The book would not have become a reality without the encouragement of Ambassador Ellefsen, my invaluable "right hand" during the most critical part of the talks. He has provided very useful advice. Without the generosity and time of my Sudanese friends on both sides, this book would not have been completed. I offer my most heartfelt appreciation to members of the negotiating teams of the SPLM/A and the Government/NCP, who spent hours with me discussing details of the negotiations. Special thanks go to Vice President Ali Osman Taha for sharing so much of his time, his thoughts and his memories with me. In the absence of our late friend, Dr. John Garang de Mabior, his information was absolutely crucial. Special thanks go as well to Salva Kiir Mayardit, President of the Government of Southern Sudan (GoSS) and Chairman of the SPLM/A, who helped me complete the picture of important events.

This book is not the authoritative history of the CPA negotiations. It is my story, and needs to be read as such. In telling my story I have had invaluable assistance from Dr. Øystein Rolandsen. His excellent advice, additional research and source checking has been critical throughout. A steering group of Sudan researchers and experts have been an important sounding board: I am indebted to Dr. Gunnar Sørbø, Dr. Endre Stiansen and Dr. Kjell Hødnebø. In the last phase, Dr. Martin Daly provided editorial assistance.

Finally, this book has been written in affiliation with Chr. Michelsen Institute (CMI) in Norway. Without the support and financial assistance of CMI and access to the archives of the Royal Ministry of Foreign Affairs of Norway, this book would never have been possible. My thanks are owed to both institutions.

While I sincerely thank all of these friends, advisers and institutions for their unstinting advice and help, I must of course take full responsibility for any slips or errors that remain. When dealing with Sudan, they will always occur, as there will be different versions and interpretations of what unfolded. The views and assessments expressed in this book do not necessarily reflect those of the United Nations or UNICEF. The story of this journey is therefore fully and solely my own.

About the Author

Hilde Frafjord Johnson served as Minister for International Development of Norway for two periods, 1997–2000 and 2001–2005. She played a pivotal role in the Sudan peace process, leading up to the signing of the Comprehensive Peace Agreement (CPA) between the Government of Sudan and the Sudan People's Liberation Movement (SPLM/A) in January 2005.

In 1998 Hilde F. Johnson formed the so-called Utstein-group, comprising four development ministers from the UK, Germany, Netherlands and Norway, spearheading crucial changes in development policy and practice.

As Minister and in subsequent capacities, Johnson has been engaged in peace building efforts and post crisis transition in relation to several countries in Africa. Hilde F. Johnson is currently Deputy Executive Director of UNICEF.

Hilde Frafjord Johnson was born in Arusha, Tanzania. Before being elected to the Norwegian Parliament (1993–2001), she earned a post-graduate degree in Development Anthropology.

Note on Transliteration

In the transliteration of Arabic I have deferred to forms by which prominent public figures, places, tribes, and so forth have become generally known. Thus, for example, "Omar [not 'Umar] Hasan Ahmad al-Bashir" ("President Bashir"); and "Ali Osman Mohamed Taha" rather than "'Ali 'Uthman Muhammad Taha"; "El-Fasher" rather than "al-Fashir"; "*Sharia*" rather than "*shari'a*". Otherwise I have systematized spellings, as in "*janjawid*" rather than "janjaweed" or "janjawiid".

Map by Ivar Windheim (based on United Nations Map No. 3707 rev 10, April 2007).

Map 1   Sudan and Neighbouring Countries

Map by Ivar Windheim (based on United Nations Map No. 3707 rev 10, April 2007).

Darfur   Southern Sudan

Map 2 Southern Sudan and Darfur

Map by Ivar Windheim (based on United Nations Map No. 3707 rev 10, April 2007).

Abyei   Nuba Mountains   Southern Blue Nile

The borders of the three areas indicated in the map are only indicative and do not
reflect any opinion on demarcation of disputed borders.

Map 3   Abyei, Nuba Mountains and Southern Blue Nile

Introduction
Africa's Longest Civil War

The Call

It began, on 31 August 2003, with a telephone call. The First Vice President of Sudan, Ali Osman Mohamed Taha, was on the line. He was concerned because his government's negotiations with the Sudan People's Liberation Movement and Army (SPLM/A), the Southern Sudanese guerrilla movement, had come to a halt. We had met before in Rome when he was foreign minister, and now Taha, who was widely seen as the "strongman" in Khartoum and usually operated behind the scenes, told me that the time had come to negotiate at a higher level. He would be attending the funeral of the Kenyan vice president in Nairobi, and asked whether I was willing to approach Dr. John Garang, Chairman of the SPLM/A, about meeting him there. It should be kept confidential.

After a breakthrough in July 2002, the peace talks had indeed stalled. Since it had long been my view (and many others') that progress would depend on the personal involvement of the two sides' top political leaders, I told the First Vice President that I would see what I could do. As Norway's Minister of International Development I had formed a close relationship with Garang. But when we spoke, on September 1st, the Chairman was reluctant: in negotiations, the principals should come in towards the end, to wind things up, he said; the SLPM/A's talks with Khartoum were nowhere near that stage.

Dr. John (as he was universally known) was concerned not only for his own position but also about what such a meeting might imply about the Sudanese president, Omar Hasan Ahmad al-Bashir. Whether or not Ali Osman Taha was calling the shots in Khartoum (as many thought), the tensions between the two were well known. In any case, leading figures within the SPLM/A thought rather poorly of Taha at the time, and an intense debate ensued. A major conference of some 1,250 SPLA officers was under way at Rumbek in Southern Sudan; members of the Norwegian "Sudan team" urged various SPLM/A officers and officials to influence the Chairman, but the majority of them shared his reluctance. We also mobilized the Americans, and they too weighed in. More phone conversations followed, involving others on our side as well as me. Taha's arrival in Nairobi with a large delegation on September 2nd added to the pressure. Although, according to eyewitnesses, only three members of the SPLM/A leadership spoke in favour, the advice of Salva Kiir Mayardit, Garang's deputy, may have proved decisive.[1] Dr. John finally agreed to a meeting, and I conveyed the message to Ali Osman Taha.

What the SPLM/A Chairman had insisted would be only a short meeting began a process that lasted more than sixteen months and ended in the 2005 Comprehensive Peace Agreement (CPA) for Sudan. The talks were highly personal, largely conducted between the two leaders and their teams, often alone behind closed doors. This book tells the story of those negotiations. As a minister of the Norwegian government I had helped facilitate the peace talks, but it was the personal contact with both leaders that gave me unique access and provided the basis for my own engagement in the negotiations; over time the relations I developed with the Sudanese First Vice President matched those I already had with Dr. John. The telephone calls in September 2003 inaugurated a "hotline" connection between the two that lasted until the CPA was signed. I was included in their personal and direct discussions and deliberations, both through continuous calls and frequent visits to Nairobi and Naivasha, the Kenyan town where most of the talks took place.

This most intense period of the negotiations involved great personal commitment and tenacity and the transformation of a unique relationship – from enemies to partners in peace. This book is my version of events. The only people with more detailed knowledge were the two leaders themselves. Whether Ali Osman Taha will present his account remains to be seen; he is still a Vice President of Sudan. John Garang's version will never be told: after twenty-one years of war and twenty-one days as Sudan's new First Vice President, he was killed in a helicopter crash in the Imatong Mountains on 30 July 2005. It is with this in mind that I have undertaken this book, in order to ensure the preservation of an eyewitness's historical record and to share it in the context of the momentous events continuing to unfold in Sudan.

At the time when Taha and Garang agreed to meet, the conflict between North and South had been under way, with varying levels of intensity, since before Sudan's independence in 1956. The only period of relative peace and tranquility was between 1972 (when, under terms of the Addis Ababa Agreement, the South began a period of limited autonomy) and 1983, when Southern soldiers of the national army mutinied at Bor. Sent from Khartoum to negotiate with the mutineers, John Garang, then a colonel, instead defected and went with them to Ethiopia. He was the founding Chairman of the SPLM/A, and remained in that position for the rest of his life, as civil war laid waste the South. By the year 2000 the international community had almost given up on Sudan: only the Inter-Governmental Authority on Development (IGAD), comprising seven countries of the Horn of Africa, remained engaged. The conflict resembled the Israeli-Palestinian conflict in complexity and animosity; few thought that there was much chance of a negotiated settlement. Even fewer were making a serious effort.

Since 1998 I had been working to win international support for the IGAD-sponsored talks and, with others, to raise the negotiations to a more serious level. We had little to show for all our efforts. The talks had gone on for years, but largely without results. In 2001 the new American administration of President Bush demonstrated renewed interest, and this intensified after the events of September 11.

At the same time both the SPLM and the Sudanese government came to realize that a military victory was impossible. While both parties sent officials to the IGAD talks, neither had taken them seriously. The most significant breakthrough came with the Machakos Protocol of 20 July 2002, which provided for *Sharia* law in the North and self-determination for the South. By then a much stronger negotiating framework had been put in place, with important international support and a skilled Kenyan negotiator, General Lazarus Sumbeiywo. Still, the process suffered reverses when new fighting flared up in the field and new rounds of negotiation ended inconclusively. It was only then that Ali Osman Taha and John Garang decided to take the big leap, meeting face to face in Naivasha.

Decades of Conflict

Sudan is the biggest country in Africa and among the largest in the world, with a multitude of ethnic groups and languages. Southern Sudan alone is as large as Germany and France together; Darfur is bigger than Spain. But more than sheer size, Sudan's contrasts and complexity are what strike a visitor. Overlapping the deserts and savannas of the North and the lush greens of the South, blending Arab and African cultures and traditions, whether bare-breasted Dinka dancers or the veiled secluded women of the Rashaida, paying allegiance to Islam, Christianity and traditional beliefs, the country is a conglomerate of contrasts. In many ways Sudan epitomizes Africa. It captures you with its diversity, its contrasts, its colours, its smells.

Sudan is also where the White and Blue Niles meet, physically and symbolically at the capital, Khartoum. It was there – at his Palace by the Nile – that General Gordon famously met his fate in January 1885, when the army of the Mahdi won its most spectacular victory against the Sudan's foreign rulers, an event that shook the British and Ottoman empires. It was there, too, in September 1898, that the British and Egyptian flags were raised, signalling the defeat of Mahdism and the advent of a new imperial era, the Anglo-Egyptian Condominium. Sudan would not be independent again until 1956.

Disturbing events have more recently brought Sudan to the top of the global agenda. The atrocities of the *janjawid* in Darfur burst into the global consciousness in late 2003, and brought world leaders to the table at the UN Security Council in 2004. At that very time the top officials of Sudan, north and south, were in the middle of negotiating an end to a civil war that had gone on for twenty years and caused the deaths, directly or indirectly, of as many as two million people and displaced four million more.

Thus the travails of Darfur, though more widely publicized abroad, were not unknown to Southerners. Many had experienced similar atrocities at the hands of Arab militias, the *murahalin* from Kordofan, sometimes abetted by government soldiers or the bombing and strafing of government aircraft. Countless villages were destroyed, girls and women raped, whole families brutally killed, children abducted into forced labour or even sold as slaves. Indeed the conflict in the South was much more entrenched than that of Darfur, with deeper ethnic, political, and religious roots.

To understand the peace process, some knowledge of the history of Sudan and its many conflicts is essential. Even that history is a battleground, where Southern and Northern intellectuals struggle to institutionalize their own versions of the background and events. Accuracy and neutrality have been victims of this struggle. Northerners blame the policies of the Anglo-Egyptian Condominium, and later foreign interference in Sudanese affairs, for much of the violence since independence. Southern politicians and intellectuals spread the blame more widely, but with most of it reserved for the ruling elites in Khartoum.

Southerners date their animosity towards Northern Sudanese to the nineteenth century, when Northern merchants (and even officials of the Egyptian regime) were prominent among those involved in the massive slave trade that devastated the South. Far from easing conditions there, the Mahdiyya (1881–98) made them worse, for it raided and conquered but did not govern. Under the ensuing Anglo-Egyptian regime the South was "pacified" and neglected; while the North was in some ways prepared for independence, the South was not, and the reins of power passed to a tiny Arab Muslim elite in Khartoum. A conference in Juba in 1947 is often referred to as sealing the fate of the South; London's imperial interests in Egypt and elsewhere trumped local British officials' concerns for Southern Sudanese. A mutiny by Southern soldiers in August 1955, and the widespread killing of Northerners that ensued in the South, is regarded as the beginning of open hostilities.

During the period 1956–62, however, actual violence in the South was sporadic rather than intense. But Southern politicians signally failed to win the federal constitution that many thought was the only way to protect Southern rights. Foreign Christian missionaries who, during the colonial era, had by default played a leading role in educating Southerners, were widely seen by Northerners as a fifth column inimical to Sudanese nation-building. After 1958, when the national government was ousted by a military coup, efforts to get rid of these missionaries, propagate Islam, and spread the use of Arabic were intensified. This policy further alienated the small but important Southern educated elite, many of whom were Christians. By the early 1960s armed resistance had escalated to the level of civil war. After the overthrow of the military regime in Khartoum, a peace conference in 1965 disappointed Southerners' hopes of a Northern change of heart, and during the period 1966–69 the war was fought with increasing intensity. Leadership of the resistance movement, the Anya-Nya, was consolidated under the ex-army officer Joseph Lagu.

Another military junta, under Col. Jafar Mohamed Nimeiri, took power in

Khartoum in 1969 and, after months of continuing stalemate, hopes rose again for a negotiated settlement of what, however, was still widely called "the Southern Problem". Secret contacts eventually led to formal negotiations, at which a southern lawyer, Abel Alier, was Nimeiri's representative. A peace agreement was signed in Addis Ababa in March 1972. Abel and Joseph Lagu took important positions in the new structure of governance, but soon became bitter rivals. Important terms of the Agreement were never honoured, however, nor did Nimeiri resist the temptations, multiplied by feckless Southern politicians, to interfere in the affairs of the autonomous South. Promised economic development did not take place. Advantage was taken of rivalries within the South to "re-divide" the region into the old provincial units, the better to control them all from Khartoum. The balance was finally tipped when Nimeiri, as a sop to growing opposition from the Northern religious right, declared *Sharia* the law of the land – including in the South. In 1983 the SPLM/A was founded and a new civil war broke out.

The failure of the Addis Ababa Agreement was an important factor in the negotiation of the 2005 Comprehensive Peace Agreement for Sudan. The SPLM/A's "red lines" in the protracted negotiations were largely results of perceived shortcomings of the 1972 arrangements and the way in which those had – or had not – been implemented. The Addis Ababa Agreement was a rather short document with few specifics and no international involvement or guarantees. It granted self-government for the South, but not self-determination. The rebels were supposed to be integrated into the national army, but were not. Enshrinement of the Agreement in the Sudanese constitution had meant nothing. The SPLM/A leadership were thus determined not to repeat the mistakes of the previous generation.

The second civil war was different from the first in several respects. It was much more deadly, it had a much greater impact on the civilian population, and it engulfed a much larger territory. Neighbouring countries were more actively involved, in particular Uganda, Eritrea and Ethiopia, and a huge international aid effort was mounted to provide relief assistance to civilians. After Nimeiri was overthrown in 1985, hopes for peace were dashed again and politics-as-usual resumed. The civilian government that took office in 1986 relied on local militias to harass the SPLM/A and civilians alike. Backed into a corner by military failure in the South and a collapsing national economy, that government was on the verge of signing a preliminary peace deal with the SPLM/A when it was overthrown in 1989.

The army officers under the leadership of Omar Hasan Ahmad al-Bashir and the spiritual guidance of Hasan al-Turabi soon adopted a radical Islamist policy. Taking on its domestic opponents and associating with the world's most notorious regimes and shadowy non-state groups, the government soon acquired pariah status. From a struggle for pre-eminence with Turabi President Bashir eventually emerged the victor, but skirmishing between the two became a permanent feature of the regime. Nevertheless a more pragmatic attitude aimed at staying in power was discernible in the government's poli-

cies. Securing oil revenue was all-important; peace in the South now had virtually existential rationale.

During the 1990s the SPLM/A was itself riddled with factionalism and
infighting. A major split occurred early in the decade, ostensibly precipitated
by dissatisfaction with Garang's leadership but with undercurrents of the
ethnic and personal rivalries characteristic of the Southern Sudanese elite. As
typical was Khartoum's ability to exploit (even when it did not foment) such
splits, and this episode was no exception. The disastrous result was now a
North–South war around which orbited various warlords, whose gravita-
tional pull ebbed and flowed in relation to such variables as materiel, foreign
support, access to relief supplies, and shady deals with the national government and at times with Garang's dominant faction of the SPLM/A. The main
victims of this development were Southern civilians, millions of whom fled
to the North, across the international borders, or elsewhere. Those who
remained were often at the mercy of undependable relief agencies, which
themselves were toyed with by the various sides for political or military
advantage.

During the late 1990s Garang's SPLM/A regained the initiative in the war
and reunited the movement. Garang could therefore negotiate from a position
of strength, as the South's undisputed leader in control of important Southern
towns and large parts of the countryside. The SPLM/A and their northern
allies in the National Democratic Alliance had support from most of the neighbouring countries, including Egypt. This, combined with an intensified
international effort to kick-start a wide-ranging peace process, made 2001–2
a rare window of opportunity.

It need hardly be said that old myths, on both sides, have not only survived
but been reinforced by this disastrous history of large-scale violence. Sudanese
nationalism, largely an elite product of the colonial period, has long been pred-
icated on a sense of the gradual, but inevitable, spread of Arab-Islamic
civilization from the urban centres of the main Nile valley. In this view, the
pax britannica of the colonial period deliberately retarded that process in the
South and introduced a significantly different element of European Christian
missionaries. But even Europe had been unable to stop the advance of Arabic
and Islam, both of which were certainly more widespread at the end of the
colonial period than they had been at its outset. This only reinforced the
Northern Sudanese elite's sense of a nation-building, civilizing mission in the
South. Rather than harp on the unfortunate history of the nineteenth-century
slave trade, as do foreign enemies of the Arabs and Islam, they argued that
Sudanese should look to the future of their resource-rich country, and seek
"unity in diversity".

Viewing the same history, Southerners have tended to reach different
conclusions, most importantly about what that history portends for their and
the region's future. Islam had condoned the slave trade, only foreign intervention had ended it, and Arab tribesmen had lately resumed it; many
Southerners were now Christians: why should Islam (whether constitutionally

or even unofficially) be the established religion of the state? Southerners had their own languages, and English was as useful as Arabic as a second language: why should their education system not reflect this? When, since independence, the Northern political parties could have conciliated, developed, and nurtured the South, instead they had triumphantly imposed their own culture, neglected the region's undeveloped economy, kept the Southerners in abject poverty and were now exploiting its resources of oil and water. Successive Khartoum governments, both military and civilian, had treated the South like a colony. Northern parties' promises before independence had been broken; peace talks during the first civil war had always foundered over fundamental issues of citizenship, religion and governance; the 1972 Addis Ababa Agreement had not been worth the paper it was written on. The SPLM/A's manifesto, calling for a "New Sudan" with equal rights for all, had little apparent appeal for Northerners, whose parties, even when suppressed by the National Islamic Front of Bashir and Turabi, still hewed to their old, largely discredited policies. Self-determination was therefore the irreducible demand of Southerners. Most people familiar with Southern Sudan knew that when they were allowed to exercise that right, they would opt overwhelmingly for independence.

The Freedom Fighter and the Islamist

I had first encountered Dr. John Garang de Mabior in 1998. The guerrilla leader and freedom fighter – as he saw himself – was a revered but reclusive figure. For security reasons his whereabouts were kept secret, and one needed very good contacts with the SPLM/A in order to secure an appointment. Even then, the time might change, the location shift, and one could end up waiting for a very long time somewhere in the bush of Southern Sudan until he appeared.

Long before that first meeting I had sympathized with the victims of war in Southern Sudan, and had wanted to learn more about the reasons for the continuing conflict. Now, as a humanitarian crisis unfolded, I had two points of entry to the SPLM leader. Norwegian People's Aid (NPA) had since 1987 been working closely with the SPLM's humanitarian arm, the Sudan Relief and Rehabilitation Agency. Unlike most humanitarian organizations, NPA worked only in SPLM/A-controlled areas of Southern Sudan, outside the UNICEF-led "umbrella" of relief agencies called Operation Lifeline Sudan. NPA had a lot of credibility with Southerners, an extensive network of contacts, and staff willing to help me. Norwegian Church Aid, a non-governmental organization on whose executive board I had served, worked in both rebel and government-controlled areas, and thus also had access to the SPLM/A leadership.

In my capacity as Norway's Minister of Human Rights and International Development I was on the way to hunger-stricken areas in the southern region of Bahr al-Ghazal, and it made sense to combine that mission with a meeting with John Garang. We had received reports of hundreds of thousands of people suffering from hunger owing to a terrible drought, a situation exacerbated by the war. Because of the fighting, people had had to flee from their home areas and were unable to use their normal coping mechanisms during the period called "the hunger gap". I wanted to understand the situation better, and to galvanize international attention and support; there had been little media attention to the situation, and humanitarian agencies were short of funds to help. By the time I flew to Bahr al-Ghazal in early June 1998, almost half a million people were at risk.

As the plane landed, the ground was dark with thousands and thousands of Dinka, all of them waiting for food. They were stretching their necks towards the sky, their walking sticks in hand, wondering whether the assistance under way would be enough. We walked into the crowd. Aid workers were labouring non-stop to manage the supplies and organize the distribution. Sacks of maize were loaded on bony shoulders. In the feeding centres many hundreds of malnourished children were receiving treatment.

I sat down and talked with men and women, old and young, all worried about the fate of their children and grandchildren. One boy made a particularly strong impression, standing in line at a feeding centre, waiting for his ration. It was not his bony figure or bloated stomach that drew attention – those were the rule, not the exception. There was something about the way he stood there, determined and focused, with dignity and a sense of confidence, despite his suffering. He looked about five years old; I asked, and was told he was seven. Malnourished children are typically stunted. I was told he had been separated from his family and had arrived at the feeding centre in a desperate state, seriously malnourished and weak. Now, after rich, nutritious food, he was already much better. An attentive little boy, he noticed what was going on around him, and looked at these foreigners. Different from so many children I had met in similar situations, his face was not empty and remote, revealing fatigue and despair. He smiled at me, a big smile that reached his eyes and met mine. I was moved, and smiled back, wishing I could help.. The hundreds of thousands of hungry were personified in him, a boy with his own name, his own history, and – I hoped, as I stood there watching him – with a future. I still remember him.

It slowly dawned on me that such hunger crises would come again, year after year, until the war ended. We were providing life support now, but this was only a band-aid to help people survive. We had the choice of either pushing for peace or continuing to pour aid to starving Sudanese – basically just keeping them alive. The people I met in Bahr al-Ghazal opened my eyes to the real cost of the war. Could we accept such disaster over and over again, year in and year out? For me the answer was simple: I made a commitment to myself – this war had to end, and I would do what I could to help end it.

Dr. John[2]

From the famine areas I flew to the appointment our contacts had facilitated with the Chairman of the SPLM/A, Dr. John Garang. We had been told to wait for further notice about where to go, and when. The original plan had reportedly been to go to Nimule near the Ugandan border, but that area was subject to aerial bombardment by the Sudanese Air Force and was deemed unsafe for a meeting. We got a message to go instead to Chukudum, in Eastern Equatoria near the border with Kenya.

We flew in to Chukudum on June 8, landing on a grass field guarded by SPLA soldiers. They were armed with AK 47s, some on their shoulders, others leaning on them, one foot against the other leg, in the characteristic pose so typical of cattle herders with walking sticks. They had grown up covering long distances on foot, tending their cattle in the Dinka tradition. Now their occupation was different. They told me that the Chairman was waiting, and invited me to a civilian Land Rover. A pick-up full of soldiers drove ahead, leading the way through high elephant grass to a dusty track and a pot-holed road full of twists and turns. We soon approached the Chairman's compound. It was near the airstrip, and consisted of a square of simple houses with thatched roofs, of which the surprisingly modest main house would be our meeting place.

Garang came out to greet us, a tall, broadly-built and rather heavy man in his fifties. He was an impressive figure, not only physically, with an aura of natural authority, the kind of person, regardless of rank, who commands attention when entering a room. At later encounters I had with the Chairman, leading figures of the SPLM/A would often be with him. At this first meeting, however, only a few were present, among them Dr. Justin Yak, one of Garang's close advisers; Martin Okurok, responsible for information; Mario Muor Muor of the SPLM/A's relief organization; and, I believe, Kuol Majak. Garang apologized for the change of venue, explaining that air raids just a few days ago had made it impossible to meet at Nimule, which was far too dangerous for any foreign dignitary. He expressed concern about the situation in the Bahr al-Ghazal, and asked for our assessment. We told him that a humanitarian crisis was unfolding before our eyes; I was committed to help mobilize more international support for the emergency response. We also stressed the need for a humanitarian ceasefire to allow distribution of aid and the return of people to their communities. (Such a ceasefire was later brokered by UN agencies.) We then discussed the status of the IGAD-sponsored talks between the Sudanese government and the SPLM/A. For four years there had been little progress; it was time for change. I brought up the need for serious commitment on both sides, and a strengthening of the negotiation framework.

This was the first of many meetings I had with Dr. John over a period of more than seven years. He was often underestimated: this apparently crude guerrilla leader and freedom fighter was an intellectual with a PhD in agricultural economics from Iowa State University. He also had a very strong political mind, sharp on both theory and tactics, and he had a solid military background. I quickly discovered another feature of the feared Chairman of the SPLM/A – his sense of humour: I seldom left a meeting without roaring with laughter. Garang was particularly good at networking, regionally and internationally, and especially in the US – where he had lived during years of study, research, and, while an officer in the Sudanese army, training at Fort Benning. His long military career had begun when he joined the Anya-Nya guerrilla movement during the last years of the first civil war.

It was Abel Alier, twice president of the Southern regional government during the regime devised under the 1972 Addis Ababa Agreement, who had given Garang the opportunity to go to the US to study.[3] Garang had opposed the agreement, and Alier had him transferred from his home area of Bor to Rumbek. His network was just as good there, however, and Garang continued his political activities among Southerners in protest against the agreement. Alier decided to send him abroad, making sure that Garang got a scholarship to Iowa State and that his stay in the US was as long as possible, including military training. Garang finally came back, well educated and unreformed. He had stayed in touch with his network while abroad, and the time had come to make use of it.

When a rebellion was mounted among Southern Army officers in 1983, the so-called Bor Mutiny, Garang was ordered there to control the situation. Little did the authorities know that he had been engaged in planning the mutiny, but that it had started ahead of schedule. Instead of calming things down, Garang joined the rebels. Abel Alier was in Bor at the time, and Garang urged him to leave immediately, offering the Southern leader a safe escort out. But the latter chose to remain, and Dr. John and the other rebels headed northeast for the Ethiopian border. He would soon emerge as the leader of the rebellion, the nucleus of what would be the Sudan People's Liberation Movement and Army.

By the time I met Dr. John, he had led the SPLM/A for more than fifteen years. Who was the person behind the uniform? Very few knew Dr. John personally, and gaining his trust and confidence took a very long time. His inner circle of confidants was small: the Chairman of the SPLM/A had to be careful. During the 1990s several coup attempts had been mounted, two major splits had weakened the movement, and significant human-rights abuses had occurred. To trust people from the outside was no safer; Garang measured strangers carefully, and over time. Confidence came only slowly, usually after years. Once admitted to his inner circle, however, one could really count on him. He had stamina, and once he had set his mind on something he was not easily moved. But although he would not give way under pressure, he was susceptible to argument after careful analysis. As Ali Osman Taha said recently, "Dr. John had a deep command of the issues. He knew what he was talking about and possessed the art of dialogue and discussion, of argumentation. Dr. John was a leader, it was very clear. He had the qualities that leadership needs."[4]

As Chairman, Garang was reputed to command obedience. In his view, a liberation movement and army could not take decisions by consensus. The buck stopped with him. As one member of the leadership said: "He may have been authoritarian, but he had to [be]. His survival was dependent on not leaving anything to chance." While some members of the leadership would later complain about decisions taken without adequate consultation, and even about being kept in the dark, others disagreed. While some claimed he did not delegate enough, others said they were given the authority to do their jobs and were not subject to micro-management. If people did not perform in the way he expected, Dr. John would often take over and do the job himself. During the negotiations at Naivasha, he consulted regularly with his colleagues in the SPLM delegation, and ensured that they were informed. And when he set them a task, he did so with clarity about the main points but was flexible about the rest. Not everyone admired his leadership style. Disagreements with Salva Kiir, his deputy, led to conflict in November 2004 and the most serious leadership crisis in the movement in more than ten years.

Those close to Dr. John always spoke of him with the highest respect and warmth. In 2010 Salva Kiir himself told me movingly about their long friendship.[5] From a more personal perspective, his wife Rebecca recently said how different Dr. John had been from traditional Dinka men in the respect he showed her, treating her as an equal, unwavering in his support.[6] Together they had six children. Garang was proud of his background as a Dinka from Bor. The place meant a lot to him. He was not one to hide his rather simple upbringing, and was the first to praise the beauty of the traditions he grew up with. He explained some of them to me over the years, and these were occasions that I, as an anthropologist, truly enjoyed. Dr. John had fun springing a Dinka surprise on me, such as jumping over a slaughtered cow as the guest of honour in a village. But in one important way he broke with tradition. On a visit to Bor years later, I was told how the Dinkas had teased the Chairman repeatedly for having only one wife, and had urged him, as a proper chief, to take more. But he always responded that this was out of the question. While he regarded himself as a Christian, the faith was more important to his wife.

Although outside his inner circle Garang was very careful about who he engaged with and how, and what he said, he was a very social person, gregarious and charismatic, and fun to be with. He loved to tell stories, crack jokes, and talk late into the night or even morning. He was a master of crowds, mobilizing thousands with speeches that could go on for hours. He spoke in the popular idiom, with analogies and stories the people knew. People would roar with laughter, and cheer in anticipation and appreciation, "SPLM Oyeeee". Even during his first visit to the Nuba Mountains, at Kauda, Dr. John got everyone's attention with his knowledge of Nuba history and use of old myths, proverbs and traditions.[7] He was an entertainer of sorts.

But the entertainment was never frivolous. John Garang's vision was a united Sudan with justice and equality for all, where no one was treated as a second-class citizen. Since independence, there had been no meaningful sharing of power and resources with those regarded as Sudan's African peoples in the South, the West, the border regions and the East. Although he was often accused of being a secret separatist, Dr. John strongly believed in uniting and transforming the country into a "New Sudan".[8] Rather than focusing on the Southern cause only, Dr. John's demand was that all marginalized peoples be included and given a fair say in the governing of the country. Not only the Southerners had suffered from what he regarded as the elitist structure of successive Khartoum regimes. This vision would build on Sudan's multi-religious, multi-cultural and multi-ethnic society, respecting diversity rather than privileging an elite.

Garang outlined this vision in books, articles, and speeches. He would always draw two overlapping circles on a piece of paper, one for the South, the other for the rest of the country. The small overlap represented the area of administration to be shared with the national government: foreign affairs, finance, defence, Customs, and border control. This model obviously involved a great degree of autonomy for Southern Sudan. Dr. John called his model a confederation, and he enjoyed educating foreign observers and counterparts on the blessings of confederative arrangements. His New Sudan implied that Southerners would largely be running their own affairs, and that sufficient change at the centre would provide justice for all marginalized peoples.

At the same time, Southerners' right to self-determination gradually became a cornerstone in his thinking. The South should, through a referendum, decide whether to remain part of a united Sudan or to be independent. His thinking was therefore that the SPLM/A should negotiate an agreement that would secure the fundamental right of Southerners to self-determination, meanwhile making unity as attractive as possible. If their counterparts in the North implemented such an agreement to the letter, unity would be worth fighting for, and the CPA would be the basis on which a united Sudan would be governed. Building on Southerners' experience of "Too many agreements dishonoured", as Abel Alier's famous book is entitled, Dr. John knew this would be very difficult.[9] And if it proved impossible, then Southerners would opt for secession.

There was no contradiction in Dr. John's thinking with regard to a "New Sudan" based on "One country, two systems", and on self-determination for the South. In his view, the "New Sudan" was an incremental process; Garang had his feet in the South and reached the North with his hands.[10] Even if he was unable to get the perfect peace agreement, his strategy was to secure the South and acquire enough leverage in Khartoum to push transformation of the whole country from within.[11]

When I met Dr. John in Chukudum for the first time, he actually welcomed me to "New Sudan". This was what the SPLM/A called all areas they controlled. While to the rank and file this meant their own liberated areas, the Chairman and others in the leadership used the term to reflect his vision for the country as a whole. This would be the slogan on huge posters all over Khartoum when Garang arrived for his inauguration as First Vice President of Sudan seven years later; most of the posters showed him alongside Ali Osman Taha, who by then had vacated the position for him. Hardly anyone, let alone Dr. John himself, would have thought this possible.

A New Acquaintance: Ali Osman

On the surface John Garang de Mabior and Ali Osman Mohamed Taha seemed as different as night and day. Dr. John was charismatic and outgoing; Taha was cautious, even shy at times. His aura of quiet authority[12] derived from his role behind the scenes of government and the Islamist movement. If Garang sometimes came across as an entertainer, Taha seemed more like a judge (which indeed he had been). I first met him in Rome, in the autumn of 1997, when he, as Sudan's Foreign Minister, and I, as Norway's Minister of Human Rights and International Development, attended a meeting of IGAD and the IGAD Partners' Forum, its international support-group. This was my first meeting about Sudan. Even at this juncture Taha emphasized the need for direct negotiations with the SPLM/A Chairman himself. Ali Osman reminded me of that conversation several times over the next decade. Little did we know then that he would be the one negotiating with Garang, and that the two of us years later would be spending more time on the phone with each other than with our closest associates or even our families.

During my first trip to Sudan in 1998, seven months later, I went to Khartoum and met the new Foreign Minister, Mustafa Osman Ismail, and other high officials. Taha had by that time become First Vice President. A meeting was scheduled with Vice President Riak Machar, however, the former SPLA commander and recent foe of Dr. John Garang. It was a surreal experience to meet Machar at the time, the signing of the Khartoum Peace Agreement a year earlier having had no apparent impact on government policies nor on the status and influence of respective Southerners. Riak was operating from a small office separate from the Palace, and I still recall its atmosphere of isolation and paralysis. While Machar had a formal position with hardly any influence, another leader had significant powers but operated in the shadows. That was Hasan al-Turabi, the famous shadow leader of the one-time National Islamic Front and National Congress Party, about whose reputation for eccentricity I was well aware. We met at his house. He was considerably smaller than I had thought, a seemingly frail old man. As a young European woman I was not expecting much respect. Of course, I had my speaking points ready, on human rights, peace with the South, the importance of inclusive government, and so on. Turabi was probably fully aware of this, and spoke non-stop for more than forty minutes, never giving me a chance to say more than hello. Worse, I had trouble understanding him. His English was good, but the message was confused. I sat there wondering whether this famously

intelligent man was crazy, or was it just rambling to prevent me from getting
a word in. Dutiful minister that I was, I did not wish to leave before delivering
my message on behalf of my government.

When finally the time allotted for the meeting had nearly expired, I decided
to interrupt, as politely as I could, to make my three most important points.
Turabi's response was not at all satisfactory. I brought up another issue, which
he ignored before resuming his diatribe. As he showed no sign of letting up, I
looked at my delegation, and at my watch, and he got the point. We politely
thanked His Excellency for giving us so much of his time. Leaving the house,
however, we shook our heads in wonder at the prominence of such a man. He
was obviously very intelligent, and we knew of his ability to navigate in tricky
political waters. Were we missing something? When, a year after this bizarre
meeting, Turabi was forced out of the ruling party, I was not surprised. More
astonishing, however, is that to this day he remains a major figure in Sudanese
politics, whether under house arrest, in the shadows, or out in the open; whatever his nominal position, he is a force to reckon with.

I did not meet Ali Osman Mohamed Taha on this trip, nor President Bashir,
an omission I would make up for during numerous future visits to Khartoum.
I did not know at the time, but learned later, that relations between Taha and
Turabi had long been souring. To me, that was a positive sign. Ali Osman told
me recently that negotiating peace with the South would have been impossible
had Turabi still been in a position of power.[13] Indeed, when the IGAD summit
in 1997 reconfirmed its Declaration of Principles, including the right of self-
determination, a text that Taha, as Foreign Minister, had negotiated and
committed to, he became the target of Turabi's fury. Only after Turabi was
out of the picture would it be possible to make progress.

Taha was elected to the leadership of the national Islamist movement in
Sudan after the ousting of Turabi in 1999.[14] He was a devout, conservative
Muslim whose identity was strongly anchored in Sunni Islam. Since his university days, Taha had been active among the Islamists. After completing a law
degree he had started a private law practice, was appointed a judge, then
entered politics as a National Islamic Front MP in the 1980s. Taha was a
member of the inner circle of former Muslim Brothers behind the coup against
Sadiq al-Mahdi's government in 1989. Although the coup was led by Bashir
(who would assume the presidency), Hasan al-Turabi, Major General Zubair
Mohamed Salih, and Taha emerged as the leaders of the NIF and remained so
for years.

As the NIF took full control of the institutions of government, including
the Army, a policy of Islamization was pursued. *Sharia* law had been introduced in 1983 under President Nimeiri when Turabi was Attorney-General,
but the Revolutionary Council of the NIF went further. Ali Osman Taha, as
Minister of Social Development, coordinated the activities of a number of
ministries (education, health, social affairs) in pursuit of the Islamist agenda's
so-called "civilization policy". He became Minister of Foreign Affairs in 1995,
and was widely regarded as the leading figure in the government. Taha's inter-

ests were not circumscribed by his nominal position; he pulled strings behind the scenes, often quietly and invisibly.

In 1998 Taha succeeded Zubair Mohamed Salih, who was killed in a plane crash, as First Vice President of Sudan. Salih had been a crucial link between the Sudanese army and the National Islamic Front. Several sources claim that Taha was never really close to the Army in the same way.[15] On the other hand he had been affiliated with the irregular Popular Defence Forces. Until the NIF split in the 1990s these militia were linked to Hasan al-Turabi and Ali Osman Taha.

In person, Ali Osman Taha was rather withdrawn. Resolute when he wanted something done, he was a careful political planner and had stamina and staying power. He did not take risks, was never in a rush, and preferred to pull the strings and lead from behind. Reflective by nature, Ali Osman was a very good listener; he gave people space, preferred to hear people out, assessing them, before saying anything himself. An intellectual, he saw issues from different angles, discerning what was possible and what was not; he was a pragmatist. Taha rarely raised his voice, and hardly ever showed a temper.[16] He was patient and consensus-oriented, consulting widely before taking decisions. Interestingly, Taha led the youth wings of the party and the Islamist movement, and even today retains a strong position among the young.

As with Garang, so with Taha confidence and trust had to be built slowly over time. Eventually I got to know him well through our numerous phone calls and tête-à-têtes. Taha did not hesitate to convey appreciation when due or indeed disappointment and dismay when concerned about the direction of the negotiations; I appreciated his openness. But he remained a rather private person. Although he would tell me about important family events (he was married, with five children) and, as we got to know each other, he would call during breaks just to chat and update me, our discussions were still usually related to the negotiations.

Like John Garang, Ali Osman had a vision for Sudan. In his case that was the Islamic agenda of the National Islamic Front. Taha shared this vision with passion. Given the diversity of Sudan, the obvious question he and others confronted was whether the Islamist vision was sustainable for the country as a whole, or whether a more pragmatic approach was necessary. Whatever the extent to which this question was ever seriously debated within the leadership of the government or National Congress Party, it is clear that Taha in the peace talks took a conscious decision to move into uncharted waters, knowing that some compromise on this fundamental issue would be necessary. This was a courageous decision. The First Vice President could read the political and external landscape well, and he knew what was at stake. But at critical junctures in the negotiations there were limits to the compromises he was ready to make, and especially over issues related to religion. Taha would make one understand when one was pushing a red line. There was an intensity there that one would not forget. Deep down, he held his political ideology very dear.

In a way that is characteristic of Sudanese politics, Taha and Garang had

much in common. In the early 1970s, student strikes at Khartoum University
had got out of control. The government conducted an investigation, and
expelled those students deemed to be the main culprits. When the rioting
continued, another investigation found that the organizer of the whole movement was a recent graduate, Ali Osman Taha, who, as president of the Student
Union in the late '60s,[17] had played the same role. At that time, another
student, Col Ding had also joined in.[18] John Garang and Col had been similarly active when students at the Rumbek secondary school struck to protest
the policies of the Nimeiri regime. Ali Osman confirmed this common trait:

> Dr John and I talked about this. We had both had a rebellious past,
> rebelling against the institutions of the time, one way or the other. We
> also discussed whether it was right or wrong to take up arms, from an
> ethical point of view, and in relation to the events in our country in the
> seventies. We realized that both of us had resorted to arms in support of
> our political claims. So – there was a lot of similarities between us.[19]

Although the differences between the two leaders were obvious, Garang
and Taha were well matched in many ways. Both were intellectuals, thinkers,
and strategists. Their academic background aside, it was the sharpness of their
minds and the tactical talent they mustered that truly impressed me. Taha was
admittedly surprised by the true nature of his counterpart: Garang was not at
all what he had expected.[20]

What must have been a new experience for both of them was that they
ended up becoming pragmatists, showing an unexpected ability for compromise. A lot of events preceded their meeting, though; among the most
important ones the developments in the US and within Sudan.

Political Gymnastics

Individual leaders' choices on whether to engage seriously in a peace process
always involve their respective domestic political agendas. In the Sudanese
case the political scene in Khartoum was an important factor. Political
alliances can be very fluid. They can shift overnight, in an instant. But in
Khartoum, as elsewhere, there are some constants, and these have not changed
for the last twenty years. Power has remained within a core group of the
former National Islamic Front, virtually all originating from the Danaqla,
Ja'aliyin and Shayqiya tribes, and all pursuing an Islamic agenda, but with
nuances of emphasis and depth of engagement. Maintenance of this position
has depended on control of the party, the Army, the security apparatus, the
Islamist movement, and oil revenue. Internal power struggles have stemmed
less from ideological differences than from competing personal ambitions.

There have usually been several factions or tendencies within the ruling
National Congress Party, principally a military-intelligence emphasis and an

Islamist emphasis. President Bashir leads the former, Ali Osman Taha (informally) the latter. Bashir, with his military background, was long seen as a mere figurehead for the coup of 1989, and was never regarded as either the regime's strongman or as much of an ideologue. Perennially underestimated, he has managed very well: a much shrewder political player than anyone had expected, he has exhibited an impressive ability to survive and indeed to strengthen his position. Control of the Army and strong relations with the intelligence services have been critical for Bashir's ability to remain in power. Ali Osman Taha's long leadership of the Islamist movement, always ripe with potential for mobilizing the Muslim community for political purposes, has made his relations with Bashir highly competitive and subject to almost continuous speculation.

In addition, there are several smaller factions within the ruling elite and the party that wax and wane depending on shifts and turns in political alliances and personal relations. There are constant changes. In early 2001, for example, Taha seemed to be in a very strong position. In June, the focus in Khartoum turned to a Joint Libyan–Egyptian Initiative for peace in Sudan, which had begun in 1999 as an Egyptian project, seemingly in competition with the IGAD process.[21] Its "Recommendations for Reconciliation in Sudan", submitted on June 26, upset the political equilibrium, not least by calling for the establishment of an "Interim Government". Taha and Bashir took differing positions, and both rallied supporters.[22] The President met senior military officers, and even visited Juba for this purpose, suggesting to some observers that he was "fearful for the security of his position."[23] The tensions subsided at this juncture, but would flare up from time to time. It is likely that they have been one factor in Taha's decision to move on the peace front.

John Garang's challenge in 2001 was to ensure that the major Southern constituencies were behind him, and that the Northern Sudanese opposition parties in exile, the National Democratic Alliance (NDA), were in alignment. The SPLM/A was under pressure from a major conference of Southern leaders in Kenya, organized by the New Sudan Council of Churches. This was the latest development in a "People-to-People" peace process that the SPLM/A had previously been able to control, and that indeed served partly as a mechanism for reuniting Southern communities under SPLM/A leadership. Now, however, the conference had gone ahead independently. Meanwhile the southern Bishops had been increasingly vocal in calling for peace, indirectly criticizing the SPLM/A. In other words, while Dr. John had consolidated his power, and was confident in his position, civil society in the South was growing impatient.

At the same time, several of the Northern opposition parties were tempted by the Libyan–Egyptian demarche that, if pursued, would undermine the SPLM/A's irreducible demand for self-determination. This threat was averted this time around at the NDA meeting, but it illustrates the SPLM/A Chairman's constant need to manoeuvre, lest he be seen as blocking even mischievous peace initiatives. The best way forward for the movement was within the IGAD Framework, whose Declaration of Principles included a clear commitment to self-determination. These were the considerations when other events unfolded that would have a decisive impact on the course of events.

September 11 and the Sudanese Government

None of these political developments was decisive. External factors were. The administration of the new American president, George W. Bush, had resolved to tackle the Sudan question. In doing so it took up where the previous administration had left off, a combination of engagement and punitive measures, with somewhat more emphasis on the latter under the former Administration and much stronger engagement at the highest level under the tenure of George W. Bush. This engagement also reflected important interests in the Republican Party, both in the country at large (the Christian Right) and in Congress, where Representative Frank Wolf and Senator Sam Brownback were among those keeping the Sudan issue alive. On the Democratic side of the aisle the Congressional Black Caucus remained very active too, and on this issue had the ear of the President. Quiet dialogue between the two governments had taken place, and some exchange of intelligence. In May 2001 the Assistant Secretary of State for Africa, Walter Kansteiner, and his Deputy Charlie Snyder met secretly in Nairobi with representatives of the Sudanese government. The US wanted real co-operation, first against terrorism, and then to assess how improved relations could be used to help resolve the war in the South.[24] On 6 September a former senator, John Danforth, was appointed Special Envoy for Sudan.[25]

But it was the events of September 11 that made the biggest difference. Now the Sudanese government not only had more reason to placate the Americans, it also had something to offer.[26] As one prominent Southerner put it, while watching the planes crashing into the Twin Towers: "If we are ever going to reach a solution, we will find it in the smoke that is coming out of this building."[27] Indeed, the event created a sense of urgency within the Sudanese government; it was of the utmost importance for Sudan to avoid being seen as supporting or sponsoring terrorism. A first indication of change came when the UN Security Council met on September 17th; the US had been prepared to lift the UN sanctions on Sudan, but in the wake of September 11 a decision was postponed.

In Washington a significant lobby argued that Sudan remained a state sponsor of terrorism. It was common knowledge that in the mid-1990s Osama bin Laden had been based in Sudan, had established training camps there for his supporters and recruits, and had developed international networks and commercial activities in aid of his broader agenda. Also the alleged involvement of the NIF in the assassination attempt on the Egyptian President Hosni Mubarak in 1995 had been a case in point, a plot whose main proponent was assumed to be Nafie Ali Nafie, a hardliner with a prominent role in the state security apparatus. At that time the National Islamic Front (now National Congress Party) had also been pursuing its own Islamist programme most aggressively. Osama bin Laden had left the country in 1996, but there were reasons to believe that contact was retained with the leadership, at least until the NIF split in 1999. It was assumed that all connections with al-Qa'ida had ended by then, but commercial links may have continued.

Having previously harboured Bin Laden, the Sudanese regime was keen to reassure the international community. Dr. Ghazi Salahuddin was shocked by 9/11. He put it this way:

> The United States looked like a wounded lion. It was very difficult for us to predict what kind of action they would take tomorrow. We had to wait and see, and watch what we said and what we did – and engage. Especially in light of the fact that they at least ostensibly were trying to help us with one of the most protracted conflicts in Sudan. So, there was no other option. We said we would engage and we told them we would judge their role according to the results and to whether they would be fair.[28]

The government of Sudan had to wait while the US reassessed; and the UN sanctions were finally lifted on September 28. The US government abstained during the vote in the Security Council, saying – in the words of Ambassador Cunningham:

> Sudan has recently apprehended extremists within that country whose activities may have contributed to international terrorism. Sudan is also engaged in serious discussions with my Government about ways to combat terrorism. We welcome those steps and expect this cooperation to continue. We expect the Government of Sudan to demonstrate a full commitment to the fight against international terrorism by taking every step to expel terrorists and deny them safe haven.[29]

Senior members of the NCP admitted privately that they had feared an American attack. Sudan condemned the terrorist outrage in the US, and chose a strategy of constructive engagement. The American approach further impressed on Khartoum the need for seriousness in the peace negotiations. This created a new dynamic and energy.[30] The government used a two-pronged strategy, bilateral cooperation with the US on anti-terrorism, and strong diplomatic outreach in general. Very active cooperation began with the CIA on counter-terrorism. Highly placed sources in the American administration told me privately that – finally – the Sudanese understood that the US was not bluffing. The US would be supplied with information on suspected terrorists, and between thirty and forty al-Qa'ida suspects were arrested and sent to Egypt.

Before September 11, the Sudanese had given the Americans only information they already knew, or just a bit more. Now they started to get really interesting material, what my source called "'A'-stuff" or even "'A plus'". Given the desperate need for intelligence about al-Qa'ida operations, the US had to rely on contacts in the region to obtain information. [31] This in turn implied that President Bush's insistence on not talking to terrorists, having no contacts with them, and not relating to countries with a history of supporting such networks, had some exceptions. At least, this was the case with Sudan.

Sudan's foreign minister at the time, Mustafa Osman Ismail, worked actively to engage with the Americans. Mustafa himself was a very smooth operator, not a hardliner, and effective as the regime's international face. He had spent many years in the UK, and seemed culturally attuned to Americans and Europeans. He started a diplomatic offensive, systematically building the credibility of the government by reaching out to a number of countries in Europe and the region, as well as to the US. The objective was obvious: removal of Sudan from the US list of state sponsors of terrorism, and the lifting of US and UN sanctions. But American interest was not limited to the anti-terror front: they had a clear strategy of engagement related to the peace negotiations as well, and wanted to revive the IGAD talks.

Danforth, Kansteiner and Snyder came to Khartoum, and openly told Ali Osman Taha, Dr. Ghazi and others that the US would not be even-handed in the peace process, implying that they would lean to the side of the Southerners.[32] Dr. Ghazi says: "I was dumbfounded [by the US attitude]. Someone was barging into your house telling you that he is there to help you, but that he would not be fair to you – and you accept it. It was a strange situation."[33] What the Americans evidently saw as candour the NCP considered arrogant. This was not what they were accustomed to in dealings with, for example, European countries.

The value of the intelligence information the Sudanese gave the Americans is unknown. *Africa Confidential* reported that Khartoum's strategy was to overwhelm its US interlocutors with "grey propaganda", mixing the factual with the false and obscuring the extent to which government officials had been complicit in past terrorist activities.[34] Turning over people suspected of links to al-Qa'ida might pose a serious dilemma to the NIF inner circle. In any case, that the information provided from December 2001 was of much higher quality indicates that a shift had taken place, with decisions taken at the highest level of government. The same seemed to be the case on the US side, as Sudan was not targeted for US reprisals. Cooperation in the areas of intelligence and anti-terrorism would continue to be an important feature of their bilateral relations.

In the end, it seems quite clear that a need to satisfy the US became a factor in Khartoum's negotiations with the SPLM/A. Progress there would serve to insulate the country from sanctions and other international repercussions of past terrorist associations. There is no doubt therefore that September 11th was a factor in bringing the Sudanese government to the negotiating table in a serious way. Another factor was the economy. The government faced problems in servicing its debt. It had already borrowed fully against its oil reserves, even as oil prices were dropping and future production estimates had declined. By 2001 the external debt had reached $22 billion.[35] The war was allegedly costing as much as $3 million a day.

Regional developments also militated against continuing the war. Bilateral relations with neighbouring countries improved. Ethiopia signed an oil agreement with Sudan, and Kenya was considering one. Relations with Uganda were also improving; after supporting each other's internal insurgencies in the 1990s, and severing diplomatic relations for a while, the two countries made substantial progress. President Yoweri Museveni paid an official visit before attending the IGAD summit in Khartoum in January 2002. He brought with him a draft agreement on cross-border operations against the notorious Lord's Resistance Army. Discussions continued afterwards, and in March, Uganda and Sudan signed a military protocol. An anti-LRA liaison team, which would include both Ugandan and Sudanese military, was established in the South, and had immediate success. On 20 March 2002, the two countries issued a joint statement to a session of the UN Security Council, underlining both parties' commitment to "further foster and maintain security across their common border".[36]

Political developments within the National Congress Party and the Sudanese government also pointed toward a negotiated end to the war. As several prominent officials later told me, Sudan had "two governments" during the nineties:[37] the cabinet in office constituted the formal government, while powerful players behind the scenes, such as Hasan al-Turabi, were the "shadow government" actually taking a lot of the decisions. After 1998, with Turabi cut loose and a more coherent NCP, it was possible to take a united position on negotiations. According to leading members of the government's team, negotiations with the SPLM/A could not have happened without this consolidation.[38] Those negotiations would moreover allow the NCP to secure the system, ensure stability, and remain in power, an important motivation for talks.[39] Making peace with the South in order to expand a national power base had been the strategy of President Nimeiri in negotiating the Addis Ababa Agreement of 1972. Would the NCP, the government, and Ali Osman Taha secure their positions now through a similar partnership with the South?[40]

September 11 and the SPLM/A

The leaders of the SPLM/A believed that the September 11 attacks would precipitate a harder American line against the Khartoum government. In this they were disappointed, as we have seen. But the SPLM/A was stronger and better positioned than in the early '90s, and might therefore now negotiate from a position of strength. With new signals from the Americans, and a similar message coming from other key players internationally, it was clear that there would be a push for a serious peace effort. It was in the interest of the Movement to keep any talks firmly anchored within IGAD, whose Sudan effort was chaired by the Kenyan President, Daniel Arap Moi, who was close to the Southerners and de facto protector of Garang in Nairobi. Progress on the IGAD track would also deflect the Joint Libyan–Egyptian initiative. Garang started to work systematically towards this end.

In the early 1990s President Obasanjo of Nigeria had tried to mediate. For various reasons the so-called Abuja I and II talks had failed. Now he tried again. From the early autumn of 2001 Obasanjo worked on a plan to unite the Southern political forces. His strategy involved a reconciliation process in two stages. The first stage was directed towards achieving political consensus through a Southern Political Forces meeting in Abuja. The second stage would involve a national conference of all political forces in the country. The SPLM/A, fearing a loss of control, tried to find ways to postpone the conference. For its part the Sudanese government had no interest in promoting a united Southern front. When a decision was made to merge the two stages into one, and a pan-Sudanese conference was called for early November 2001, time was too short for preparations. Khartoum asked for a postponement, the meeting never took place, and Obasanjo's effort was abandoned. He tried again, a year later, to facilitate a meeting between Garang and Taha. That attempt was also unsuccessful, this time owing to the SPLM/A Chairman's resistance.

While Garang was in Abuja for consultations, however, a meeting was arranged with Bona Malwal, a veteran Southern leader and recent foe of Dr. John. They had fallen out in 2000 over a project to buy the freedom of enslaved Southerners. Bona Malwal, once a secessionist, had also faulted Garang for inadequate defence of self-determination, while he himself was often seen as "feeding" Southern divisions. Garang had not been informed of this meeting, but could not avoid it. The two parties agreed to pursue reconciliation through a committee of elders in London, and to withdraw from public accusations. This lopsided agreement soon failed.

But the SPLM/A was serious about its own unification process. Negotiations took place, and a series of agreements were signed. In this way a more unified opposition came about, and the SPLM/A's hand vis-à-vis the Khartoum government was strengthened. Among the most important agreements was an understanding with the Sudan People's Democratic Front (SPDF), chaired by Riak Machar. Signed in January 2002, this ended a long and very damaging split and returned leading Nuer political figures and military commanders to the SPLM/A. This was particularly significant because of the role the SPDF played in the oil-producing areas, where now the SPLA could hit strategically important targets. Further agreements followed with other disaffected commanders. The SPLM–SPDF agreement was widely seen as strengthening the call for Southern self-determination.[41] It was also clear that Riak Machar would not soon recommend his own experience under the Khartoum Peace Agreement of April 1997, when he had signed a separate peace and been widely ridiculed for getting little in return.

The SPLM/A also approached the Northern opposition, negotiating political agreements with both the Umma Party of former Prime Minister Sadiq al-Mahdi, and Turabi's Popular National Congress. More important in military terms was the strategic partnership developed with the Sudan Alliance Forces (SAF), the most significant armed opposition group in the Muslim north. The merger of the SPLA and SAF, under Garang's command, also emphasized the "New Sudan" agenda. The SAF agreement was signed immediately before Garang set out on an international tour, during which he visited both the US and the UK in March 2002. Just as the Sudanese government wanted an exclusive partnership with the SPLM/A, the latter wanted to strengthen its own hand by winning over other internal opponents of the regime and making friends in foreign capitals.

The international community's involvement in pushing for serious peace talks played a significant role in the SPLM/A's calculations. Prominent among these were the US and Norway, also joined, as we will see, by the UK, the so-called Troika. Garang tried to anchor their support. In the US he met the Secretary of State, General Powell, the Special Envoy, John "Jack" Danforth, and other officials. In connection with these meetings, he stated publicly that he now saw a "window of opportunity" to end the Sudan conflict.[42] Subsequent meetings in London with the Foreign Secretary Jack Straw, the Secretary of State for Development Clare Short, and Alan Goulty, who by then had become the UK's Special Representative to Sudan, were also successful. After these meetings, Goulty was quoted as saying he was "upbeat on Sudanese peace prospects."[43] Garang also had several meetings with members of the Sudanese diaspora during these foreign visits, including long-time critics of his leadership. The Movement emerged stronger and more confident from these initiatives. As Dr. John said at the time, the SPLM/A needed to "bring Khartoum to the brink of peace."

Strength in one's own home base usually makes a negotiating party more willing to compromise. This was the case in Sudan, as both parties had gone through a process of either consolidation or reunification that resolved internal tensions. This ensured that both were more coherent and confident in their positions, and hence more ready to deal with a negotiation process of this magnitude. Importantly, neither side felt military weak or "on the defensive". Developments in the late 1990s had laid the foundation for a serious effort to make peace in Sudan. But the most decisive factor was September 11.

CHAPTER ONE

The Troika

The Organisation of African Unity and a regional body of the Horn of Africa countries, IGAD,[1] had tasked Kenya to mediate peace talks between the Sudanese government and the SPLM/A. Since then there had been little progress. The negotiating structure was very weak, and neither side treated the infrequent meetings seriously. The only achievement during this period was a framework agreement for the talks, the Declaration of Principles, which was negotiated in 1994 and finally agreed upon in 1997. This would be the basis for all later negotiations; it committed both sides to uphold the right of self-determination for the Southern population through a referendum on their future status. An IGAD Partners' Forum grew out of a "Friends of Sudan" group founded by Norway and the Netherlands in the mid-1990s, chaired by the Dutch Minister of Development Cooperation, Jan Pronk. One of its most important contributions was strong and continuous support of IGAD and the Declaration of Principles. I took over from Pronk in 1998.

Egypt, with its strategic interest in the Nile waters, feared any exercise of self-determination that might lead to partition of Sudan. Attempts were made to create an alternative to the Declaration of Principles as the basis for negotiations. The so-called Joint Libyan–Egyptian Initiative was one such attempt, seemingly intended to undermine IGAD's efforts. Its "Nine Points" included many of IGAD's principles, but notably omitting self-determination. The Initiative was intended to include the SPLM/A, the National Democratic Alliance, and others in a Sudanese national peace conference in Cairo.

The conference was initially scheduled for mid-September 2001. The Sudanese government, with nothing to lose, agreed to attend. The SPLM, however, saw the Egyptians and Libyans as potential spoilers, and John Garang agreed to take part only in order to keep the sponsors happy. But the SPLM/A Leadership Council declined to endorse his participation, lest it imply willingness to compromise on the principle of self-determination. The conference never took place. The Initiative would be revived, however, when Libya and Egypt found it opportune to try to sidetrack IGAD efforts. For its part the US had very early impressed upon the Egyptians its support for the IGAD Principles, a stance Jack Danforth reiterated to President Mubarak. According to US officials,[2] the Egyptians seemed to accept this, and the Americans would later brief them after every visit to the region. In spring 2002, however, the Egyptians were piqued by an offer of observer status at the first Machakos round, and stayed away, a decision I am sure they later regretted.

Egypt's machinations did not go down well with the Kenyan government, or with IGAD and its member countries' heads of state. Egypt continued to press for inclusion in the international support structure for the negotiations, known as the Sudan Committee of the IGAD Partners' Forum. As Co-Chair of this coordinating group I had to deal not only with Egypt's agenda but also with those of the other member countries of the Forum. By the late 1990s it had become clear that the Forum was too unwieldy to play an active and supportive role. Together with the Italian Deputy Foreign Minister, and a "Core Group" of Americans,[3] British, Dutch and Canadians we tried to revive the peace talks. Joint missions to Sudan were conducted and international Partners' Forum meetings convened, including one in Oslo in March 1999 with twenty countries present, but to no avail. As I left office in March 2000, after several negotiating rounds, little had been achieved. It was out of this acknowledgement that the idea of establishing a "Troika" was born.

By the time I was back in office in October 2001, it was clear that the "Troika" – as the partnership that Norway forged with Britain and the US to revive the Sudan peace talks came to be called – had great potential for moving the process forward. As early as October 2000, when the Partners' Forum met in London, Alan Goulty, then Director of Middle East and North Africa in the Foreign Office, John Prendergast from the US State Department, and Hans Jacob Frydenlund from the Africa division of Norway's Ministry of Foreign Affairs began to consider informal coordination. By the summer of 2001, after the transition to the new US administration had largely been completed, it was evident that the Bush team was interested in a more formal relationship. Cooperation intensified with a meeting at the officials' level in London on October 24th, where Goulty and Frydenlund were now joined by the Americans Robert Oakley and Charlie Snyder.

With a new American administration in place, I had to start building relations. Walter Kansteiner, the new Assistant Secretary of State for Africa, was my new counterpart, and John Danforth was President Bush's Special Envoy on Sudan. Kansteiner and I soon met in Washington, and there were a number of consultations at the officials' level. We began to coordinate contacts with the Sudanese government and SPLM/A. After September 11, the US had greater strategic interest in Sudan, not least from an anti-terror perspective. In the Congress there was continuing interest too, fortified by the Black Caucus and, on the Republican side, by Evangelical Christians. Bush became personally involved, and became the first US president to engage directly with the Chairman of the SPLM/A.[4] The reason for British membership of the Troika was obvious: as the former colonial power the UK had taken a strong interest in the country. At the political level there had been less British engagement in ending the conflict, but this was changing, not least among development officials.

The Troika

Upon my return to office one of the first people I got in touch with in the UK was Clare Short, the Secretary of State for International Development, by then an old friend. We had worked together on a number of issues relating to development and Africa since my first term as Minister in 1997. In 1998 Eveline Herfkens became Dutch development minister, and Heidemarie Wieczorek Zeul (known as "Rote Heidi") got the development portfolio in the new German cabinet. I saw the possibility of a progressive team of female ministers making a difference in international development, and invited them all to Utstein Monastry, an island in my constituency off the coast of Stavanger, for a couple of days. Our strategy was to pursue reform in development policies and practice on the basis of a global partnership with mutual accountability – "we do our bit, you do yours" – a line of thought later anchored and codified as Millennium Goal 8 in the Monterrey Consensus. This meeting began a close working relationship and friendship among the four of us. The so-called "Utstein Group" would make a big difference in international development during the next four or five years, both in the OECD context and in relation to the Bretton Woods institutions.

This alliance also became important in relation to Sudan. As part of a division of labour in our group, I took on more of the Sudan portfolio, and Eveline Herfkens instructed her officials in the Netherlands Ministry of Foreign Affairs to take their cues from Norway. This tended to give our positions more weight. The friendship, partnership and trust between Clare Short and me were critical for the negotiations. While I was more engaged on a day-to-day basis, I knew I could call on Clare at any time for support. She proved to be a real team player, and was fully behind what was later agreed as our common approach to achieving a peaceful resolution to the Sudan conflict. Her position on self-determination would be particularly important. When I first discussed Sudan with her in London in 1998, after my initial trip to the country, Clare asked in jest whether I had become a supporter of the SPLM. No: favouring a just solution for Southerners and other marginalized peoples, within an agreed negotiating framework, was something else; I also underlined the importance of good relations with Khartoum. But the thrust and parry gave me reason to reflect on what it takes to maintain impartiality in a conflict while holding strong views on certain issues. For me the latter related to overarching principles and values, regardless of the circumstances and positions of either party.

During my eighteen months out of office, I had kept in touch with key players on Sudan and I knew that little progress had been made. Clare and Eveline were still ministers. We were immediately back in official touch and decided to continue our work on a broad development agenda. The Norwegian Sudan team agreed that it was the right time to start moving on the peace process. September 11 had also given impetus to such an effort. The

Sudanese government knew that cooperating against terrorism and making peace with the South could improve relations with the US. This provided an important incentive to negotiate seriously, as we shall see.

The rationale for the Troika was the need for a small and cohesive team of countries with their own strengths in relation to both parties in Sudan. As the former colonial power, Britain was important. The Foreign Office had extensive knowledge of Sudan and a lot of contacts among important people in Khartoum. Norway had close relations with the Southerners; Norwegian NGOs such as Norwegian People's Aid that had been working in the South for decades, and Norwegian Church Aid, which had worked on both sides throughout the conflict. Our involvement would give Southerners confidence in the role of the Troika and in the peace process. I built a team that consisted of people with long experience of – and longstanding contacts in – the country, including notably Halvor Aschjem, who was well known and respected throughout the region. The role of the United States was even more vital. We knew that no peace effort on Sudan would have any chance of succeeding without the Americans' close involvement. The US had the broadest and most powerful set of carrots and sticks at their disposal, and as a Troika we decided to make full use of a range of these. We would do our utmost to revitalize the peace process and make a peace agreement a reality.

Danforth: Testing the Water

The American Special Envoy for Sudan, the former senator Jack Danforth, was an Episcopal priest and seasoned politician firmly placed at the centre of the Republican Party. He was also a pragmatist, and wanted to see results. Danforth was on a short-term mission, partly for personal reasons. He had little African experience and limited knowledge of Sudan, but decided to move quickly. During his first visit in early November 2001, and without much international consultation, he presented Khartoum with a set of tests designed to gauge its level of commitment.[5] Some were of particular interest to American constituencies; others were designed as models for comprehensive arrangements as negotiations proceeded. The Nuba Mountains Ceasefire, for example, was intended to show the parties that if cessation of hostilities was possible in one area, it could be achieved generally. Monitoring arrangements were another example.

The four tests involved (i) humanitarian access to SPLA-held areas of the Nuba Mountains, and a ceasefire there; (ii) allowing humanitarian delivery and immunization programmes, including through days and zones of tranquillity; (iii) cessation of aerial bombardment of civilian targets; and (iv) a commission to investigate cases of enslavement, and the release of people so held. The SPLA-controlled Nuba Mountains had been largely inaccessible to outsiders, and Danforth's securing permission to visit was a major breakthrough. But on November 11th, just before the first UN flights were due there, government forces shelled the airstrip, with the apparent intention of delaying or preventing the visit of the Special Envoy. But Danforth was undeterred.

Danforth's demarche took the British and Norwegians by surprise. We were worried that a focus on humanitarian issues might divert attention from – and thereby delay revitalization of – the peace negotiations proper. Not all the American "tests" seemed necessary or immediately pertinent to the collective effort. In the end, however, several proved useful in the later talks.

Although obviously pleased with US engagement, the Sudanese government, for its part, was also apprehensive about Danforth's approach. Lest they be seen as foot-dragging, however, they accepted the four tests; the mission was a success, although aerial bombardment of civilians would continue. The SPLM/A responded positively to the tests relevant to them. En route from Sudan in December, Danforth visited London and Oslo to consult Troika colleagues and explain the rationale behind the tests. He promised that the US would monitor performance on the ground, and that he would pay regular visits to keep up the pressure. In Oslo Danforth met the Swiss Sudan Envoy, Ambassador Joseph Bucher, and they discussed the possibility of inviting the parties to Burgenstock for talks on the Nuba Mountains. Danforth would return to Sudan in January, when both Clare Short and I intended to visit; we agreed to try to link up there. Appreciative of Danforth's engagement, we emphasized the need for a collective effort to revitalize the negotiating process.

By early January 2002, progress had been registered in three of the four areas: humanitarian access in the Nuba Mountains, a temporary ceasefire, and arrangements for cessation of hostilities (or "areas of tranquillity") for immunization. Similarly, agreement was reached for a commission to investigate abductions and enslavement. At the same time, however, the Sudanese government began its dry-season offensive on several fronts. These included the Nuba Mountains, where ground attacks and arrests were carried out, Western Upper Nile, the Bahr al-Ghazal and Southern Blue Nile. Plans for these attacks were likely the government's reason for declining to halt aerial bombardments. As so often before, it seemed that they too had tests – of how far they could go, and of the extent of the Americans' commitment.

The US strategy indeed remains the subject of debate. It "tested" the parties' willingness to implement humanitarian and human rights standards, but not their political will or readiness for peace. Since the tests did not necessarily reflect the variables driving both sides' calculations, failure to comply could be misinterpreted as a lack of political will. But there is no doubt that the tests galvanized US attention to Sudan and engagement in the negotiating process.

Danforth's most controversial views involved the SPLM/A position on self-determination. His repeated statement that independence was not a realistic outcome, a conclusion reflected in his report to President Bush a few months later, implied that the SPLM/A demand for a referendum was seen as only a bargaining chip to be traded for concessions in other areas. The SPLM/A and other Southerners found these statements offensive; they would never abandon the principle of self-determination. This was a "red line" for them, and it would remain so throughout the negotiating period.

Danforth eventually developed a strong knowledge of and affection for Sudan. Over time he quietly adjusted his positions and refrained from public statements prejudicial to the outcome of the talks. In the end he proved quite effective, working closely within the Troika and playing an important role at some critical junctures in the negotiations. Danforth was also instrumental at a later stage. As US Ambassador to the UN he refocused attention on the Sudan peace agreement and, when chairing the Security Council, he organized its session on Sudan in Nairobi in November 2004, when a firm timeline for completion of the negotiations was set. This was critical in forcing the parties to agree on the last Protocol on Implementation by the deadline of 31 December 2004. But although the role of the US, with its political clout and carrots and sticks, was essential for the success of the Troika, the Americans were less effective when operating alone, without the cooperation and advice of other countries. Combining the assets of all three countries proved to be the best approach.

The Troika and the Summit

Jack Danforth, Clare Short and I all visited Sudan in January 2002. This was my first opportunity, since returning to office, to meet the key players on both sides. The IGAD Summit in Khartoum on the 8th–9th marked the culmination of all Sudan's diplomatic efforts to escape from isolation. It was a great success, in terms of both the level of participation of regional heads of state and in the outcome of the meeting itself.

The summit requested President Moi to find a way to accommodate the Libyan–Egyptian Initiative within the IGAD process. A key issue in this regard was whether to modify the statements of principle on which both initiatives were based. Just as the SPLM/A would oppose any change that weakened the IGAD Declaration of Principles' paragraph on self-determination, Khartoum might prefer re-wording that achieved precisely that. In the end, the Egyptian and Kenyan leaders made no serious attempt to merge the two initiatives, a default that sustained the IGAD track's pre-eminence. As co-chair of the IGAD Partner's Forum I was quite satisfied with this outcome. In my address to the Summit, I called on the Sudanese parties to use the "window of opportunity" now available to them to negotiate peace, and to do so seriously and urgently. I committed our full support to their efforts.

The host of the IGAD Summit was President Bashir, then widely considered a figurehead. Contrary to what many think, not least in light of the indictments by the International Criminal Court, Bashir is neither the hardest of the hardliners nor among those most strenuously pursuing an Islamist agenda. Having risen through the ranks of the Army, he is first and foremost a military man and not adept at small talk or diplomatic niceties. (This would later become evident to the world during the Darfur crisis.) At the same time, having survived many ups and downs as president since 1989, Bashir was clearly abler at political manoeuvring than first impressions implied. Discussing sensitive issues with him was never easy. On the Norwegian side we had major concerns, but I knew instinctively that confrontation would backfire; I conveyed our views in such a way that Bashir, although not always happy, remained respectful in dialogue. Nor was *amour propre* a problem: even though meeting him and his deputy, Ali Osman Taha, during one visit breached protocol, for example, I repeatedly had access to them both when they were in town.

Before the summit, a sensitive issue had been outsiders' support for and presence at the negotiations. While the Kenyans were somewhat apprehensive, both sides had discreetly communicated to us that such external support was needed. And although formally the Partners' Forum would provide the assistance, the Troika would be the most critical players. The IGAD initiative was weighed down by historical baggage. One SPLM/A official was blunt: "IGAD can't do it alone."[6] Sudanese government officials echoed that view. Formal recognition would be the best way of anchoring our role. The IGAD Summit's final communiqué therefore welcomed international support, thus accepting the Partners' Forum's role as observers in the negotiations. That text was the formal basis for the Troika's negotiating effort. A lot of expectation was in the air.

Clare Short in "Rebel" Territory

Clare Short had just returned from the South, and her first meetings with John Garang, when we met in Khartoum. We discussed the situation, the outcomes of our respective meetings, and what could be done to kick-start the peace process. Clare had already commissioned a Defence Security review of the Sudanese conflict, which basically concluded that it could go on indefinitely. But she still thought it possible to achieve a "package deal": the government, with international engagement and debt relief, would agree to peace; the South, after an interim period, would exercise self-determination in a referendum.[7] Well known for impatience and straight talking, she thus cut to the core of the issues; putting both President Bashir and the SPLM/A Chairman on the spot, she wanted to know what they would settle for, and tabled the "package" as a way forward. She was pleased with the outcome of her discussions.

Clare Short had no notion then of the effort John Garang had made just to meet her. Alan Goulty had originally tried to ensure that the meeting with the SPLM/A would be at a lower level.[8] But Col Ding, a leading figure of the Movement in the UK, realized the significance of what would be the first meeting ever between the Chairman of the SPLM/A and a Minister of Her

Majesty's Government and insisted. Garang, constrained by tight schedules, duly asked a trusted intermediary to hire a plane for him. For security reasons he never flew in Southern Sudan, and was now willing to make an exception. He ordered everything to be kept secret. When someone else, whom Garang did not trust, came to inform him that the arrangements had been made, the Chairman, detecting a plot, feigned ignorance. Remonstrating with the aide who had breached confidentiality Garang lifted a finger to represent one person, himself, then lifted two fingers and said: "What is the difference between 2 people and 11? I am not using the aircraft. I will drive."⁹

Garang then rescheduled a meeting that had been planned in Nairobi to mark the merger of Riak Machar's organization and the SPLM/A, and drove for some sixty hours, arriving during the night to meet Clare Short, who flew into Rumbek a few hours after he got there. Clare was joined by Alan Goulty and the aptly named Ambassador Richard Makepeace from Khartoum. The meetings were lengthy, and Clare was impressed with the SPLM/A Chairman's intellectual capacity and commitment. More pleasing still was his enthusiasm for the package they discussed. She invited Garang to visit London, which in itself would be another breakthrough in the Movement's relations with the UK government.

Short's discussions with Ali Osman Taha and other government officials had been equally encouraging. In her view, which I fully shared, the government's keenness to end its isolation gave us a real chance to move forward. Clare now became a passionate ally in the peace process, influencing the thinking of the prime minister, Tony Blair, and driving key changes in the UK's Sudan policy. She was quite clear that a referendum of the Southern Sudanese was the key, and that this had to include the option of secession. I too was very pleased with the outcome of the summit and the discussions in Khartoum, and set off for Rumbek myself to see Dr. John and the SPLM/A leadership.

A flurry of Troika activity now took place. From Sudan I went directly to London for talks with the British and Americans on January 14th. Walter Kansteiner, the American Assistant Secretary of State for Africa, Alan Goulty, and I had detailed discussions on Danforth's four tests, and we went over so-called "non-papers" drafted from our end on issues related to revitalizing the negotiations. On February 4th we met again in Washington. Talks at the officials' level ensued only ten days later in Oslo. By this time Troika cooperation was well established, with close coordination of the capitals, UN missions, and embassies in the relevant countries. At this stage, however, no public reference was yet made to our activities, lest these give rise to tensions with the member countries of IGAD and the Partners' Forum.

Meanwhile Clare Short had consulted closely with the Foreign Office and 10 Downing Street. Clare and I also continued our consultations with the Americans. These efforts culminated on February 7th during Tony Blair's visit to Nigeria. In an address to the Nigerian parliament the British prime minister said that

Sudan had been mired in conflict for all but ten years since independence in 1956. We and others continue to provide extensive humanitarian aid, but that is no substitute for a lasting peace. I believe there is now a chance for peace. I want to announce today that I intend to appoint a Special Envoy to work with others in the search for peace. Britain will show the necessary political commitment and tangible support. In June I will call upon the G8 to redouble its efforts to bring peace to these two conflicts.[10]

Alan Goulty's appointment as Special Representative came soon after.

The Nuba Mountains and the First Signs of Peace

The people of the Nuba Mountains have a modern history similar to that of Southern Sudan. During the second half of the 19th century, slave raiding in the area was intense. When the British arrived they resorted to large-scale military operations including aerial bombardment to subdue the local population. The area was put under a separate administration for a time, and attempts were made to close it off to Northern influence. The region remained a backwater, undeveloped, on the borderlands of North and South but belonging neatly to neither.

Since independence, disputes over land and resources had led to increasing alienation of the local population. In the long-running disputes between the Nuba and the neighbouring Baggara Arab nomads the Khartoum government favoured the latter. During the early phase of the second civil war Khartoum began to arm the Misiriya Baggara against incursions by the SPLA, tilting the local balance of power further against the Nuba. When representatives of the SPLA appeared in the Nuba villages in 1985, they easily found recruits. The government responded with violence, either directly or through the Misiriya militia. By the late 1980s the war in Southern Kordofan had gained its own momentum.

Situated far from international borders, the Nuba Mountains remained sealed off during long periods of the war. Burning crops and villages, and denying trade and access to humanitarian aid were part of Khartoum's counter-insurgency strategy. The aim was seemingly to starve people out of the mountains and drive them into "peace villages", where they could be controlled. Massive abuses took place in these camps, where people died from mistreatment, malnutrition, and disease. (Some have cited this as part of a policy of forceful assimilation of the Nuba into mainstream Northern Sudanese culture – the so-called "civilization project".) A little outside aid was provided in government-controlled areas through local and international NGOs, but this was inadequate. Khartoum managed to stymie international aid efforts for SPLM/A-controlled areas, even during the worst famine in 1991–92. Operation Lifeline Sudan managed to provide assistance later, but the first UN humanitarian assessment mission to SPLM/A-controlled parts of the Nuba Mountains took place only in 1999. At the time of the renewed peace effort, resistance in the border areas was mounting and becoming quite significant.

Following Jack Danforth's "test", the Americans asked the Swiss to help negotiate a cessation-of-hostilities agreement. (This was done without Troika consultation, again taking the British and Norwegians by surprise.) Talks took place in Switzerland over a period of three weeks, and concluded in a signing ceremony on 19 January 2002. This marked the first time the Americans had engaged in negotiations between the Sudanese parties, and that they did so in a way that both sides saw as even-handed strengthened the possibility of further US engagement. The Swiss role was appreciated, and they were keen to do more. But enthusiasm for expanding the Troika was limited: where would it end? Besides making the group more unwieldy, expansion risked the confidentiality of the talks and of the level of our engagement. The UN was to be represented from time to time; the AU had the right to observers, as had the IGAD countries; as co-chair of the Partners' Forum, Italy would also have an observer at the talks.

That a Nuba Mountains ceasefire agreement had been negotiated came as a surprise to most observers, and was very promising. If successful, this could become an important basis for cooperation between the parties and for international support for the peace process. Through the IGAD Partners' Forum we therefore mobilized support for monitoring the ceasefire, asking many countries for contributions, both financial and material, and including equipment and the deployment of police and military personnel. The response was positive. The US, Canada, and several European countries supported the mission with personnel and resources. A Joint Military Commission of the two parties was established, and integrated units were deployed in the region.

The monitoring operation was ably led by the Norwegian General Jan Erik Wilhelmsen, based in Kadugli, whose appointment had resulted from discussions within the Troika. He had previously participated in a range of international operations under UN auspices and been in charge of monitoring missions in several countries, including the Temporary International Presence (TIPH) in Hebron in the Palestinian Territories and for the UN in El Salvador. Although he had limited African experience and no knowledge of Sudan, doubts about the appointment soon proved unjustified. Wilhelmsen quickly took charge of the mission, and invested a lot of time and energy in understanding the situation in the country and the Southern Kordofan region, and in gaining the confidence of both parties. The Joint Military Commission was a great success; several elements of the Security Protocol of the Comprehensive Peace Agreement of 2005 would be modelled on the Nuba experience.

Soldiers of the Sudanese Armed Forces and SPLA constituted the main asset of the monitoring operation. They were trained to patrol, observe, and intervene together. International observers took on support functions. A new and groundbreaking model was thereby created, a small, "light-footed" international contingent, with no weapons, which focused on the need to build trust between the parties locally.

When I visited the area on 19 February 2003, I talked with several joint observer teams deployed in the field. I was amazed to hear how well these worked. Both parties confirmed this. After initial hesitation in dealing with former enemies, they had managed to establish good working relations in the field. Approaching a post not far from Kadugli, I sat down with the two policemen, one from each side at one outpost. After we had chatted for a while, I enquired about why their uniforms were the same. "You see", the SPLA soldier, turned policeman, said, "we have been promised new police uniforms, but they have not arrived yet. In the meantime, my brother here lent me one of the government uniforms. It works well for me, and after all – we are on the same mission".[11] We all laughed. For me, these were first signs of peace.

The unique monitoring and governance arrangements helped to create an atmosphere of peace and hope in the Nuba Mountains. Throughout the monitoring period, very few serious incidents or violations of the cessation of hostilities were reported. The success of the Joint Military Commission led to intense discussions with the UN Department of Peace Keeping Operations about the later Peacekeeping Operation in Sudan. Throughout 2004–05 the parties and countries behind the Nuba Mountains model urged adoption of a similar, "light footed" model for the whole South, but to no avail. A traditional peacekeeping operation was to be deployed, the effectiveness of which would be called into question on a number of occasions.

Other Civil Wars

There were other conflict zones of importance equal to that of the Nuba Mountains. In Southern Blue Nile, Eastern Sudan and Abyei – the last an area of great contention on the border between Northern and Southern Sudan – armed resistance to the Khartoum government was supported by the SPLM/A. In all but one of these regions (Abyei), SPLA forces were present. The SPLM demanded – and the government resisted – inclusion of the Nuba Mountains, Southern Blue Nile and Abyei in the IGAD negotiations. The Southerners had tabled almost exactly the same demand in the negotiations for the Addis Ababa Agreement of 1972, and been similarly rejected. Now the SPLM position reflected Garang's vision for a New Sudan, in which all marginalized areas would have a fair say in the affairs of the country and a fair share in its resources.

The area referred to as Southern Blue Nile is mostly east of the northernmost part of Southern Sudan. Parts of it were "closed districts" during the Condominium, when there was some exposure to Christianity and Western education. As in the Nuba Mountains, the introduction of large mechanized farming schemes and the use of forced labour had alienated much of the population. Resistance against Khartoum policies mounted. The SPLM/A first came to the area in 1985, but its influence had ebbed and flowed during the war. The Movement recruited across religious lines; the local SPLM/A strongman and current Governor of the state, Malik Agar, was a Muslim. Other local people regarded as "Arabs" had allied with the government. Since 1997 the SPLM/A had controlled significant areas, which it defended successfully, in part with support from neighbouring Ethiopia, against repeated government offensives.

The background of the conflict over Abyei is unique.[12] Abyei is a smaller area than the other two. The people of the area, the Ngok Dinka, are "Southerners" living in a "northern" province, Kordofan. The area concerned was the traditional territory of the nine Ngok Dinka chiefdoms, as transferred to Kordofan in 1905. During the last phase of the colonial era the paramount chief of the Ngok, Deng Majok, rejected the idea of attaching Abyei to the Bahr al-Ghazal, and it remained an anomaly. The first civil war reached the Abyei area in 1965. The Ngok sided with the rebels, while neighbouring Miseriya Baggara Arab groups assisted the government. The result was a civil war within a civil war. Deng Majok's son, Abdalla Deng, was among the many killed.

Under the terms of the 1972 peace settlement a referendum was promised to decide whether Abyei should be attached to the South. This never took place. But Abyei had a special status, Southerners took up administrative positions in the area, and former Anya-Nya soldiers manned local garrisons. Now ethnic enmity flared anew. The Baggara herds had greatly increased since independence, even as the carrying capacity of their lands diminished owing to drought, and mechanized farming schemes encroached. Responding to this marginalization, the Baggara began to organize into militias called *murahalin*. Clashes with the Ngok and local police increased in frequency and intensity. The Ngok, denied their referendum, started to arm and organize into militias of their own. Several local leaders became senior figures in the SPLM/A, and Abyei, with its "Southern" population and newly discovered oil, became an important issue for the Movement. The Ngok were brutally displaced; the region came to epitomize successive Khartoum regimes' exploitation of Southern resources, apparently no matter the cost. The Abyei issue proved intractable during, and indeed after, the peace negotiations, and ultimately was referred to the Permanent Court of Arbitration in The Hague.

From the SPLM/A's point of view the situation in the border areas required their inclusion in any peace negotiations. The Movement had never defined itself as "southern", and in any case the peoples of the border regions were "northern" only in the formal sense of arbitrary political boundaries dating to colonial days. The government, however, did not acknowledge an SPLM/A right to negotiate on behalf of the border peoples. Nor did the agreed Declaration of Principles, which provided the mandate for negotiations, include the border areas. When the Machakos Protocol was seen to promise a referendum for the South, pressure on the SPLM/A from the Nuba

Mountains and Southern Blue Nile mounted. Representatives wanted their issues included in the talks, and recognition of their own right to self-determination; they feared abandonment in a separate peace. The SPLM/A decided to include leaders from the Nuba Mountains and Southern Blue Nile in its negotiating team. When the parties convened for a second round in mid-August 2002, the SPLM/A pressed the issue very hard: the three areas needed to be part of the negotiations. The government was as adamant, understandably concerned that loose talk about referendums for other regions would lead to "balkanization" of the country. They had made their concession on self-determination for the South, and that was that.

Darfur – a Different Story

Inter-ethnic tensions in Sudan's western region of Darfur dated back to pre-colonial times. The issues, which often related to water and grazing rights and political power, had largely been managed in peaceful ways. The Fur, Masalit and Tunjur were mainly sedentary farmers. The Baggara Arabs were mainly nomadic cattle keepers, and the Abbala Arabs mainly camel nomads. Relations had been fairly good, and much social interaction solidified the feeling of communality. Many villages in Darfur were ethnically mixed, and indeed ethnic identities were fluid. All the people were Muslims.

As much as Southern Sudan, Darfur suffered from neglect during and after the colonial era. That era had in fact been particularly brief in Darfur: the independent Fur state had been conquered, and the territory annexed, to the Egyptian Sudan only in 1874, and after the collapse of the Mahdist State in 1898–9 the new Anglo-Egyptian Condominium had acquiesced in the revival in Darfur of an autonomous sultanate. This reflected no solicitude to the local people but, on the contrary, determination not to take administrative and financial responsibility for them. When, during the first world war, the Condominium regime invaded and annexed the region, that attitude had not changed: Darfur was relegated to a system of Indirect Rule, by which local tribal leaders' authority was recognized (and to some extent regularized), in order to avoid the "bureaucratic" administration that, in the Nile Valley (and elsewhere in the British empire) had seemed to encourage the rise of a "class" of deracinated local officials susceptible to nationalism and inimical to colonial rule. Because of its remoteness, moreover, sparse population, and lack of any high-value resources, the region remained almost entirely undeveloped; in indices of social advance, for example – health, education – Darfur lagged even the notoriously neglected South.

Even before independence, however, the economic and social pressures that would later create what would be called "the world's worst humanitarian disaster" were already building. Darfur, like much of the sub-Saharan region, was drying up in a century-long drought. At the same time, demand for the region's dwindling water resources continued to increase, as the human population – but much more importantly the size of its vast herds – continued to grow. Now the distribution of land became a major source of tension, particularly as grazing land became ever scarcer, and the pressure for acquiring land thereby increased. Ethnic groups that had in the past migrated seasonally, or during emergencies, now wanted to settle permanently away from their desiccated homelands. In ethnic terms this generally meant the migration southwards of camel nomads into the grazing areas and settled agricultural areas of the Fur and Masalit. The potential for applying an ethnic match to this economic tinder was obvious, and local troublemakers, abetted by Khartoum, took full advantage.

Never a land of plenty, Darfur had a history of drought, famine, and recovery, by which its human and animal populations had waxed and waned in uneasy response to environmental pressure. But when one of the worst famines in Darfur's history occurred in 1984–85, times had changed. The Khartoum government was particularly weak, and its inability to administer (rather than repress) the province was reflected in the rise of Fur and Masalit self-defence forces, and of ethnic militias. These easily acquired arms from Chad and other neighbouring states, where various insurgencies were under way, and from Libya and other sources. The activities of some militias, notably in the nomadic north of the province, approximated mere banditry; these forces came to be called the *janjawid*, by now infamous for their murderous rampages. Their atrocities acquired an overlay of crude chauvinism, which uncritical observers have abbreviated as "Arab" versus "African". As two experts on the crisis have pointed out, the combination of the movement called the "Arab Gathering" – based on Arab supremacy, extremist Islam, recruitment of frustrated members of ethnic groups that had seen their livelihoods undermined or destroyed – and the influx of arms, proved particularly toxic.[13]

Under the NIF regime, which in 1989 took power in a coup, the use of Arab militia would become systematic. So-called Popular Defence Forces became increasingly difficult to distinguish from ethnic militias and the *janjawid*. An Aballa Rizeigat chief, Musa Hilal, rose to prominence by facilitating military training for hordes of young men in Libya, transporting weapons, and mobilizing recruits for the Arab militia in Darfur. The idea of Arab supremacy now gave a spurious ideological basis for a movement to eject the African population altogether.[14]

Darfur's Resistance and The Black Book

Parallel to conflict on the ground, policies originating in Khartoum strengthened the hand of the groups claiming Arab origin. After an abortive SPLA foray into southern Darfur in 1991, a decision was made to take control in the West. The government divided Darfur into three states, and formalized a discriminatory "tribal hierarchy". The Fur people were divided among the three states, and instantly became a minority everywhere. New administrative positions were established to ensure a majority of Arab origin, and some appointees were not even Darfurians but individuals originally from Chad. This changed the balance of power entirely. Together with already simmering ethnic conflict, the flood of arms, the growth of Arab militias, and the noxious notion of Arab supremacy, this precipitated a reaction. From 1997 more organized armed groups were formed among the non-Arab population. Abd al-Wahid Mohamed al-Nur came to prominence at this time; Sharif Harir, a lecturer at the University of Bergen who went to Eritrea to help build the Sudan Federal Democratic Alliance, would later become an important figure in the Darfur opposition.

The Zaghawa of northern Darfur had been seen as potential allies of the Arab Gathering, but events undermined any such proposition. As early as 1991 Zaghawa elders complained to the president of nascent "*apartheid*". Sporadic outrages continued, and after several local peace agreements were dishonoured, armed resistance began. Contacts were established with the Fur, and in mid-July 2001, as conditions in Darfur continued to deteriorate, agreement was reached to establish a joint resistance movement. This took Khartoum's political and security elite by surprise. In due course, the experience of the Zaghawa fuelled the rebellion of the Justice and Equality Movement (JEM), under the leadership of Khalil Ibrahim.

It was against this background that *The Black Book: Imbalance of Power and Wealth in Sudan* was published anonymously in May 2000. Photocopied and stapled together, it avoided government censorship. It outlined in detail the monopoly of economic and political power in the country by a small group of people from three ethnic groups, the Shaiqiya, Ja'aliyin and Danaqla, all from the Nilotic north. Virtually all important positions, from the Cabinet to the police and military forces, the judiciary and the provincial administrations, were held by "the riverain people", and most of them from the same ethnic nucleus. The book showed how all other regions had been marginalized in comparison. This was not news, but until now no one had put all this information on paper in a systematic way and for political purposes. Exact authorship was disputed, but a core group of the Justice and Equality Movement engineered dissemination; it was even alleged that Hasan al-Turabi was behind the whole thing.

The Black Book certainly struck a chord in Darfur. Some people joining armed groups had been in government jobs, but had been denied promotion. Some had experienced systematic discrimination over benefits, lower salaries, frequent arrears, and fewer rights in the workplace than colleagues of "Arab" origin. Some saw their gifted children suddenly failing exams that others, theretofore less bookish, mysteriously passed with ease. *The Black Book* now tied all of this together in a way that made sense, too, of the far more serious outrages of recent years.

A peace conference attended by representatives of both sides at Nyertete in August 2002 briefly achieved consensus on all key issues. The ease of agreement belied the intentions of some of the participants. The Arab Gathering, allegedly in league with State Security, convened its own conference of militias a month later. Many Fur interpreted this as a "declaration of war".[15] Meanwhile, the forces around Musa Hilal and the Arab Gathering had been scaled up significantly. What had previously been militia operating partly on their own were now becoming more organized forces, with external support, training, and transport of weapons, apparently in systematic preparation for large scale operations. From the year 2000, when an Abbala Rizeigati was appointed Governor of North Darfur, materiel was flown in directly from the capital.

Gunship Attacks in the South

As international partners, we had been aware that something was brewing in the Western region in early 2002, but our focus had been on Africa's longest civil war, the conflict in the South. Just as the Kenyans and international observers were preparing for the first round of negotiations within the IGAD framework, consulting with the parties after the summit in January 2002, government helicopters suddenly roared into action in Southern Sudan. On February 9th Nimne was attacked; on the 20th a helicopter gunship attacked the UN feeding centre at Bieh and killed at least two-dozen women and children. Before that attack, the foreign minister, Mustafa Osman Ismail apologized, blaming a "technical fault" for the earlier bombing. Later explanations included the need to respond to an SPLA ground offensive, and a lack of coordination by field commanders.

In Europe and North America fierce criticism and massive protests ensued. Fall-out was greatest in the US, where the anti-Khartoum lobby seized on the incidents to put pressure on the Administration for a tough reaction. The US government condemned them as part of a "pattern of senseless and brutal attacks by the government against innocent civilians". Rather than withdraw completely from the peace process, however, as some in the Congress demanded, President Bush "suspended" US participation.

To be sure, although three of the Danforth "tests" had had positive results, the test regarding aerial bombardment and protection of civilians had not. Such bombardments were an essential part of Khartoum's military tactics. As one expert put it: "If Khartoum were to forego attacking civilians, it would have to abandon its current military strategy in the oil fields. Its entire strategy is based upon displacing the population that lives around the oil fields."[16] Indeed, air dominance had been one of the main advantages of the Sudanese Armed Forces throughout the civil war. But although government officials expressed regret for the helicopter bombing incidents, the timing of the attacks called into question Khartoum's commitment to the peace process itself.

There was much speculation that certain quarters in Khartoum were trying to undermine the negotiations even before they began. Who were they, and how high up? There were rumours about the First Vice President, Ali Osman

Taha; senior army officers; members of the security apparatus; and Dr. Ghazi
Salahuddin whose role, despite his outreach to the international community,
also was subject to speculation. But none of us really knew.

John Garang, perhaps unexpectedly, was emboldened by the Bieh incident
to visit the US and UK to galvanize support. I updated Clare Short in March
on the initiatives we had taken and briefed her ahead of Garang's visit. We
had learned of movement on the Sudanese government's side in relation to the
fourth Danforth test, and we hoped that Danforth would be able accordingly
to report positively to President Bush, thereby winning resumption of
American involvement. I told Clare that following this we should push for
direct negotiations as soon as possible, and ease the pressure in Washington.
Walter Kansteiner suggested a meeting with Clare and me, to discuss ideas for
strengthening the negotiating framework and to set strategy for approaching
the talks.

The Bieh incident was a typical setback. Similar episodes would occur later.
Several months would go by before we were able to revitalize the process.
Norway and the UK could not proceed without the US, but we needed a credible entry point for the Americans to resume involvement. Meanwhile we
focused on galvanizing broad international support for implementing the
Nuba Mountains agreement. It was reaction to the incident that forced
Khartoum to take the final Danforth test seriously. In early March it signalled
willingness, and talks were convened very soon after this. The government
ended up conceding, and at the end of the month both parties signed the agreement on the protection of civilians. International observers were to monitor
the agreement; there were plans to set up two monitoring teams, one in the
South and one in the North. After this achievement, and Jack Danforth's
report to President Bush on May 14th, the Special Envoy got the green light
to re-engage.

The international community was by now engaged in several monitoring
operations. The Joint Monitoring Mission of the Nuba Mountains Ceasefire
was an early success. The Civilian Protection Monitoring Teams, set up for
quick deployment in cases of attacks on civilians, was primarily supported by
the US. As international assistance was mobilized for these efforts, and for the
IGAD secretariat, the Troika continued trying to get the IGAD negotiations
off the ground. We focused on practical support for the negotiating framework and ensuring the presence of our observers at the talks.

As co-chair of the Sudan Committee of the IGAD Partners' Forum I was in
frequent contact with the Kenyan government and with General Sumbeiywo,
whom we believed was the right person to mediate the negotiations. He had
been a member of the Kenyan delegation at my first IGAD meeting, and I
remember vividly how impressed I was. Even then I had talked to him about
the possibility of a mediating role, given his familiarity with the conflict and
several of the leaders. Having declined an invitation in 1998, Sumbeiywo had,
in October 2001, agreed to succeed Daniel Mboya, the previous negotiator.
The general's authority derived not only from his military background and

closeness to President Moi, but also from a strong personality and independence. He was firm, and would not easily cave under pressure. These qualities
were critical for the success of the negotiations.

Sumbeiywo was eager to get started. The parties were not ready, however,
and in our view there was no point in holding a round of talks that would
merely proceed from previous failures. A different, more dynamic negotiating
format was needed, and was being prepared. After the summit in January,
moreover, IGAD had been slow in reorganizing itself, and valuable time was
lost during this period. Nevertheless in early March 2002, General Sumbeiywo
started to consult the parties. He presented to the SPLM Chairman a paper on
the major issues, which was interpreted as very one-sided by the Movement,
and was leaked to the public. This led to much speculation about whether
IGAD, under European influence, was abandoning the right to self-determination. This was clearly not the case: the paper was a product of the Chief
Mediator himself, and none of us had seen it or been consulted about its
contents. The upshot, in our view, was that the IGAD secretariat and negotiating team needed more support. We decided to give the talks a major push.

CHAPTER TWO

The Watershed Agreement on Self-Determination

Washington, London and Oslo took a decision to engage in the peace negoti-ations between the Government of Sudan and the SPLM/A at the political level and give them a significant thrust forward. The Troika (the US, UK, and Norway) was from January 2002 represented by Walter Kansteiner, Clare Short, and me, all of us personally committed to the peace process. In late April 2002, just before the American decision to re-engage, we met in New York at the American Mission to the UN, to explore ways to kick-start the moribund talks. At the meeting, which was attended also by our principal advisers, we agreed on key principles, some positions for the talks, and a roadmap to strengthen the framework for the peace negotiations, including Troika support for IGAD mediation. A main point of discussion was whether we should insist on a strong, visible role – a Coordinator from one of the three countries, working with General Sumbeiywo as a co-negotiator. For the time being we decided instead to send our own envoys as observers to the negoti-ations and to support the talks with technical experts. Meanwhile we would work behind the scenes to influence the parties to make the commitments needed to reach an agreement. This meeting, and the agreed approach to the talks, would later prove to have been critical for our collective efforts in the negotiations.

Although it was clear that without outside involvement progress was very unlikely, we took care lest this support seem to threaten a Western take-over, not only by General Sumbeiywo personally, but also by Kenya and the other leaders of the region. The IGAD secretariat was ready to start the negotia-tions, and given the agreement of the IGAD summit our role was broadly accepted.

The talks began with preparatory technical meetings in Nairobi in May 2002, focusing on the agenda and modalities for the negotiations. These talks were contentious, and the Sudanese government refused to sign the prepared draft. Agreement was reached only when the unity of Sudan was moved to the top of the agenda, self-determination put further down, and ceasefire removed altogether. This last was in accordance with SPLM/A wishes, since the mili-tary card was its highest trump, and not one it would give up easily.

Both sides sent stronger delegations and negotiating teams than to previous rounds under the IGAD negotiating framework. The new Chief Mediator, General Sumbeiywo, was supported by a better secretariat with more international and technical experts, funded by the Troika and other countries. Rather than sporadic negotiating sessions, convened for shorter periods of time, the IGAD secretariat now outlined a strict agenda for continuous talks, and specific deadlines, to be pursued for the next four or five months. They wanted to create a "do-or-die" effect. It was also clear that the Troika observers would be intimately engaged in the negotiations. On the American side, Jack Danforth, Walter Kansteiner, Richard Armitage and Colin Powell were mobilized to urge agreement and push the counter-terrorism message. Alan Goulty used his good relations with Khartoum to contact Dr. Ghazi and others, and I talked to the SPLM/A leadership.

Given the Egyptian-Libyan initiative and the importance of Egypt's relations with Sudan, the Kenyans looked for ways to integrate Egypt into the negotiation framework. IGAD therefore proposed observer status, which Egypt rejected. The Egyptians wanted a much more substantive role. Numerous invitations were sent to Egypt, including vague signals of a somewhat larger role, but without success. These approaches worried the SPLM/A, for Egypt's views on self-determination for the South were well known. It was against this background that the first round of talks was conducted.

The first round commenced on 17 June 2002 at Machakos. The leader of the Sudanese government's delegation was Dr. Ghazi Salahuddin Atabani, as Adviser to the President on Peace Affairs, whose strong team included Chief Negotiator Idris Mohamed Abd al-Kader; the Minister of State in the President's Office, Yahia Husein Babikir; Under Secretary in the Ministry of Foreign Affairs, Mutrif Siddiq; Said al-Khatib, a prominent NCP strategist; and others. On the SPLM/A side, Garang's Deputy, Salva Kiir Mayardit, headed a delegation that included Commanders Nhial Deng Nhial, as Chief Negotiator, Deng Alor, Dr. Justin Yak, Samson Kwaje and others. Pagan Amum and Yasir Arman would join the team later.

The Key Players

Dr. Ghazi Salahuddin Atabani was a member of Khartoum's Islamist elite. He was Advisor to the President on Peace Affairs, a prominent leader of the National Congress Party, and a shrewd politician. His father's family came from Egypt, his mother's from Morocco. A medical doctor with a British Ph.D. in biochemistry, he was an intellectual with great analytical ability, and could easily be taken for a person who would craft well-balanced compromises and cut deals. Usually eschewing the *jallabiyya* for an impeccable suit and tie, he effortlessly received international figures, and in polished French and English conveyed the policies of his Government. He was the only Sudanese politician I knew who, from the very beginning, communicated by e-mail and was always a prompt correspondent. He was, in short, someone many thought they could do business with.

But many Western politicians and high-level officials misread Dr. Ghazi.

They did it then, and they still do. He could be taken for a pragmatist, but was fundamentally an Islamist, with loyalties firmly anchored at the core of the former National Islamist Front, the current National Congress Party. Without a traditional northern Sudanese tribal background he has yet managed to retain a position at the very centre of the NCP, no small achievement. He has competed several times for the leadership position in the national Islamist movement with Ali Osman Taha. Dr. Ghazi knows the political game, and should not be underestimated. He does not easily accept compromises that would threaten the status quo. As head of the delegation he was seldom present at the negotiations proper, did not negotiate personally, and preferred to stay in the vicinity somewhere, providing guidance and ready to come if called upon.

Salva Kiir Mayardit had been in the bush with John Garang since the very beginning in 1983, the only survivors of the first group that defected. He was first and foremost a soldier, with his origins in the armed forces and experience in military strategy and intelligence. He was quiet, strikingly deferential, with an aura of dignity, integrity, and humility. He was respected rather than feared. Salva Kiir lacked the academic background of the intellectual Chairman, to whom he was deeply loyal, but was more of a "doer". For this reason Salva was also less concerned with negotiating processes and international diplomacy, preferring to remain in the background and dealing with military affairs. He led the talks at Machakos on occasion, but was not present on a day-to-day basis. Since Dr. Ghazi also kept a distance from the talks, he and Salva never faced each other directly in real negotiations during this period. Much of the "heavy lifting" on the SPLM/A side was left to Nhial Deng Nhial and Deng Alor, who later alternated with Pagan Amum as the real drivers in the negotiations.

The observers from the Troika were Jeff Millington, charge d'affaires at the US embassy in Khartoum; for the UK, Rachel Sisk; and for Norway, the Sudan expert Halvor Aschjem. During later rounds Special Envoy Alan Goulty of the UK; the US Special Envoy or his ambassador, Michael Ranneberger; and Ambassador and Special Envoy Vegard Ellefsen from Norway would become key players in the negotiations. From our side, Kjell Hødnebø also played a very important role. The focus during this first phase of "round one" was development of practical proposals for constitutional arrangements of what could be called a "one country, two systems" model. Asymmetrical federalism, granting the South significant autonomy and representation at the centre, was seen as one way forward.

General Sumbeiywo cooperated with the Troika. He consulted the observers at least once per session, and had daily formal meetings with them to discuss strategy. On Sumbeiywo's team at this juncture were Nicholas "Fink" Haysom from South Africa, a constitutional lawyer with long mediation experience who was present throughout and played a key role; and later Julian Hottinger of the Swiss Federal Department of Foreign Affairs would join him. The IGAD secretariat had recruited several other professionals, and technical experts were employed for the various negotiating areas. A number of other experts and negotiators joined the team, depending on the subject at hand. Among other observers at times was Ambassador Mohamed Sahnoun on behalf of the UN.[1]

Despite high-powered teams from both sides, the negotiations got off to a slow start. During the first three weeks there was much uncertainty and anxiety among participants. Prior to the IGAD summit General Sumbeiwyo had drafted a paper on "One country, two systems" which he had discussed with the two parties. Both had summarily rejected it. Garang, upset that it did not deal with self-determination, had told the general that Southern Sudan would not be a "bandage" on Sudan.[2] But although the paper was dead before the negotiations commenced,[3] the SPLM/A continued to refer to it as a matter of grave concern. Thus, despite all the years of talks, the parties started from scratch. Instead of entering into real negotiations, focusing on the key issues, they reiterated longstanding positions. The IGAD team deliberately let the parties vent their frustrations, then vainly tried to focus discussions on "one country, two systems". Deng Alor later told me diplomatically: "The discussions were not fruitful, but they were educative. At least we managed to clarify the positions of both parties".[4] But Mutrif Siddiq of the government delegation was blunter in saying that "The talks were going in a vicious circle."[5]

Initially, at this very early stage, the government insisted on a federal structure and the SPLM/A delegates were not happy about this. The government delegation was cautious: without tabling concrete proposals they made general points about a range of possible federal structures. Early on Dr. Ghazi called for a think tank to be used to study options. To the SPLM/A, "one country, two systems" meant confederation, preferably secular and with a rotating Presidency. For the Government, "one country, two systems" had to be a federal system, and they objected to confederation because it implied a country composed of two equal units. More, in a federal Sudan their concept of an Islamic state had to be retained. Significant disagreements arose between the negotiation teams.

Shifting the Agenda: Self Determination Up Front

The positions of the parties were far apart, and while the SPLM/A seemed rather inflexible, the government seemed to be "beating around the bush". The mediators had looked at previous IGAD negotiations on Sudan, and concluded that these had all failed over the issue of religion and the state. They therefore decided to focus on this, since a breakthrough in this area might make it easier to resolve other issues later. Fink Haysom's team undertook a series of informal discussions with the parties, individually and together.[6] They developed a text they thought could "fly" with both parties, and tabled it in a workshop. While the substance seemed very close to what both parties could accept, neither side would commit to the text. The government claimed few objections to it; the SPLM/A insisted that the question of self-determination had to be addressed first. For them, the two issues were linked.

The SPLM/A, frustrated and aggrieved, feared a trap – extensive talks on governance arrangements, federal systems, and state and religion, without ever getting to the core issue of self-determination by referendum. It was the sequencing of. issues that upset them most. In their opinion, General Sumbeiywo deferred too much to the Sudanese government, giving short shrift to the issues fundamental to the South.[7] They had been critical too of Senator Danforth's efforts, which created tests for the parties that were not linked to the key issues of contention between the North and the South. And to them his public statements against secession as a viable option seemed to prejudge the issue of self-determination. Thus while the SPLM/A favoured the Troika's role in the negotiations, they continued to worry about the Americans. The Americans, moreover, were getting impatient: in mid-July they contacted Khartoum at the political level, and said they wanted a deal within a week.

On July 16 I met Jack Danforth in Oslo. He was pleased with the four tests, and declared the monitoring mechanism ready to go. But he was worried about the humanitarian crisis, which was getting worse. I was surprised at how little informed he was about the tensions in the negotiations. I told him that the SPLM/A was losing confidence in the talks, and that both John Garang and Abel Alier had expressed dismay. I referred to General Sumbeiywo's old paper, in which self-determination was formulated within a context of a united Sudan, which in the SPLM/A's view was not in accordance with the IGAD Declaration of Principles; the issue of state and religion was not even covered. It therefore seemed that the discussions premised a special solution for Southern Sudan along the lines of the Addis Ababa Agreement of 1972. Signals from the Troika countries had also created suspicion and frustration within the Movement's leadership, as I knew from their calls to me. Whatever the status of Sumbeiywo's paper, it was now imperative to change the negotiating strategy and get the sequencing right: governance arrangements could not be discussed separately from state-and-religion and self-determination; otherwise the talks would never get off the ground. The Movement also needed to know that the international community stood by the IGAD formula on the right to self-determination.

Because of the South's experience of broken agreements, I knew that the SPLM/A would never give up that right and the explicit option of independence. The SPLM was, however, susceptible to pressure on the length of the interim period and on state and religion. Danforth responded that the US was in a position to use carrots and sticks with Khartoum, but had less leverage with the SPLM/A. But he doubted whether Khartoum would ever accept secession of the South, not least because of its oil. Nor would the government negotiate away the unitary system of governance and *Sharia*, only to see the South disappear later. It was critical, though, that the talks move forward: how could we make that happen? Walter Kansteiner and Clare Short had agreed to travel together to the region with a joint message. I was ready to go at any time if there was a need. We agreed to coordinate our messages, and to work over the phone and through our envoys. The US would draft a strategy note on carrots and sticks in relation to both parties, and this would be discussed at a Troika meeting at the end of July.

I learned at about this time that the SPLM/A's concerns had reached the level of its commanders in the field. I received information from my own contacts, as well as indirectly. John Prendergast, an old friend and Sudan expert in a senior position with the International Crisis Group, told me in mid-July of talks he had had with several SPLA commanders. Now he reported that the SPLM/A would leave the negotiations if issues important to them – particularly self-determination – were not addressed very soon. (This was recently confirmed by members of the SPLM/A leadership.)[8] It seemed we had only a few days, at most a week, to get things back on track.

There was a long history behind Southerners' demand for self-determination. They insist that a promise of self-determination was made after World War II by the departing colonial rulers, Britain and Egypt, a commitment later broken by the northern Sudanese in connivance with Egypt. Although such undertakings may in fact have involved "self-government", this perception has prevailed among Southerners until today. In any case, the Southern view was refined, and redefined, from the 1960s onwards, after which self-determination became a core demand for all Southerners and a main point of contention between North and South. The Addis Ababa Peace Agreement of 1972 was, in many Southerners' opinion, too weak, particularly on self-determination, security arrangements, and international guarantees (of which there were none). These flaws led to its collapse, and to the resumption of civil war in 1983. The right to self-determination – and thus at least implicitly to independence – had even been accepted by the government in previous agreements, notably the Khartoum Peace Agreement with Southern parties in 1997, and was imbedded in the constitution.

After talking to John Prendergast, I understood the seriousness of the situation, a view reinforced by my trusted advisor, Kjell Hødnebø, who had picked up similar signals from his own discussions with key people in the SPLM/A. It was clear that we were heading for a crisis. Kjell told me that we needed immediately to contact our representative at the negotiations, Halvor Aschjem, with clear instructions. I had been in touch with him almost every day already, getting reports and providing guidance when warranted, and I agreed.

In the opinion of the negotiation team and observers, the SPLM delegates were being difficult. This was not the first time my interpretation of events differed significantly from that of others involved in the talks. In this case I warned that a complete breakdown of the negotiations was likely unless the sequencing of issues was changed. The principle of self-determination, including the option of an opt-out, or independence, had to be part of the negotiation text and be addressed at once. I asked Halvor Aschjem first to discuss the situation with his Troika colleagues, and then with their agreement approach Sumbeiywo, the Chief Mediator, and convey the need to change course. No one would benefit from a breakdown in the negotiations now: they had just started, and it was critical to show at least some progress to both the parties and international supporters. After our phone conversation Halvor, with his Troika colleagues' agreement, talked to Sumbeiywo and insisted that the sequencing of negotiation topics should be altered.

The SPLM delegates were so frustrated that Nhial Deng and Deng Alor paid a similar visit to Sumbeiywo.[9] They had been unhappy with the Chief Mediator for quite a while, and their patience was about to run out. If one country, their preferred governance arrangement would be confederation, providing the basis for a New Sudan and unify Southerners and the Three Areas. Now Khartoum had rejected this position. This, coupled with the government's rejection of a secular state, seemed to leave the SPLM with only one option: self-determination, exercised by referendum, and with an option of independence. It was now high time the issue was discussed. Following their complaint, the intervention of the Troika observers, and also Fink Haysom's own observations, the Chief Mediator decided that self-determination and a Southern referendum should be addressed in conjunction with state and religion and the issue of federalism.

Meanwhile Fink Haysom had quietly worked on a framework for possible compromises, with input from the parties, building also on his previous work.[10] He focused on identifying each side's "red lines" in relation to the state-and-religion issue within a federal context and a referendum exercising self-determination. Although there was no agreement yet on a referendum, there were hot discussions on its possible timing. The main point of contention was the interim period.[11] The government insisted on a ten-year interim period, the SPLM/A two years. It was during these discussions that Justin Yak declared that the Arabs had always tried to cheat the South. He told this story: An emir promised his daughter to anyone who could teach his donkey to talk. A clever Arab said, "Your Excellency, I am ready to take the daughter and teach the donkey to talk, but I will need 10 years". If he failed he would be killed. His friends said he was crazy, but he answered that within ten years the emir might die, he might die, the daughter or the donkey might die. And maybe the donkey in the end would speak? Everyone laughed. General Sumbeiywo did some simple math, and split the difference: a six-year interim period was proposed between the signing of a peace agreement and a referendum.[12] But the parties would not commit. This was on Monday or Tuesday July 16–17.

Haysom continued to develop a text covering the key issues. In the plenary session, however, not much progress was made. The parties were far apart. The government delegation had circulated a paper that showed some latitude on state and religion. Haysom used this, integrated some of the language in a draft text, and shuttled between the parties again. He reminded the government delegation that resisting an exercise of self-determination was problematic, since Khartoum had signed on to this in previous agreements and even embedded the principle in the constitution.[13] But there was not much progress.

The government delegates were getting tired. In their briefings to Khartoum and to Dr. Ghazi, who was in Nairobi, they reported as late as Wednesday July 18th that the talks were going nowhere. On Thursday they started to watch TV and play cards: "Everyone thought that the only thing we could do now was to try to find a way to make sure we got a "decent departure".[14] On the margins of the meetings there had been some informal discussions between the parties. Said al-Khatib and Deng Alor had sat together a few times, and discussed the two sides' red lines and the need to respect them. A comment to the same effect by Nhial Deng on Monday or Tuesday had been noticed by government delegates. This was important, for it acknowledged that "political suicide" had to be avoided on both sides, whether by abandoning *Sharia* on the government side or giving up the option of secession on theirs.[15] These were the only signs of any hope of finding a solution.

The Red Lines

On Thursday the 19th, discussions focused on state and religion within a federal system, and on the exercise of self-determination through a referendum. While the SPLM insisted on the South's right to self-determination, they also wanted a religiously neutral Sudan in the meantime. But the current Khartoum government would never countenance a secular state or the abolition of *Sharia* law. Strengthening Islam as the state religion and enforcing the *Sharia* was the stated *raison d'être* of the party behind the coup of 1989, the National Islamic Front. The Sudanese government's delegates to the negotiations were adamant: Islam and *Sharia* had the highest priority. The outstanding question was whether they could make a Southern exception to the Islamist agenda.

The issue of federalism was at the heart of the matter. The government insisted on keeping the current system. But a federal system would be acceptable to the South only if the region was treated as a whole, and if self-determination, with the possibility for an opt-out through a referendum, was guaranteed. These were the "red line" issues. Addressing them at the outset was a way of testing the willingness to compromise. If the two sides could get over these two hurdles, there would be a much stronger chance that an overall agreement could be reached.

For both parties there were significant risks. This had become even clearer to me when in early January 2002 I visited the town of Yambio in Western Equatoria. The area was under SPLM/A control. I visited a secondary school for girls, supported by UNICEF. The teenagers put on an impressive show for us. Dancing in a circle, they pointed their fingers at us in a warning gesture. Their singing was loud, but I could make out only the words "Addis Ababa". Curious, I asked for a translation. As they continued to wave their fingers, I was told they sang, "Don't betray us again!" and "Remember Addis Ababa!" – the song was about self-determination. Even teenage girls deep in the bush wanted to prevent history from repeating itself.

Sumbeiywo understood what was at stake, and he exerted considerable pressure on the parties, supported by the Troika representatives. Both played an important role at this juncture. I frequently phoned Halvor Aschjem and Sumbeiywo. The Troika had agreed on a few fundamentals at the April meeting in New York, one of which was support for the right of self-determination in the IGAD Declaration of Principles, so the team had a pretty clear collective negotiating mandate. Even then we had known there would be no peace agreement without the guarantee for an opt-out for the Southerners. As the issue of self-determination got more attention at Machakos, the Troika's pressure increased. Team members were in close touch with their capitals, Washington, London and Oslo, and alerted them that the moment of decision was approaching very quickly. I followed the discussions closely.

The American observer, Jeff Millington, could not get final instructions cabled from Washington. This was an inter-agency decision on the American side, involving the National Security Council, and time was too short to clear an instruction in writing across the agencies. In the end Jeff got oral clearance from the political level at the State Department to support the proposed position on self-determination, with options of unity and independence.[16] I knew from other sources of President Bush's personal engagement in the Sudan issue, and that he was not always happy with the role played by the State Department. Bush wanted the US to take a much more active part in the talks, and was also clearly leaning towards Southern positions. The issue of self-determination was never tabled for the President's consideration at this juncture, but for those familiar with his views, there was no doubt about where he would stand. He was a staunch supporter of the Southern cause.[17]

Decision Time

At this stage, on July 19th, General Sumbeiywo played a critical role. Building on previous discussions, Fink Haysom had prepared a lengthy text on the key issues. This covered governance arrangements, including an asymmetrical federal system wherein the Southern states would constitute one region, while the Northern states would relate separately to the federal government. On the questions of *Sharia* law and the referendum, Haysom had ensured that each party's red lines were honoured. Text on the interim period and other arrangements, such as establishment of an Assessment and Evaluation Commission, was also included. Sumbeiwyo and Haysom knew that in key areas the text was a carefully crafted compromise that should be acceptable to both parties. They agreed that the time had come for forcing a decision.[18]

As Sumbweiywo later said, the three-page section reflected "creative ambiguity".[19] It included language on state and religion that the two sides had almost agreed to earlier; arrangements for Southern government wherein *Sharia* would not be applicable; language on self-determination exercised through a referendum with the option of secession; and a specific length of the interim period, six years. He asked that two representatives from each side remain in the conference room and not come out until they had agreed. They were allowed one hour only, and were asked for a straight yes-or-no answer as to whether they accepted the text. As Sumbeiywo now says: "I decided that it was now or never. Either the talks would break down, or there would be a breakthrough."[20]

The respective heads of delegation named Said al-Khatib and Yahia Husein Babikir to represent the government and Deng Alor and Nhial Deng to represent the SPLM/A. These were interesting choices. Said and Yahia were key members of the government's negotiating team, with solid technical and political background. Observers regarded them as more pragmatic than some of their colleagues. Although loyal to the government's positions, and firmly anchored in the thinking of the ruling party, they were the sort of people who preferred to look for solutions rather than digging in their heels. Said also had a strong intellectual and academic background, and a prominent position in the National Congress Party, and for this reason was a real asset to the negotiation team.

Commanders Deng and Nhial belonged to the core leadership of the SPLM/A. Both were Dinka, Nhial from Bahr al-Ghazal, and Deng Alor from Abyei, and both had strong academic backgrounds. Nhial was more cautious and quiet by nature, less confrontational, and sometimes preferred to think through difficult questions for a long time before reaching a conclusion. Deng Alor, on the other hand, was more outgoing, a strong analyst and strategist who would speak his mind and make quick decisions. They complemented each other.

The four delegates were left otherwise alone in the meeting room. At the time, Garang was driving between Boma and Kapoeta, and was available only by satellite phone. President Bashir was in Khartoum. Ali Osman Taha was in Indonesia. The two heads of delegation, Dr. Ghazi and Salva Kiir, were both in Nairobi. While the assumption had been that the two teams would negotiate and agree in the room, in fact they spent most of the time ensuring that the text was within their mandates and contacting their leaders. Deng Alor and Nhial called Dr. John and Salva;[21] there was a terrace outside the room, and Nhial remained there virtually the whole time, talking on the phone. Dr. John in turn consulted a number of his leading commanders via satellite phone, including Salva, Pagan Amum, Kol Manyang and Malik Agar. Deng remained in the room.

It was more difficult for Said and Yahia to consult their superiors in Khartoum because they had to speak Arabic, in which their two SPLM/A counterparts were fluent. They laughed at this situation.[22] As many present in Machakos observed, all four were on the phone frequently. In any case, after very careful review and analysis, Said and Yahia realized that the text was something they thought they could live with. Their negotiating mandate included instructions on several options for self-determination, including the option of secession. They recognized that some of their language also had been integrated into the text. It was a well-crafted compromise.[23]

Accepting a referendum with the option of secession was seen as a very last resort. The delegation had been instructed to consult Khartoum if this was tabled – but it was not seen as a red line that could not be crossed.[24] Yahia and Said confirm that they might have made a call or two within the delegation. Idris Mohamed Abd al-Kader then called Dr. Ghazi to get his approval. Outside the negotiating room things were extremely tense. Everyone could see what was going on, and wondered why the delegates were making outside calls rather than talking to each other.[25] The mediators and others observed the calls and heard conversations in Arabic; Sumbeiywo and Haysom came to the conclusion that neither of the two delegations actually had the necessary mandate: both needed clearance from above.[26]

The four of them asked for more time, and were given another hour. (While Sumbeiywo and the SPLM/A say that the teams ended up spending four hours in the room, the government delegates claim they were there for only two.)[27] It was after 1:00 am when they came out. The government delegation declared that they could agree to the text, but they had seven reservations that needed to be addressed.[28] According to some of the people present Nhial said: "On our side we cannot say that we don't accept the text," and referred also to some minor adjustments they wanted.[29] It is not clear exactly how they sorted out the last issues,[30] but at about 3:00 a.m. Sumbeiywo called both delegations and all the observers as witnesses. He asked them what their response was. Both sides accepted the text tentatively, pending approval from their respective leaders. A major breakthrough had occurred. The government delegates and the head of the delegation, Dr. Ghazi, called President Bashir a few hours later, early in the morning on July 20th to get his formal clearance.[31] According to members of the government delegation the President's reaction was: "Congratulations. I agree"; he would immediately convene the Leadership Bureau of the NCP for final approval.[32] Yahia Husein Babikir called Ali Osman in Delhi for his agreement, and got it without delay. Later that morning, the meeting endorsed the Machakos Protocol in its entirety.

But on the SPLM/A side all was not well. Some members of the delegation had questions. Nhial Deng asked to talk to Fink Haysom,[33] and convened a meeting with the whole delegation. The problem was with the federal model. How could the interests of the South be defended in a federal system? How could they ensure the referendum? Fink described the model of "asymmetrical federalism". He used a drawing board to explain how the governance arrangements would work, ensuring one Southern region, with the Government of Southern Sudan in charge. Members of the delegation then asked which other country practiced this system. Fink gave an honest reply: none. But he insisted that the scheme would answer their concerns. The SPLM/A delegation then endorsed the Protocol. Given Garang's leadership style, it is interesting that the Southern Sudanese delegation needed an extra round of clarification before accepting a text that had already been cleared with their Chairman.

Thus the SPLM/A ended up accepting *Sharia* law in the North, as the government accepted its non-applicability in the South; and they accepted the government's preference for a federal system while the government agreed to creation of a Southern region strong enough to help guarantee an opt-out through a referendum. The Protocol contained detailed provisions for the referendum, including language of the Declaration of Principles: "That the people of South Sudan have the right to self-determination, *inter alia*, through a referendum to determine their future status [as in para 1.3 of the DPO]." The agreement went further, in paragraph 2.5, explicitly declaring:

> At the end of the six (6) year Interim Period there shall be an internationally monitored referendum, organized jointly by the GOS and the SPLM/A, for the people of South Sudan to: confirm unity of the Sudan by voting to adopt the system of government established under the Peace Agreement, or to vote for secession.

The Protocol included other important provisions. It specified the core principles of governance of the country and details for the transition period until the referendum could be held. It contained an approach to state and religion that upheld the principles of religious freedom and non-discrimination.

The deal was done. It took people by surprise. On the government side, key officials were not even aware that the talks were heading towards a critical juncture. The Foreign Minister, Mustafa Osman Ismail, who had allegedly given certain promises to the Egyptians, was with Taha in Indonesia at the time, and was informed at the last minute. Not everyone was happy. As Dr. Ghazi disclosed later in an interview:

> There wasn't unanimity within the delegation or within the government. Before I signed I had received an urgent call from a senior member of the government who advised me not to sign. But then I made my own calculations and I phoned the President of course. I discussed and I consulted with the delegation. To me it looked like a chance of a lifetime. I just could not miss it. I had before me at that particular moment the future of Sudan. No leader in his right mind would miss such an opportunity.[34]

In any case, the substance of the protocol did not differ greatly from other agreements Khartoum had signed in Frankfurt in 1992, and the Khartoum Peace Agreement in 1997, negotiated by Zubair Mohamed Salih. Self-determination was also included in the new constitution.[35] Nevertheless this time it seemed that the government and the President really meant business. Its agreement to the Machakos protocol was not intended to be used in a political game, or as a measure to divide and rule the South. It was a means for reaching an agreement with the SPLM/A. And now the parties were much closer.

The government had acquiesced in self-determination, including the option of secession, in order to preserve the religious foundation of Sudan. The SPLM/A had given up a secular, confederative state, an essential part of the "New Sudan" agenda, in order to get a referendum on unity or secession for the South. Learning from the mistakes of the 1972 Agreement, which included no international guarantees, the SPLM/A proposed an Assessment and Evaluation Commission of international representatives to monitor the agreement and help to ensure its implementation. This concern was duly reflected in the agreement.

The Machakos Protocol was signed on 20 July 2002 by the two heads of delegation, Dr. Ghazi Salahuddin and Salva Kiir Mayardit, with a prominent ceremony taking place later at State House in Nairobi in the presence of President Daniel Arap Moi. Without this Protocol, the Comprehensive Peace Agreement could not have been negotiated. And the Sudanese themselves had made the decisions, behind closed doors. This would prove to be the pattern of the talks until they concluded.

Garang Meets President Bashir

Like the parties themselves, the international community was taken completely by surprise by the Machakos agreement. Only a few of us had known that the talks were coming to a make-or-break point. Having followed them very closely, and knowing the sensitivities involved, we had kept the discussions as confidential as possible. We needed to avoid a situation where the "whole world" arrived at Machakos and tried to influence events. Highly publicized talks seldom succeed in reaching agreement.

Everyone has a different version of how the breakthrough occurred and what the decisive factors were. There is no doubt that the deadlines and international pressure imposed on the parties were very important. Walter Kansteiner thought that his enlistment of Jimmy Carter to telephone the SPLM/A on July 19 had made the difference. But Deng Alor, who received the call, has recently said that if left him nonplussed, since they were about to go into the closed session to reach an agreement anyway.[36] Others have also weighed in. But as we have already seen, the two parties themselves deserve most of the credit. General Sumbeiywo forced the timing of the decision, with a text that was so well crafted as to be almost impossible to reject. But the decision was their own.

Much of the international community regarded the Machakos Protocol as a major breakthrough. The agreement received broad support from the IGAD countries, the African region, and from the IGAD Partners' Forum. A discordant note was struck by the Egyptians. They had not been present for the IGAD negotiations, and did not support them. The guarantee of self-determination, with a referendum to choose unity or secession, caused consternation. They were furious that this had been decided in their absence, and a blame game reportedly ensued within the government in Cairo. Control of the Nile was the key issue. Egypt wanted no change in its longstanding – and very favourable – international water-sharing agreements. An independent state on the upper Nile might question these, or indeed use water in ways that would diminish the flow reaching Egypt. The Egyptians castigated the Sudanese government for allowing this to happen. But Dr. Ghazi and other officials would not be intimidated, and they referred to the numerous times that Khartoum had already accepted a right to self-determination: why should they abandon that position now?[37]

But the Machakos Protocol was different of course, with its close involvement of other countries and the guarantees of its provisions. Norway was a member of the UN Security Council at the time, and our team immediately called New York and dictated a text that welcomed the agreement and affirmed the Security Council's support for the Protocol. The British held the presidency, and the press statement on July 24 is worth quoting in full:

> Members of the Council welcomed the signing on 20 July of the
> Machakos Protocol between the Government of the Sudan and the Sudan
> Peoples' [sic] Liberation Movement, which represents a significant
> breakthrough on major issues and a major step towards the realization of
> a just and lasting peace in the Sudan. In connection with that signing,
> members of the Council paid tribute first of all to the parties, but also to
> the President of Kenya, Daniel Arap Moi, and his special envoy,
> Lieutenant General Sumbeiywo, on behalf of the Intergovernmental
> Authority for Development (IGAD), for their efforts in finding a peaceful
> solution to the conflict in the Sudan. Members of the Council appealed to
> the parties to continue to work for a successful conclusion of a global and
> definitive agreement during the course of 2002.[38]

This recognition of the Machakos Protocol as a turning point was of great importance. A flurry of activity ensued. A strong supporter of the IGAD negotiations, President Museveni of Uganda, set about facilitating a meeting between Garang and Bashir. A week after the signing of the Protocol, on 27 July 2002, he welcomed them both to Kampala. This historic event marked the first time that the Chairman of the SPLM/A, until then only "the rebel leader" as far as the Sudanese government and media were concerned, had met the President. The meeting itself was thus another breakthrough, and contributed to anchoring the Machakos Protocol. (Worried that President Bashir would make too much of it and try to embrace Garang in front of the photographers, the SPLM/A team advised Dr. John to hold his document case in such a way that Bashir would have to stretch out his hand instead.[39] He did so, and no "compromising" photos were taken.)

Immediately after the meeting Garang told me that it had gone well and built confidence. Bashir had been very positive, they had discussed the Protocol and the peace talks, including power sharing and even the possibility of two separate armies. But Garang had also warned the President that, "They should not enter into any agreements that they don't intend to keep."[40] Aware of the differences between Bashir and his First Vice President, Garang also soon spoke on the telephone with Ali Osman Taha. He told Garang that he had received the Machakos text and assured him of his support. In high spirits, Garang even joked that by the Protocol's six-year interim period "We have given you another six year chance to become the President"! His private assessment, however, was that Bashir would be out within two years.[41]

After the signing of the Protocol both parties took steps to defend it. Media reports and rumours had it that First Vice President Taha's support was luke-warm.[42] This was not true. Having received the text before it was signed, Taha acknowledged that it fell within the framework of the negotiating mandate. If these terms were the best the negotiators could do, and Khartoum accepted them, then so did he; he never intervened despite encouragement to do so.[43] On a previously scheduled visit to Cairo he insisted that Egypt respect the agreement. The Americans also contacted the Egyptians at the political level to calm them. In mid-August Danforth reported that the situation in Egypt was now improving, and indeed was better than expected.

Other potential spoilers were the old Northern political parties. The Umma party of Sadiq al-Mahdi opposed self-determination. The Democratic Unionists and Mirghani family disliked the government's idea of *Sharia* in the North. The Sudanese Communist Party opposed both provisions. None of these parties had been included in the negotiations or been consulted about the Protocol. With so many constituents of the National Democratic Alliance opposed, however, Garang worried about holding it together. He contacted them all after the signing, with full explanations.

The Norwegian side now suggested that the Troika request Alliance involvement in the negotiations or at least a mechanism for formal consultation. This would strengthen and broaden Sudanese "ownership" of the agreement and the peace process, and reduce the number of potential spoilers. This proposal reprised one we had made during a visit to Nairobi in the spring of 2002, before the talks really started, when we had asked the Kenyans and IGAD to include the Alliance in the talks. Khartoum and the SPLM/A were subsequently consulted. Nafie Ali Nafie reportedly went to Nairobi and threatened the government's withdrawal from the talks if the Kenyans pursued the idea. Garang too was unenthusiastic, preferring to negotiate on behalf of the Alliance rather than alongside it. Khartoum would not agree even to formal consultation. It was left to the SPLM/A to keep the other opposition parties informed about the negotiations. After some serious political legwork the Alliance's Council, meeting on August 7th in Asmara, strongly endorsed the Machakos Protocol and gave the SPLM/A a conditional mandate to negotiate on their behalf. The Alliance's leaders also reserved the right to review a final peace agreement before one was signed, and a small team was tasked with drafting positions on the issues ahead of the second round of talks.

Both the Sudanese government and the SPLM/A were well aware that disaffected elements within their respective ranks needed to be controlled. Hardliners on both sides were unhappy with the compromise that had been struck. But the commitment to carry the process through seemed strong. The mediators thought that agreement on state and religion and self-determination was the key to an overall peace deal, and that the talks would be much easier after this.[44] Khartoum was, if anything, even more sanguine: once power-sharing and ceasefire arrangements were negotiated, an overall peace agreement could be signed.[45]

They counted without the SPLM/A. The Movement wanted transformation of Sudan, not containment of the South. My own assumption was that agreement on the Machakos Protocol implied that about half the job was done. But even this estimate proved overly optimistic. In the end the negotiations would take much longer and become much more complicated than any of us expected. Developments soon after the Bashir-Garang meeting would moreover show that potential spoilers were closer than the two leaders had thought.

CHAPTER THREE

Peace-Making in Peril
Conflict and Confrontation

After the agreement at Machakos, expectations were high of an early conclusion of the negotiations between the government and the SPLM/A. That the
ceasefire in the Nuba Mountains was holding and the parties were cooperating well on monitoring its implementation added to the sense of optimism.
During the second round of the negotiations, in mid-August 2002, discussions
continued on power sharing and several knotty constitutional issues, including
the status of Khartoum and whether it should be subject to *Sharia* law. At the
same time, technical seminars were organized on revenue-sharing frameworks
and oil revenues, preparing the ground for negotiations on wealth sharing.

For the SPLM/A the main issue was security. But now they insisted on
discussions first about the "Three Areas", or what they called "the definition
of the South", and included the respective regional leaders in their delegation.
Malik Agar from Southern Blue Nile was particularly tough.[1] Discussions
were so heated that the talks almost broke down, and the mediators wondered
what had happened in the interim.[2] The leaders of the Three Areas disliked
aspects of the Machakos Protocol,[3] including acceptance of the 1956 borders
without provisions for the marginalized areas. They had expected the
Movement to fight for their rights, and now they demanded redress.

The government delegates were equally unhappy. Key members tried to
push for a speedy deal,[4] and accused the SPLM/A of trying to re-open issues
already resolved. In their view, the Three Areas were outside the agreed negotiating framework, and the Machakos Protocol had already dealt with the
status of the capital: Khartoum was in the North. At the same time, two
SPLM/A documents, one on wealth sharing and one on power sharing,[5]
revealed a long way to go on a number of issues. Just as the government was
preparing to suspend the talks, new fighting erupted in the South. The parties'
commitment to peace would now be tested away from the negotiating table.

The Battle of Torit

Despite recent government reinforcement, the SPLA had for a while been in a
position to threaten the strategically important town of Torit in eastern
Equatoria. The town was symbolically important for Southerners as the place
where the 1955 mutiny had broken out and where John Garang had been

headquartered in the early 1990s. On September 1st the SPLA took the town. It was a hugely embarrassing development for the government, where losses involved also high-ranking officers. The government had been taken completely by surprise.[6] Although the exact sequence of events was unclear at the time, I expressed serious concern to the Chairman of the SPLM/A. Garang said that the government had provoked the attack by building up its forces in the area. Whatever the case may have been, I called for an immediate halt to the fighting. The same message was conveyed from the US and the UK.

At the time, I wondered whether the government had wanted an SPLA attack as a reason for suspending negotiations or to get ceasefire talks started. Previous provocations had led to the SPLA's capture of Kapoeta in early June, and there had been a significant build-up of government forces in the area around Torit.[7] After examining the sequence of events and interviewing members of the SPLM/A leadership, however, I am certain that there had been no specific provocation for the attack on Torit;[8] the Movement had used military force to make a point in the negotiations. Since the government in their view seemed to want only a quick, limited deal and a ceasefire, and not a broader agreement, the SPLM/A was sending a message that they had the power to back up their demands. (This has been confirmed in recent interviews.)[9] Garang said the same thing to President Moi at the time. General Sumbeiywo, who was present at that meeting, quotes Garang as saying:

> "Mzee . . . These people don't understand anything but the barrel of the gun. I was showing them that it was not out of weakness that I was negotiating. If they want us to go back to war, we would ably do so."[10]

The day after the SPLM/A attack on Torit, the government withdrew formally from the talks. The government delegation handed a letter to General Sumbeiywo, dated September 2nd, stating dissatisfaction with the direction the talks were taking,[11] and accusing the SPLM/A of introducing issues outside the framework of the Machakos Protocol, specifically power sharing, relations between state and religion, the structure of government, and the boundaries of the South. The government was particularly unhappy with the SPLM/A's insistence on including in the talks the Three Areas, which they saw as a clear departure from the agreed agenda, and (accurately) claimed that the IGAD Secretariat supported this approach. Less than diplomatic in tone, the letter did not refer directly to Torit, but did call for an immediate stop to the fighting.

Thus the talks had been in serious trouble before the fall of Torit. It was difficult for outsiders to assess what exactly was behind the government's decision to withdraw. We picked up a lot of rumours from Khartoum at the time, including stories of a potential coup. A contemporary Justice Africa report states that the First Vice President, Ali Osman Taha, supported by other important figures in the government and security institutions, demanded a full SPLM/A withdrawal from Torit before the talks could proceed, and that

President Bashir had already made the decision to suspend participation in late August.[12] Whatever the case may have been, this was the most significant crisis in the peace process so far.

Relations between the parties continued to deteriorate. President Bashir's meeting with Garang had led to hope of a budding partnership. Now Garang had gone on the attack, and the government was mobilizing for *jihad*. Dr. Ghazi explained in retrospect: "We were ready to go all the way in a military campaign . . . It [the mobilization, and recapture of Torit] was the most massive operation the Sudanese army undertook."[13] Fighting continued for weeks in and around Torit. There was heavy fighting on other fronts as well, and aerial bombardment. Reports reached us of as many as a thousand people killed in Western Upper Nile around the oilfields. We all knew that military action was a way to gain an advantage before further negotiations – but it was still indefensible, and as a tactic it risked a complete unraveling of the situation. We were really worried. The Troika issued new appeals for restraint.

The ostensible positions of the two sides were clear. The government wanted a ceasefire before resuming negotiations for which, moreover, the commitments made in the Machakos Protocol must serve as the basis. The mediators approached the SPLM/A about a ceasefire in September, but Garang said no; armed struggle was a card they would not give up before the end of negotiations, when they had a deal. A ceasefire agreement therefore had to wait.

It was clear to most observers that negotiating peace while fighting continued would be very difficult, if not impossible. Without an agreement on at least a cessation of hostilities the process was extremely vulnerable. It was in this regard that Abel Alier, highly respected in both North and South, was ready to assist. As the key negotiator of the 1972 peace agreement, Vice President of Sudan in 1971–76, and President of the High Executive Council in the Southern Region in 1972–78 and 1980–81, he had a special stature. A lawyer, Alier had never participated in Southern armed resistance movements, preferring instead to work from within for change, and was therefore regarded somewhat sceptically by die-hard SPLA cadres. We on the Norwegian side had close relations with him; I had met him a number of times, first in Khartoum in 1998. With his quiet, yet natural authority, he was a person one would always listen to carefully. As a young minister I immediately felt I had a lot to learn. Alier would always speak with civility, wisdom and direction. He seemed to combine generations of African oral tradition and transfer of knowledge with an incredibly sharp and current brain, and an ability to navigate tricky waters. I would often turn to Abel for assistance, and he would prove very valuable to our collective peace efforts.

Cessation of Hostilities

A couple of weeks after the government walked out of the negotiations, Vice

President Taha invited Abel Alier to a private meeting to discuss the situation. On his own, Alier had been drafting an agreement for a ceasefire that would start with a "period of tranquillity" during negotiations. Taha was receptive. At the same time, fighting continued on a number of fronts, with heavy losses on both sides, and the atmosphere in Khartoum seemed fraught.

Events now moved quickly. On 17–18 September I called Alier and then Garang, who wanted a day to think about the idea of periods of tranquillity. The latter approach was building on the Danforth tests, where periods and zones of tranquillity were used. Abel then asked for a secret meeting with Taha to share a draft, and again received a positive response. I approached Dr. John about meeting Alier, emphasising the importance of an agreement of some kind to stop the fighting. I said that Alier would come with important proposals, and I asked him to keep an open mind. Norway facilitated Alier's secret travel from Khartoum to Nairobi to meet Dr. John, who subsequently acquiesced in the proposal for a period of tranquillity while negotiations were under way, and in a mutual agreement to show military restraint. After word of this reached me on the 24th I called Garang to confirm what had been agreed, and later that day reached Dr. Ghazi with the news. It was time to inform the British and Americans that an agreement seemed possible.

For the Sudanese government, however, a "period of tranquillity" was not enough. They still wanted something more substantial, preferably a formal ceasefire. Because the fighting had by now raised major humanitarian implications, the Troika too appealed for an agreement firmer than the "tranquillity" approach. Another flurry of activity ensued. I discussed the issue with Walter Kansteiner on September 27th. While I called Dr. Ghazi, Secretary Powell called President Bashir. I also contacted Garang again. On behalf of the SPLM/A Salva Kiir wrote to the Chief Mediator, General Sumbeiywo, outlining its position, which was pretty much in line with our expectations. At the beginning of October the Norwegian Special Envoy, Vegard Ellefsen, arrived in Khartoum with Halvor Aschjem, our representative there. Halvor was not a diplomat by training but had a lifetime of experience in Sudan, where he was widely admired and respected – equally by both parties – no small achievement, and in East Africa generally. Ellefsen had worked in the cabinet of the Minister of Foreign Affairs when I was Political Advisor to the Minister, and he had later been *chef de cabinet*. He had now just ended five years as Norway's Deputy Permanent Representative to NATO. This was hardly the prescribed training for work on Sudan, and I had had a hard time convincing him to join my team.

Together with the rest of our Sudan team (Halvor, Kjell Hødnebø and Endre Stiansen), Ellefsen had met representatives of the Troika in London in September after the SPLM/A attack on Torit. While preparing for that meeting, Vegard Ellefsen confronted my doubts about a formal ceasefire by simply asking, "Are you prepared to face the Norwegian Parliament and tell them that Norway has been working *against* a possible ceasefire in the longest running civil war in Africa?" Yet the choice was not an easy one. I knew that the Americans were close to my position but that the British wanted a cease-fire, and I was unsure that my group could strike the right balance. I called Vegard from Oslo and told him I would not accept language calling for a ceasefire now. After a brief but heated discussion we settled on the term "cessation of hostilities". Vegard had negotiated NATO ministerial communiqués for the last five years and knew perfectly well that this term in practice was close to a ceasefire agreement, but an intermediate solution. A ceasefire agreement would normally include permanent arrangements for monitoring performance and for integration and demobilization of forces. "Cessation of hostilities" implied a freezing in place: interim arrangements that would depend on renewal if it was to last. The value of a cessation of hostilities agreement was the appearance of compromise between the two sides' opposing positions. As expected, the Troika aligned behind it.

This triggered a number of events. The IGAD Special Envoy, General Sumbeiywo, on a shuttle between the parties, arrived in Khartoum at almost the same time as the Norwegian diplomats. A few days into his stay, Vegard Ellefsen and Halvor Aschjem met Sumbeiywo and his aide, and the American chargé Jeff Millington, at the residence of the British ambassador William Patey. Sumbeiywo had been talking to the government and found them receptive. In order to get things moving, Patey suggested drafting a more detailed text for Sumbeiywo to present at his next day's meeting with the government. The team went to work. Patey and Ellefsen typed out the text on Patey's home computer.

The next evening, Aschjem and Ellefsen coincidentally left on the same plane for Nairobi as Sumbeiywo. Earlier that day they had met at the Hilton, where Sumbeiywo was staying, for a briefing on his talks with the government. He was optimistic. The government was still fuming over Garang's "deceit", but they were ready to move forward with the text proposed by the little party the night before. As they were parting at the airport in Nairobi, Sumbeiywo agreed to stay in touch with Aschjem and Ellefsen after his discussions with the SPLM/A. The next day, while I was sitting in my office in Oslo with my colleague, Vidar Helgesen, the State Secretary for the Foreign Minister, a call came through from Ellefsen. "Put me on the speaker", he said. "Vidar needs to hear this too."

Ellefsen briefed us about a call he had just received from Sumbeiywo, whose contacts had revealed that the SPLM/A were ready to accept the formula for a cessation of hostilities that had been proposed in Khartoum. This meant, he said, that we might have managed to bring about a stop to the fighting in Sudan. "And, by the way, Vidar", Ellefsen asked, "how many ceasefire agreements have *you* produced this week?" (The joke was a reminder of the competition between the two parts of the Ministry over peace and reconciliation issues: Vidar had been central to the efforts to bring an end to the fighting in Sri Lanka; to achieve a cessation of hostilities in Sudan would give my team an edge.) But uncertainties lingered: would agreement on paper result in implementation? I had my doubts, and in the end I was not entirely wrong. The fighting continued in the field as each side tried to gain the upper hand before the weapons were silenced.

For the government to return to the negotiating table before retaking Torit would have conceded weakness. The SPLM/A had to hold on to Kapoeta for the same reason. They did so. The government re-took Torit in the second week of October. The parties were ready to resume negotiations, and a Memorandum of Understanding for Cessation of Hostilities between the Government of Sudan and the SPLM/A was signed on October 15th, effective from the 17th until the end of December. It was "blessed" by the IGAD subcommittee on Sudan, chaired by the Kenyan foreign minister, Stephen Kalonzo Musyoka immediately after. The Memorandum would be renewed regularly until the end of the negotiations, when the SPLM was ready for a formal ceasefire. The longest civil war in Africa had been brought to an end, at least on the battlefield. Could this be the starting point for serious negotiations on a lasting, comprehensive peace agreement?

The Troika followed up with high-level calls to both parties to move on to the next round of negotiations. A technical agreement formalizing humanitarian access was soon signed with the UN, and the negotiations (dubbed "Machakos II") resumed. The negotiations would focus on power sharing and on holding elections during the interim period. The latter was important, lest the two sides be seen to be shutting out from future governance those parties not involved in the negotiations. Many important power-sharing issues remained unresolved.

The Three Areas and the Fourth: Darfur

It was during these discussions that the issue of procedure for negotiations on the three contested areas was resolved. General Sumbeiywo provided an elegant solution. Instead of negotiating the issue under IGAD auspices, which the government rejected outright, he proposed talks under Kenyan leadership and at a different venue, Nairobi. Sumbeiywo would request a separate mandate from his government for negotiations starting in January 2003. This was very important, as any agreement between the parties would have to deal with the Three Areas. The issue proved to be among the most contentious of the negotiations, eventually having to be resolved in May 2004 by John Garang and Vice President Taha. Machakos II concluded on November 18th owing to the forthcoming elections in Kenya, after which President Moi would leave office. This was close to the deadline IGAD had set for completion of the talks on all issues, but that had proven completely unrealistic.

Towards the end of the year, a delegation of the National Democratic Alliance visited various capitals, including Oslo, soliciting support for inclusion in the IGAD negotiations. Both the SPLM and Arab League endorsed that participation. The Secretary General of the Arab League, declaring the Libyan–Egyptian Initiative "dead", wanted observer status too. The Alliance delegation told us that its armed member-groups had taken defensive positions all over the country as a consequence of the October 15th Memorandum of Understanding. They also called for attention to the situation in Darfur, where a new front might be opened if the peace talks did not deal with their concerns. We on the Norwegian side took note of this, and pointed out that we had called for expansion of the IGAD process to include other political forces in Sudan, so far without success. We encouraged the Alliance to work with the SPLM to find ways to represent their views and influence the negotiations. This was an issue I brought up with both sides, calling for proper consultation mechanisms to avoid an impression of exclusivity. Insistence on national elections in the interim period was another way of ensuring inclusiveness, accommodating more of the concerns of the opposition, and preventing the peace agreement's resulting in a duopoly.

The National Democratic Alliance's delegation was right. Conditions had started to deteriorate in Darfur, as we have seen. Although the situation there was significantly different from that in the three contested areas, both the government and the SPLM/A knew that Darfur had to be addressed one way or the other. The same was the case for the eastern Sudan, where SPLA troops were already deployed. These were not North–South "border" regions in the same way as the Three Areas. The government regarded the conflicts in these regions as its business alone, and nothing for the SPLM/A to deal with. They reacted as negatively to SPLM/A claims to speak for the peoples of the Three Areas; the SPLM/A was holding what were seen as provocative conferences in the Nuba Mountains and Southern Blue Nile. In Khartoum's view the IGAD negotiations were intended to solve the Southern problem, and nothing else. The SPLM/A, on the other hand, negotiated to transform Sudan, and to serve the interests of all marginalized peoples of the country, including the East and the West. But even the SPLM/A feared that explicit inclusion of Darfur and eastern Sudan would complicate the negotiations and make agreement more difficult to reach. The SPLM concentrated instead on a solution for the Three Areas, and on negotiating an agreement that would provide enough change at the centre to serve the interests of the other regions as well.

The SPLM/A and Darfur rebels had been in contact for years. Accounts are garbled. The Nuba leader, Abd al-Aziz Adam al-Hilu traced his origins to western Darfur, and during the 1990s Yasir Arman and his brother, both senior members of the SPLM/A leadership, actively recruited Darfurians to the Movement. Under the auspices of the National Democratic Alliance, Darfurians were trained in camps in Eritrea; a Masaliti unit was formed within the SPLA. As the Darfur rebellion grew, and the movement under Abd al-Wahid al-Nur's leadership got better organized in early 2002, formal contacts with the SPLM/A began.[14] Yasir Arman and Abd al-Aziz were designated to work with the Darfur rebels. One account refers to Dr. John's sending envoys to Abd al-Wahid in Jabal Marra, who organized a telephone conference with the SPLM Chairman.[15] In this version the Darfurians rejected an invitation to join the SPLM/A, for both political and tactical reasons: Abd al-Wahid supported the concept of New Sudan, but opposed self-determination for the South. In another account, several members of the SPLM/A leadership and Col Ding say, however, that the Darfurian rebels in their very early days wanted to join the SPLM/A, but that Garang disapproved.[16] Instead, he wanted the rebels to strengthen their own movement, make sure they had a national agenda, and work with the SPLM/A behind the scenes. The first meeting between the leaders of the (Darfurian) Sudan Liberation Movement/Army and the Chairman of the SPLM/A allegedly took place secretly in Brussels in 2002, when Dr. John was on his way to Norway.[17] This was apparently also the venue of his first meeting with the leader of the Justice and Equality Movement, Khalil Ibrahim.[18]

In November 2002 Sharif Harir, a Darfur rebel leader, came to Machakos to ask for Darfur's inclusion in the IGAD negotiations. He was turned down by all parties. The Darfur militants likely concluded that they would be taken seriously only if they were seen as a significant military factor. Armed resistance in Darfur had its own history and rationale, but the talks at Machakos and the response to Harir probably exacerbated a rift. Several statements at the time, by leaders of the Darfur rebels and of the Beja Congress of eastern Sudan, indicated their support for a comprehensive negotiating framework encompassing all marginalized areas of the country.

The SPLM/A and the Darfur groups agreed to cooperate, however, with the Southerners assisting with organization. On the political side, engagement with the Sudan Liberation Movement/Army was strong. Abd al-Wahid and Minni Arkoy Minawi visited Rumbek and New Site in South Sudan with a delegation in early 2003.[19] It was in this context (according to one source) that they were promised weapons and training.[20] The SPLM/A leaders worked with the Darfur Liberation Front, developing its manifesto and political strategy, and even recommending a change of name to reflect a national agenda. Yasir Arman claims that these SPLM/A allies virtually wrote the manifesto and helped with the political declaration; even the Chairman himself took part.[21] The influence of the SPLM/A is obvious in the wording of the manifesto. Several sources in the SPLM/A leadership confirm that the Darfur groups were assisted with military training at Eri and Chukudum. Two very credible SPLM/A sources confirmed that military support and supplies – both logistics and weapons – were provided over several years.[22] The main supply routes to the SPLA were through Uganda and Eritrea, and one can assume that weapons passing westwards had similar origins. The role of Eritrea in supplying Darfur has not been confirmed by SPLM/A sources.[23] Government intelligence services monitored this engagement very early, and claim they had solid documentation of the supplies to the rebels in the West.[24]

The attacks and clashes in Darfur in 2002 and early 2003 attracted little attention in the outside world. Things moved quickly, however, and by this time the Fur resistance had become better organized. In February 2003 the Darfur Liberation Front claimed responsibility for an attack on the government garrison at Golo. Many observers see this event as the real start of the organized Darfur rebellion. The declaration that the DLF had been renamed as the Sudan Liberation Movement and Army, in March 2003, indicated the assumption of a national role, beyond Darfur.

The SPLM/A wanted to speak for all the rebel groups at the negotiating table. When Garang had discussions with Sharif Harir and suggested that the Darfurian join the SPLM/A, he was rebuffed.[25] The same had been proposed to Khalil Ibrahim, but the ideological differences on state and religion prevented their alignment.[26] The Justice and Equality Movement had a national agenda of regime change and thus differed from the other rebel groups in Darfur. The SPLM/A's concern was that inclusion of the Darfur rebels in the talks at Naivasha would make the overall negotiating process much more complicated, and nothing would be achieved. Garang explained his position to the Sudan Liberation Movement/Army in early 2003.

No Progress

Several rounds of negotiations convened during the first half of 2003. The first, which began at Karen on January 23rd, included an observer from the National Democratic Alliance. At the same time, serious fighting in Central and Western Upper Nile between government-aligned Southern militias and the SPLA endangered the talks. A meeting in Nairobi of the committee tasked with overseeing the Memorandum of Understanding on cessation of hostilities was particularly stormy. The SPLM/A listed a series of violations in Western Upper Nile that the government's representatives insisted were episodes of "tribal fighting". Our Special Envoy, Vegard Ellefsen, took the floor, and referred to the grand old man of Norwegian politics, Prime Minister Einar Gerhardsen, who once, when preparing a speech, famously wrote in the margin: "Weak argument, raise your voice!". Ellefsen called for calm, and proposed an independent verification mechanism to monitor implementation of the agreement.

Although at Karen the agenda called for discussion of power sharing, wealth sharing, and the Three Areas, the parties focused instead on the violence. At the Troika's suggestion, they negotiated an Addendum to the cessation of hostilities' agreement, giving the previously established Verification and Monitoring Team a wider mandate and composition. This was signed at Karen on February 4th. The Addendum required both parties to facilitate such a team, which could include personnel and aircraft from an expanded Civilian Protection Monitoring Team and international observers. On 29 January a team already deployed had confirmed attacks on civilians by both militia and Sudanese Armed Forces. Humanitarian access was also being restricted. The Troika coordinated a response to these violations; I conveyed our concerns to the Sudanese Ambassador in Oslo and called for withdrawal of forces.

Meanwhile the Karen negotiations ended without other significant results.

Discussion of the Three Areas, for example, had been relegated to a "seminar" when the government declined to negotiate more formally. Dr. Ghazi and Salva Kiir had started discussions about a possible meeting of President Bashir, the SPLM Chairman, and General Sumbeiywo to move things along. But as the parties dithered in negotiations, it seemed quite clear that re-armament was under way. The government strengthened its position in Western Upper Nile and in Abyei, in the latter area with militia rumoured to be under direct orders from Khartoum. Our sources reported that the government had also made significant new purchases of weapons, helicopters and armoured vehicles from Russia, at least some of which may have been destined for Darfur. Members of the government delegation at Karen, however, claimed that the SPLM/A was suffering from "buyer's remorse", uncertain how to proceed after the unexpected breakthrough of the Machakos Protocol.[27]

The time had come to assess the willingness of the parties to move on some of the critical issues. In mid-February I decided to go to Sudan. General Sumbeiywo would arrive after me, and we agreed to coordinate our messages and to brief each other. I visited Nairobi first and had long meetings with John Garang and his team. They insisted that, far from having dug in their heels, they had adjusted their positions on several points. Having in the past called for a confederation with a separate, secular constitution for the South, for example, they now accepted federation but with a referendum to exercise self-determination. The SPLM had given up its demand for a short (two-year) interim period, and agreed to one of six years before a referendum would be held. The SPLM was prepared to accept the position of First Vice President instead of a rotating presidency, and secular-enclave status for the national capital. Garang stated that the people of Abyei should decide by referendum where their area belonged – North or South – and that this should take place before the overall Southern referendum. As far as security issues were concerned, the SPLM Chairman continued to argue for two armies; the government should withdraw its forces to north of the 13th parallel and the SPLA to south of the 12th. We discussed the government's positions on the issues, and I got a good sense of the red lines and possible trade-offs.

Regarding the way forward, Garang was receptive to the idea of a summit with Bashir in order to accelerate the peace process, but stressed the need for not overloading such a meeting with unrealistic expectations. A second summit might sort out the most difficult issues after more progress had been made at the negotiation table. Garang was also open to considering a hotline for clarifications and handling urgent situations, but not for negotiations. Yet the Chairman expressed great doubt about the government's sincerity. In this regard he referred to what he regarded as its "divide-and-rule" tactic of supporting militias in the South and his serious questions as to whether they would be willing to implement a peace agreement. He still emphasized the SPLM/A's strong commitment to complete the peace negotiations.

Impatience in Khartoum

I was quite optimistic after the discussions and felt I had something to bring to Khartoum. There on the 17th I met President Bashir, First Vice President Ali Osman Taha, and the Advisor of the President for Peace, Dr. Ghazi. Mustafa Osman Ismail, the foreign minister, was out of the country. The meetings with the President and Vice President were positive, although I had hoped for more. I conveyed Garang's expressed willingness to meet President Bashir "anytime, anywhere", and that the Kenyan foreign minister, Stephen Kalonzo Musyoka, would be happy to organize a meeting as early as the end of the month. Bashir was receptive to this, but wanted a well-prepared summit, with a substantial outcome: he complained of previous occasions when the SPLM/A Chairman had failed to appear; the Kampala meeting would not have happened without the Machakos Protocol. I replied that the significant progress made recently – agreement on cessation of hostilities and the verification mechanism – was something the parties should build on, and I outlined possible issues for discussion as an agenda for the meeting. Bashir reiterated that a summit needed to be a "landmark" in the process, with significant results.

The President mentioned an incident in December, when Vice President Ali Osman Taha, at the invitation of President Obasanjo of Nigeria, had gone to Abuja to meet Garang, who was on vacation there and refused even to greet him. I conveyed what Garang had told me, that he had not been informed of any meeting and thus felt "ambushed" by the Nigerians. There was more to this than meets the eye. Dr. John at this juncture regarded Ali Osman as a hardliner, and on several occasions referred to his history as an Islamist and his alleged links to the security apparatus and Popular Defence Forces. Besides, the SPLM Chairman considered President Bashir – not a vice president – as his counterpart. Bashir, for his part, stressed the importance of Garang's getting to know Taha better: "They need to, they are going to work together in a new government". The President ended our meeting on an optimistic note, but warned that the government had a "red line" that they would never agree to cross; anything within this red line they were prepared to accept. But what was it?

The talks with Dr. Ghazi went into details. After a formal meeting of an hour or so we talked privately for three hours. I wanted to get a clear picture of the "red lines", and of where compromises could be found. Dr. Ghazi said that they had thought the negotiations would be "an easy ride" after Machakos, and that they had been surprised by the difficulties encountered. He talked about war fatigue and the urgency of reaching agreement (a message the SPLM/A Chairman had also conveyed to me). Khartoum's first preference clearly was unity, in default of which, however, there was a strong element within the government reconciled to secession, without even a transition period. The deal on the table, he said, would not be there six months from now; the government had clear red lines, and the question was whether the SPLM/A was ready to accept them. He said that the SPLM/A should settle for what they could get, and leave after six years.

In our private discussion the Presidential Advisor for Peace expressed irritation with the SPLM/A who, he said, tabled unrealistic proposals and revisited settled issues. He warned that any attempt to re-open the issue of *Sharia* in relation to the capital would be rejected: this had been dealt with in the Machakos Protocol and was now "untouchable". Regarding governance Dr. Ghazi dismissed the SPLM/A's position as totally unfounded: they constantly introduced new elements of a confederate model, even as, in his view, the Machakos Protocol adopted a federal solution and was clear both about the borders of the South in relation to the Three Areas and about power-sharing arrangements. Dr. Ghazi said that the SPLM is behaving like a contractor, ready to get a share of the cake and leave. They are not a partner, and do not seem to want partnership. And he continued, if you put yourself in their shoes, what package would make them remain in the Sudan? I really don't know, he said. I got a clear feeling that there were limits to the compromises the government would make, and that if the SPLM/A was completely "unreasonable", they might as well just secede.

Dr. Ghazi thought that security and the Presidency would be decisive issues. He revealed that the government was planning to submit to Sumbeiywo a paper on how to deal with the Three Areas; I got the impression that a distinction would be drawn between Abyei on the one hand and the Nuba Mountains and Southern Blue Nile on the other: over the latter two there would be less flexibility. I now also heard for the first time that the government would be willing to accept standing SPLA forces in the South during the interim period. Dr. Ghazi stated that wealth sharing was among the easier issues and could now be settled quickly, and that the issue of the Presidency could be resolved as part of a total package towards the end of the negotiations. I reverted to the proposal for a summit, in two rounds: one to reaffirm what had already been agreed and to set the course for continued talks; and, after progress had been made, another to sort out final issues. The response was the same as in my previous meetings.

Based on the lengthy discussions with Garang and Ghazi, I concluded that the gulf between the parties was not narrowing. The problem areas seemed quite clear, though. For the SPLM the Three Areas and security were the most difficult issues, while for the government the status of the capital and of the Nuba Mountains and Southern Blue Nile seemed to be red line issues, with the presidency and security somewhat less crucial. It was also obvious that there was a lot of impatience in Khartoum, and that the forces that were ready to "let the South go" appeared to have become stronger. I recall being somewhat disappointed with Khartoum's reluctance to move on the summit issue.

Upon returning to Norway on the 19th I briefed Clare Short by telephone. When I mentioned what Ghazi had said about secession, Clare stated that it would certainly be legitimate for the South to secede if a referendum favoured that. To me the possibility of secession had been very clearly a core element of the Machakos Protocol, but this was the first time I had heard a British minister accept it in such a way. Clare was the principal driver of the Sudan portfolio during this period and her views were critical.

I called Dr. John in early March and briefed him about my discussions in Khartoum. By then talks on the Three Areas had started but had been largely procedural. I urged the SPLM/A Chairman to show flexibility in order to move the negotiations forward. Referring to my own visit to the Nuba Mountains, Garang said that "the arabization process", as he called it, had been stopped in all SPLM/A-controlled areas. About the key issue of "self-determination" in the Three Areas I said it was important to be creative: this could be referred to in many ways, including through terms such as "popular consultations". Dr. John agreed, so long as the democratic rights of the people were upheld.

Prolonged Talks

On April 2nd a second meeting between Bashir and Garang finally took place. President Moi never managed to get the summit he had so wanted: it was his former opponent and successor President Mwai Kibaki who hosted it. The meeting was a success. The two leaders agreed on a timetable to finish the negotiations by the end of June. (They chose not to publish the deadline in case more time proved necessary.) A few days later President Bashir for the first time publicly referred to Garang as the "SPLM-leader" rather than by an epithet, a gesture interpreted very positively in SPLM circles.

The fourth round of negotiations, on security arrangements, was conducted on 6–16 April. A later session, on the Three Areas, chaired by Kenya, ended in late May. Considerable progress was made on wealth-sharing issues during this period, with assistance from the IMF, the World Bank, the Troika and others; a technical, factual and educational approach really helped to narrow the gap between the parties. The talks were led by the Norwegian advisor to the IGAD mediator, Endre Stiansen. Agreement seemed very close. On most other issues, a lot of text had been negotiated and cleared, but key issues still remained on the table, unresolved.

Later in April Dr. John telephoned me with an account of the meeting, in Asmara, of leaders of the National Democratic Alliance. The SPLM had used the opportunity to brief them on the negotiation process, and to start discussions on how an inclusive government could be established after a peace agreement. In this way, constitutional issues had also been addressed. Dr. John reviewed some of the negotiating issues with me, and stated that the principle of two armies during the interim period needed to be accepted before the SPLM could compromise on other questions. He also expressed dissatisfaction with the IGAD team's management of these particular negotiations. Regarding militias (called "other armed forces" in the negotiations), Garang rejected outright any notion of their representation in the talks. The SPLM regarded these groups as Khartoum's proxies in destabilizing the South, and saw the idea of including them in negotiations as completely cynical. Overall Dr. John was relatively optimistic, but warned against artificial deadlines and doubted that the talks would be completed by July. He was clearly not in a rush.

It was during this period, at the end of April, that we received reports of a surge in fighting in Darfur. We were increasingly worried. Information reached us also that the SPLM/A might be involved in supplying the rebel groups in Darfur with weapons. An SPLM/A statement expressing support for the rebels did not help. We on the Norwegian side warned that such support would be destructive of the IGAD negotiations and that their statement undermined the Memorandum of Understanding on cessation of hostilities, which was supposed to apply to the whole country. Garang denied that the SPLM/A had provided support to the rebel groups.

By that time Clare Short, my friend and colleague, had been through a very difficult period of discussions on Iraq within the British cabinet and directly with Prime Minister Blair. In early March Clare told me she had threatened to resign if certain conditions were not met and a decision to go to war in Iraq was made without the backing of the UN Security Council. Her conditions included making a major effort to resolve the Israel–Palestine conflict and ensuring that the UN had overall responsibility for the reconstruction of Iraq.[28] Realizing that her conditions had not been met, on 12 May 2003 she resigned as Secretary of State for International Development. This was a great setback both for the development community and for cooperation on Sudan. Baroness Amos took over the development portfolio in the British government. Despite attempts to establish close working relations, cooperation with the UK suffered from the change of leadership. Sudan was never high on the agenda of the new Secretary of State.

Clare Short's departure occurred at a critical stage of the negotiations. Just before this, on April 30th–May 1st, she and Jack Straw, the Foreign Secretary, received in London the Sudanese First Vice President, Ali Osman Taha; State Secretary Yahia Husein Babikir; and Under Secretary Mutrif Siddiq. Walter Kansteiner came from Washington to discuss with Taha both the terrorism agenda and the peace talks. As Taha himself said recently:

> It was in the meeting with Kansteiner I gave the main message, that we were ready to accept two armies in the country, SAF and the SPLA. Kansteiner came to London to talk to me specifically about this issue. I understood that this was the main focus of his visit. I also used the press conference to give another important signal: When asked about the position of the Vice President, and whether I was ready to step down if an agreement was reached, I said yes.[29]

Taha has confirmed that his object in giving these assurances was to show the SPLM/A that the government meant business. Asked whether he saw the London visit as a turning point, he said: "Yes, it was."

From Walter Kansteiner we also heard that the two armies would need a coordinating body of some kind, a Joint Defence Council or Board. The two armies' functions, including the role of the Sudanese Armed Forces in the South, would have to be clarified. Details of the future integration of the two armies after the interim period could be negotiated later. Regarding red lines, Taha had been very clear in London that arrangements during the interim period must not prejudge the outcome of a referendum. The role of militias and "other armed groups", and possible guarantees from the SPLM side, were also discussed. The Vice President had no objection to international monitoring of the ceasefire and security arrangements. Taha had also talked about the peace process in general: a much stronger and direct engagement of the parties was needed than the IGAD talks had so far provided.

Furthermore, from a contact in the UK, Col Ding, we heard that Taha had been very concerned about the situation in Darfur. He was worried that fighting could spread to the east and Kassala. The First Vice President had said he was committed to finish the talks by June 30th. Another meeting between President Bashir and the SPLM/A Chairman was apparently under discussion, this time with Ali Osman Taha taking part. Taha had repeated his willingness to vacate the First Vice Presidency for the Chairman of the SPLM/A. At this juncture, he did not want to delay elections in the interim period, as the SPLM/A had requested.

In the Shadows: Col Ding

One of our best informants during the whole peace process was Dr. Col D. Ding[30]. He was an old friend of Dr. John and, as the SPLM/A's de facto representative in the UK, an important operator behind the scenes. The two men came from the same area north of Bor, but first met while attending Rumbek 2 School during the early 1960s, when Col was two years ahead of Garang. The school strike throughout the South in October 1962 led to their expulsion, but they kept in touch over the years. After they both returned from their studies abroad Dr. John married Rebecca, a relative of Col, and they became close friends. As a medical doctor who had lived in Cairo, Col had high-level contacts in both Egypt and in Sudanese government circles, including the Armed Forces, which were useful to the movement. When Col visited Dr. John at Gambela, Ethiopia in 1984 they agreed on his informal role as the "hub" of the SPLM/A's network in Europe, mobilizing political and military support, providing information, giving political advice, and acting as a go-between with important contacts. Over the years Col was on the phone with the Chairman very frequently, normally several times a week, and became one of his closest advisors.

The Norwegian side had its own contacts within the SPLM/A, and diplomatic representation in Khartoum, giving us most of the information we needed. If we wanted to understand more of what was really going on behind the scenes, however, Col Ding was our contact. From his office in the hospital at Norwich he often had better knowledge than almost anyone else. It was natural, then, that Col Ding was approached when Ali Osman Taha wanted to meet the Chairman of the SPLM/A. Interestingly, this was not in May or June 2003, but in November 1990. An intermediary had told him that Ali Osman wanted to visit him in Norwich. Taha had no government position; Col Ding did not know who he was, nor did Dr. John. Col called Abel Alier, who told him that Ali Osman was the most important person in the NIF movement, second only to Turabi, and operating primarily behind the scenes of the newly established government. Col agreed to meet, and Taha came to his house in Norwich. He brought three security guards and two advisors with him, one of whom was Mathiang Malual Mabur, a Southerner who was Sudan's ambassador in Romania. Ali Osman Taha began the meeting by acknowledging the massacre of the Chiefs in Bor and Jonglei in 1967, and at his request Col told the full story behind the SPLM/A. They talked for six hours. Taha explained why he wanted to meet John Garang: only direct talks would yield results in the South. Col Ding replied that the SPLM/A wished to talk only with a formally mandated government representative with cabinet rank.

When Col reported this conversation, Garang asked him to maintain the contact. Six months later, as Minister of Social Affairs (an omnibus ministry with many portfolios), and with the Sudanese ambassador to London in tow, Taha returned to Norwich. The Abuja negotiations were going nowhere, and Taha believed that Garang's direct involvement was needed. He repeated his request for a meeting with the Chairman. Dr. John was still skeptical: he had no interest in a media event. After this Taha visited Col in Norwich twice more, in 1993 and again in 1997, by which time he was Minister of Foreign Affairs. Each time he had the same errand. And each time Col Ding had reasons why a meeting with the Chairman could not take place.

In 1997 Elijah Majok went as a secret envoy to Taha on behalf of John Garang, and arrangements were made for a rendezvous at the Hilton Hotel in Norwich. Now it was Ali Osman Taha who allegedly "dodged" a meeting, according to Ding. It was indeed later confirmed that his excuse – delay in getting a visa – had been a pretense. Taha went instead to Nairobi to meet Lam Akol, and tried from there to arrange a meeting with Garang. Taha was evidently uninterested in seeing another middleman.

After Taha had become First Vice President, Col Ding met him in London at least twice, in 2000 and in April or May 2003. Again, the same discussion took place. But at the time of the latter meeting the IGAD peace talks seemed to be on the verge of collapse. It was during this London visit, in discussions with the Americans and with Col Ding in private, that Taha gave new and important signals to the SPLM/A. The two of them discussed the situation for five hours. Col told Taha that Dr. Ghazi should be removed as the government's chief negotiator and that he should take over himself. Col said: "Better you than President Bashir".[31]

Even more people were involved in this process. Col Ding and Abel Alier were in-laws of long acquaintance. They had met before Col went to Cairo to study on a scholarship arranged by Nhial Deng's father, and had kept in touch throughout the years; the relationship would prove useful long before the talks and later for both sides in the negotiations. Col often turned to Abel for information and advice. Abel could reach Ali Osman Taha and other government officials, if convenient through Ambassador Mathiang, who was also a relative of Col. Virtually all communication was by telephone, and since the lines were tapped this involved risk. But they were all Dinkas, so Col developed code words in their own language. The word for Turabi was "malieet", meaning "dust"; for Bashir the name was "mior nang nom", "the bull that is tied by its horns". Ali Osman Taha's Dinka codeword meant "our friend", an interesting choice in light of later events, but at this time likely a reflection only of Col's assessment. There was no code word for Dr. Ghazi, but the Southerners had jokingly called him the "Mullah of the Hotels" during the talks, referring to the fact that he spent most of his time during sessions at hotels far away from the negotiation sites, and SPLM/A delegates never saw him. Contact between Col and Abel Alier would prove very important as the negotiations proceeded, not least when they moved to the higher levels. They linked up with Dr. John when need be, using the code words. In later years Ambassador Mathiang would also assist Alier in direct communication with Garang, using his own phone and a special code that had been arranged with Dr. John's nearest aide.

After Ali Osman had pursued talks with Dr. John for years, he called on the Southern leaders he had consulted from time to time, asking: "Should I give up?" Abel Alier, Ambassador Mathiang and other Southern leaders in Khartoum encouraged him to continue. It was their view that Ali Osman was the only one who for several reasons could make peace with the South. They believed that Dr. John would come around. "And eventually this happened," Mathiang said with a smile when recounting these conversations.[32] Four months later the meeting finally took place.

A Change in Tactics

The fifth round of the negotiations started in early May. The strategy this time was to find a comprehensive solution. The mediators presented an open agenda to each of the parties separately, asking for their positions on all the issues, and on which basis they would look for common ground and trade-offs. Dr. Ghazi Salahuddin, the main negotiator on the government side, liked the possibility of trade-offs between the different issues. But Garang was unhappy with the new approach and deeply suspicious of the government's positions; he viewed their expressed willingness to negotiate as a cover for very tough terms. Dr. John appealed for a much stronger role and heavier investment from the Troika.

Garang was quite emboldened, however, by a successful visit to Cairo at the beginning of May when, at President Mubarak's invitation, he had provided a briefing on the status of the talks and his discussions with President Bashir. The Chairman had taken the opportunity to express also his concern about the role of First Vice President Taha, whose alleged links to the Security forces and Popular Defence Force made trust impossible. It was his opinion that the Egyptians became more receptive towards the SPLM/A's positions during the visit. He had tried to reassure them that the SPLM/A would honour Sudan's agreements relating to the Nile waters. Observer status for Egypt in the IGAD framework was discussed, and the SPLM/A was offered observer status in the Arab League, an invitation that apparently created shock waves in Khartoum. President Bashir also paid a visit to Cairo at this time, but we got no information about the discussions that took place.

Despite Garang's *tour de force* in Cairo, the SPLM delegation to the peace talks had very little room for manoeuvre. They had no mandate from the leadership to engage in trade-offs of any kind, so they stuck to their positions. Dr. Ghazi complained that the SPLM leadership and their delegation at Machakos were playing "ping-pong", each always referring to the other when decisions were supposed to be made. In a mid-May meeting with our team he referred to the lack of movement on the SPLM/A side, questioning whether they were really into it. He answered the question himself, saying: Likely not! He signalled willingness to move on issues such as the First Vice Presidency – if the government was accommodated in other areas, such as political representation and if there was no re-opening of the *Sharia* issue. In other critical areas, such as the two armies, Dr. Ghazi indicated positions less accommodating than those that had been indicated by Taha in London. Based on the talks so far, he did not think that the end-of-June timetable would hold, but he was still fairly optimistic about reaching a deal. He agreed that a stronger role for the Troika would be useful, especially in this comprehensive phase of negotiations.

Dr. Ghazi referred ominously to SPLM/A support for the rebel groups in Darfur. This was completely unacceptable; it indicated that the Movement wanted the whole country to fall apart. Khartoum would repeat this accusation many times in the course of negotiations. The SPLM/A strategy, in this view, was to weaken the government and the ruling party by strengthening the opposition everywhere, and thus to win more concessions for itself. As we shall see, both parties may have miscalculated in this respect.

The fifth round ended on May 21st. Although the atmosphere had been less antagonistic, important issues remained unsettled: security, the Three Areas, the presidency, political representation in the government and parliament, and the status of the capital; a lot of progress had been made only on wealth sharing. The government side had appeared more flexible than the SPLM/A, for example by signalling willingness to accept two armies. But there was a collective sense that the talks had reached a point where neither party would compromise on remaining points without a broader trade-off. The IGAD secretariat, with the full involvement of the Troika, was expected to suggest a package or framework. The next round was scheduled for June 23rd. While the government wanted a quick deal, the SPLM/A was in no rush.

Building a Constituency

It was therefore not a surprise when the SPLM/A moved on the political front. In late May, Garang, Sadiq al-Mahdi (Umma) and Mohamed Osman al-Mirghani (Democratic Unionists) convened the so-called Summit Meeting of the Opposition. The outcome, the "Cairo Declaration", upheld the unity of Sudan, supported the Machakos peace process, and called for a national capital with equality for all citizens. That last point was particularly provocative, for it aligned with the SPLM/A those traditional Northern political parties that had religious credentials.[33] The government denounced the Declaration, but was put on the defensive. Its discomfiture was worsened when the SPLM/A and Hasan al-Turabi's Popular Congress Party reached a similar deal, which made no specific provision for the Islamic character of Khartoum but merely stressed that it should be the national capital.

Garang proceeded to Washington, London and other capitals. He had long meetings with the Americans. When General Powell told him that President Bush wanted an agreement by the summer, Garang replied that the lesson of the Addis Ababa Agreement was that a good deal was preferable to a quick one. From these discussions the Americans also concluded that retention of its army was a fundamental issue for the SPLM/A. On the Three Areas Dr. John seemed more flexible, although insisting that the populations must be consulted. On the capital his clear minimum was some sort of secular enclave in Khartoum. Garang still wanted the power-sharing arrangements to include a rotating presidency; the Americans recommended that he accept a Vice Presidency. They also warned that stalling while hoping for regime change in Khartoum would likely lead to the collapse of negotiations.

I had a long talk with the Chairman after this trip. He was pleased with the visit to the US, less so with his meetings in London. Clare Short had left office, the discussions were "not as conducive", and Ambassador Alan Goulty seemed to be "calling the shots" in the absence of engagement at the political level. A Foreign Office Arabist of the old school, with postings in Khartoum (twice), Washington and Cairo, Goulty had been the Foreign Office's Director for the Middle East and North Africa before becoming the UK envoy for Sudan in 2002. He knew the political elite in Khartoum, spoke fluent Arabic, and had a very good understanding of what was going on in the country – especially in the North. From the very beginning Goulty had been sceptical about the deal that Short had advocated, which included a referendum for the South with the option of secession.[34] He never directly voiced such concerns with the Troika or the SPLM/A, but he was easy to read. Leading figures in the SPLM/A jokingly called him "Mr. Guilty", apparently in reference to the legacy of the Anglo-Egyptian Condominium.[35] Dr. John therefore looked elsewhere. A visit to Sudan, including the South, by Baroness Amos, Clare Short's successor, might help.

In our conversation Dr. John reiterated a willingness to show flexibility, referring to interesting ideas for compromise that had been discussed with the Americans. He was clear, however, that any compromise proposal had to come from the negotiation team or the Troika, not the parties themselves. He wanted the Troika to approve in advance any framework that General Sumbeiywo might propose. Dr. John also wanted to discuss the issue of the capital with President Bashir directly, on the telephone. With the support of out-of-office political leaders in the North, there was now broad agreement that the capital's status should reflect the diversity of the country. Garang was impressed with the way President Bashir had avoided rhetorical references to *Sharia* in his public statements lately; in this view Bashir might be ready for a compromise. I warned that this was an extremely delicate issue for the government, but I encouraged such direct contacts between the two; the Troika had long pressed the SPLM/A leadership for such consultations. Dr. John replied that the problem was what Taha would do. Despite his early contacts with Col Ding and persistent efforts to meet, Ali Osman remained a sinister figure in the Chairman's mind, and Garang referred at this juncture to the issue of the capital and *Sharia* as a potential pretext for a military coup.

Garang did acknowledge, however, the importance of the role of the First Vice President, and knew that any agreement with the government would need at least his acquiescence.[36] Garang now told me that the SPLM would accept a Vice Presidency as part of a power-sharing arrangement, thus implying willingness to drop the demand for a rotating Presidency. This illustrates what for Garang and the SPLM/A was a constant dilemma: the tension between his vision of a New Sudan, which implied reform at the centre and a process of transformation; and the need to secure the fundamental interests of Southern Sudan, including the referendum. It goes without saying that the government position was, as much as possible, maintenance of the status quo: the object was to limit change to the minimum necessary for a deal. Which would prove more important to Garang and the Movement – the New Sudan or Southern Sudan? Difficult choices had to be made.

The parties were to convene in late June for what was meant to be a "take-it-or-leave -it" round, after which the only remaining issues would be the final security arrangements and the fate of the Three Areas. General Sumbeiywo visited Khartoum in early June, and the Three Areas and the South towards the end of the month, to consult the parties about a final deal. The plan was to present a Draft Framework Agreement at the next round.

Meanwhile the conflict in Darfur was escalating. The government had reportedly transferred ten thousand soldiers to the West. Despite this, they were suffering repeated defeats. In Dr. John's view, the government was now under great pressure; according to his information, a "siege mentality" was building in Khartoum, and this was the likely reason for the government's anxiety to conclude negotiations. I responded that, if true, this was indeed a good reason for the SPLM/A to act expeditiously. The SPLM Chairman agreed, but stressed – as usual – that any agreement had to lead to a "just peace".

Darfur Goes from Blister to Fire

When the SPLM/A issued a statement welcoming the launch of the Sudan Liberation Movement/Army's manifesto, it referred to a solution for Three Areas as a possible model for Darfur. According to one authoritative account,[37] the Darfurians rejected that idea: they deserved more substantial concessions. On the other hand an overall peace agreement between the government and the SPLM/A might provide a framework for negotiations on Darfur. For the SPLM/A the comprehensive peace agreement must come first: its principles should be applied to Darfur through a separate process. Throughout 2003 this seemed a plausible position. None of the power-sharing arrangements had been negotiated yet, so there was no model to emulate in relation to Darfur. Moreover the two principal rebel groups there had joined hands, and appeared to be growing stronger. The Darfur rebellion, more serious than the government had appreciated, now seemed to pose a greater threat than the unresolved conflict with the SPLM/A.

In April 2003 the combined forces of the Darfur rebel groups launched a spectacular attack on the capital, El Fasher. Government aircraft were destroyed on the ground, and the Air Force commander was taken prisoner. A string of successful rebel attacks took place over the next few months. The fate of the government itself seemed at stake, and it responded with a major counteroffensive. Until then it had relied mainly on proxies against the Masalit, Fur and Zaghawa, including the Popular Defence Forces (PDF), a paramilitary organization with a shadowy command structure. The use of militia to control or "clean up" areas of interest had been a feature of Khartoum's policy for decades. PDF had been recruited from among Muslim northerners for operations in Southern Sudan.

Now, the Khartoum-supported PDF and Arab militia or mere *janjawid* bandits operated on a larger scale, attacking villages, burning them to the ground, and killing people. This was, after all, a well-established counter-insurgency strategy; instead of sending in regular forces, local militia could do the job of controlling areas of strategic importance. This had been the case for years in relation to the Nuba Mountains, Bahr al-Ghazal, and areas of the Blue Nile, where Arab tribal *murahalin* had operated in ways echoing the conduct of the slave trade in the 19th century.

During the period of conflict, according to multiple sources, atrocities had been committed by these militia, in some cases on a large scale, with or without aerial bombardment, clearing large areas of civilians through a scorched-earth policy that included widespread attacks on civilians and systematic rape. Whether the purpose was to control an area of economic importance, such as the oil-exploration regions of Upper Nile, or the purpose was security, the same tactics were used. The government could remain above the fray, and dismiss outrages as episodes of inveterate "tribal" enmity. But the government's hand in this violence, through various organs (Military Intelligence, Security, the Ministry of the Interior, or other less formal entities) was common knowledge. Only the leaders were paid; their gangs seemed to be licensed to loot. In this way a low-intensity conflict could be conducted over a long time, ensuring control – though hardly "government" – without the formalities of a full-scale military operation or war. This method was also more easily veiled from the international community.

After the successful rebel attacks in Darfur in 2003, the government seemed to resort to the same counter-insurgency tactics, but the sheer scale of the operation indicated a different level of engagement and direct involvement. PDF forces and *janjawid* became indistinguishable, and worked in concert with government air and ground forces. While the PDF were under direct orders from certain quarters in Khartoum, the *janjawid* increasingly joined in without direction of higher authority. Now the time for low-intensity counter-insurgency seemed to be over. Although the methods remained the same (and were all too familiar to SPLM/A veterans from the South and the Three Areas), the scale was vastly greater. Several rebel leaders said that in the first half of 2003 Darfur was on the brink of "Southern Sudan speeded up".[38] Dr. John told me on several occasions that Khartoum had lost control over the counter-insurgency, unlike in the other areas. There would later be reason to question this assessment about loss of control: the government seemed to have deliberately opted for a more aggressive strategy over a shorter period of time in Darfur than it had elsewhere.

Janjawid was a term commonly used for bandits. Some Arabs resented this characterization of the militia, but the label stuck. In June, Musa Hilal, the notorious Rizeigat leader, was released from prison at Khartoum's orders,[39] and continued to recruit, eventually claiming to have some 20,000 men under his command.[40] These were a motley collection of local Arabs, tribesmen from neighbouring countries (Chad, Libya, even Mauritania), and outlaws – including convicts. His command centre was at Misteriya. Substantial weaponry was supplied, not only from abroad, but also, from mid-2003 onwards, in significant amounts by the government. It was after this that the *janjawid* were unleashed as part of a seemingly coordinated military operation.

Unlike the SPLM/A, which was never thought able to supplant Khartoum, the Darfur rebellion threatened the government at its core. Both the importance of that Western region, and the close if imponderable ties between Hasan al-Turabi and several of the rebel movements there, imbued the threat from the West with the potential for "regime change". This was Garang's analysis, too. Thus the Darfurian rebel attack on Omdurman in 2008 had more than symbolic importance. The spectre of overthrow, however unrealistic, had a decisive impact on the government's strategy in the West, and contributed to its anathematising of a fragmented Sudan consisting of autonomous regions.

At this stage, my own and my colleagues' focus remained on the negotiations for the South, and on creating conditions for a just peace nationally. That conflict had had by far the direst humanitarian consequences, in terms of the numbers of dead, internally displaced, and refugees. The rebel attack on El Fasher awakened us. But even then we did not apprehend the scale of what was about to unfold in Darfur. As the government and SPLM/A negotiated at full force to resolve Sudan's main conflict, the "blister" of previous decades had turned into a conflagration.

Heated Discussions

The need for progress in the IGAD talks was becoming urgent. The negotiating team, supported by the observers, had decided to move the talks from Machakos and Karen to Nakuru, the distance of which from Nairobi and the media might help to speed up the process at this decisive moment. I fully supported the move. Both delegations had expressed frustration with so many external observers and stakeholders. But we would also need to inject new ideas in order to save the talks from stalling completely.

We had agreed with General Sumbeiywo to walk through some of the remaining issues and try to take a new approach. A draft Framework Agreement was virtually ready from the secretariat. This derived from an old tactic, the "Mediator's Draft", to force the parties to take a stand. Fink Haysom had worked continuously on this,[41] in collaboration with the advisers and observers from the Troika.[42] The result was called a "Draft Framework for Resolution of Outstanding Issues Arising out of the Elaborations of the Machakos Protocol". The draft had input from both parties throughout the talks, and from shuttling between them. More than 90 percent of the draft originated from the parties themselves, who had seen elements of the text during the process. The Kenyan foreign minister's consultations with IGAD countries also contributed to the draft.

A basic question remained: How to create a unified government based in Khartoum? Why should the SPLM join it? At the very least, why should not the national capital be more neutrally located? Everyone knew that the National Congress Party would never agree: A "New Sudan" perhaps, but not a new capital! The idea of two capitals was also floated, but was also unacceptable to Khartoum. But how could the SPLM be expected to cooperate in a capital under *Sharia* law and the aegis of Sudan's numerous security services? The Troika discussed this quite extensively during the spring, on the margins of the negotiations and with the parties. My experts were clear: If Khartoum was to be the capital, it had to be made acceptable to both sides.

I thought a special arrangement was most sensible. Our object was to preserve the unity of Sudan.

At this juncture, and with larger trade-offs needed for a comprehensive deal, General Sumbeiywo expressed concern that the Troika might take full control of the negotiations. He was particularly apprehensive about the role of the Americans.[43] The events leading to this concern may be briefly surveyed.

In preparation for the Nukuru round Sumbeiywo had agreed to let the Troika examine and comment upon the draft framework. His lawyers and advisors would make their case, and the Troika would respond. We hoped that this would be beneficial not only to the negotiating team but also to the process, for there was as yet no common position even among us on some of the key issues. The preparatory meeting in London was joined by the British envoy, Alan Goulty; Mike Ranneberger from the US; and the Norwegians Ellefsen and Aschjem. From the IGAD team were Fink Haysom and Endre Stiansen, Norway's member of the IGAD team. The task at hand made everyone feel the burden of responsibility.

Substantive differences came into the open during these discussions. On important issues in the framework document the UK favoured either vagueness or positions closer to Khartoum's. The US and Norway, on the other hand, wanted clarity on all key points: the time had come for decisions, for the parties to "take it or leave it". This was the rationale also behind the "Mediator's Draft", usually a dangerous strategy but sometimes worth the risk. If the parties rejected the document, it was up to them to find a way forward. The discussions in London were very heated. Alan Goulty disagreed both on strategy and on several substantive points. On a number of the remaining issues it was pretty clear where compromise was needed. The draft included language on power sharing, and called for two Vice Presidents, one for each side, but not a rotating presidency.

Many of the points in the Nakuru document were closer to those the negotiations had already reached than most people would have thought possible. But several issues remained. Regarding political representation, the draft was based on demographic calculations and an assumption of power sharing between the two negotiating partners. Wealth-sharing arrangements largely allocated oil income on a 48/52 basis between the North and South. On the all-important question of security arrangements the document provided for two armies, but with arrangements for withdrawal of government forces from the South left for later,[44] a desideratum of obvious concern to the SPLM/A.[45] The Nakuru draft also proposed a Truth and Reconciliation process, which neither side never took up.[46]

Much of our London meeting dealt with the issue of the national capital.[47] I had given my people very clear instructions: They were not to accept anything but a solution permitting Southerners to move freely around town without fear of harassment by police or other government agents. Some kind of special arrangement had to be devised: the status quo was not an option. A capital respecting all citizens of the country would be an important way of preserving the unity of Sudan, making it a more attractive option for Southerners.

Alan Goulty now stated firmly that we must not propose or endorse a draft framework agreement that took clear positions that, for example, favoured the SPLM/A's points of view. The status of the capital was an issue that the parties needed to sort out themselves. The parties had agreed at Machakos that *Sharia* should be the law of the North, as defined by the 1956 borders. Khartoum was part of that deal and was going to be the capital. Anything that interfered with this line would be rejected outright by the ruling party. The Norwegian and American representatives argued differently. They referred to the need for each side, when in government, to conduct business without risking interference by the other party. They noted several models for neutral arrangements for capitals, and that even the US had established a capital immune to state legislation; a similar arrangement was possible for Khartoum. The talks lasted for three or four hours before a break for lunch. The usually stoic Norwegian gentleman Halvor Aschjem was fuming, and Alan Goulty did not seem to be in a much better mood. The atmosphere was tense. No one wanted to give in.

The IGAD advisors, Haysom and Stiansen, tried to be impartial yet in the end had to accept the points made by the US and Norway. What ended up being the most decisive factor was the shared recollection of mediators and observers alike that the status of the capital had not been finally resolved during the July negotiations in Machakos in 2002. It would be hard to explain – let alone to defend – a draft text that did not take into account the new situation after a peace agreement, when two parties were to govern together as a national government in the same capital. The law of the land was one thing; regulation of government business (and everyday living arrangements) had not been dealt with. The meeting ended at 5:00 p.m., seven hours after it had begun. Halvor Aschjem had left earlier to catch a plane for Khartoum. Alan Goulty looked very unhappy. Mike Ranneberger and Vegard Ellefsen left together for the Intercontinental, where Ranneberger was staying. Fink Haysom and Endre Stiansen went to their hotel to ponder the issues. Ellefsen was elated with the way the talks had gone, but was unsure how Haysom and Stiansen would tackle the issue of the capital. I wondered if I should try to reach them, but decided against it. Everyone was exhausted.

Near midnight, however, I got an e-mail message from Ellefsen copying one from Stiansen. The ominous title was, "For Your Eyes Only", and I immediately understood why. The text proposed by Stiansen and the legal experts was identical to the Norwegian-US position on the capital. I took a deep breath. Finally, things seemed to be moving in the right direction. I hoped the trend would continue when the parties met in Nakuru. Meanwhile I had a chance to read the draft more thoroughly. Some parts were perfect; others needed elaboration. I called Vegard Ellefsen as he arrived at Nakuru and suggested a number of adjustments.

Talks in Need of Life-Support: The Near-Collapse in Nakuru

Later I learned that Vegard had arrived in Nairobi without his luggage after delays and almost-missed connections. When I reached him by telephone he was in a sour mood in an Embassy car outside Nakuru lodge. While he was listening to my ideas and proposals, a monkey climbed down from a tree and sat on the hood, toying with the wiper and looking at him. The diplomat later told me that he considered whether to give the phone to the monkey; listening to me was the last thing he wanted just then.

With the reluctant agreement of the UK, the draft framework document was handed to General Sumbeiywo. The sixth round of the peace talks resumed at Nakuru on July 6th. At this juncture, a closed meeting between the general and the mediators was organized for the negotiating team to thrash out details. The general was unhappy, and initially disagreed with the negotiating strategy. The draft contained clear positions on a number of the remaining issues, including the status of the capital. Sumbeiywo thought this would only lead to a breakdown of the talks. Fink Haysom, too, had second thoughts about the issue of the capital, which he thought was a red line for the government. He did not share his doubts at the time, but later told me that he deeply regretted having given in on this point.[48] After lengthy discussions, the Chief Mediator agreed to put the proposals forward. Together the mediators made some adjustments and finalized the Draft Framework Agreement. On the 12th the mediators finally presented it to the parties. As it was distributed, William Patey, the British ambassador, stated clearly that the document reflected the Troika's position. The Norwegian Special Envoy, Vegard Ellefsen, had been the real architect of the "make-or-break" strategy – with my full approval and backing. We knew that the document would provoke heated reactions at the negotiating table, but it was better to get them all out in the open, and force the process to deal with them, than to beat around the bush. We knew that adjustments would be needed, as would serious "massaging" of both parties, before the proposals could – if possible – be accepted.

Although we were aware of the risk, there seemed no other way to move the negotiations forward. As we saw it, the Nakuru talks were the last chance to revive the negotiations and regain the momentum of the first Machakos round. But when General Sumbeiywo presented the draft, the government delegation rejected the proposals outright, threw the document on the table, and stormed out of the room. They called the draft unbalanced, biased and both a departure from and re-opening of the Machakos Protocol. The proposal gave the South far too much autonomy, too much power at the centre, and contributed to a process that could lead to secession during the interim period. Khartoum had expected the opposite: more government authority in the South and a smaller Southern role at the centre. Most unpalatable of all were probably the draft recommendations for the capital.

Having read through the document, the SPLM/A agreed to accept the draft as a "basis for further negotiation". In private, however, the leaders reacted variously. A few were calling the document "Addis Ababa plus" with reference to the security arrangements, and were glad that the government had spoken first and rejected the draft.[49] Others saw the document as generally in accordance with their views, with a few (important) exceptions[50] that would have to be dealt with later. Post-war security was the SPLM/A's biggest concern, specifically the arrangements for the Sudanese Armed Forces' withdrawal from the South. They wisely kept their reservations to themselves, and publicly said little. Privately they were not so reticent, telling us that the document had "blazing defects": besides security, they were unhappy with the sharing of oil revenues. Haysom later told me that – notwithstanding the parties' stated objections – it was the issue of the capital that had tipped the balance.[51] Whatever their real views, the question that concerned us was whether the parties were ready to finalize *any* agreement at this level, and at this time. In the observers' opinion, it was the format as much as the substance that had to be changed: "negotiation by proxy", as one member of the government delegation later put it, "was not working".[52] We wanted the negotiations to be conducted at a higher level. Still, the government walkout surprised many of us. The UK ambassador to Khartoum, William Patey, sitting in for Alan Goulty, looked at the US and Norwegian envoys with an expression that said: What now?

No one represented the government's reaction better than the President himself, who was quoted by Agence France-Presse on 14 July 2003 as saying that if the IGAD mediators did not come up with something better they could "go to Hell". The government started to mobilize support for its position. They made overtures to the old parties and to prominent individuals. There were rumours that the government would try to scrap the IGAD-framework altogether. The African Union's foreign ministers were meeting at Maputo soon after and, sure enough, a proposal was floated for the AU to take over the Sudan negotiations. We got the Norwegian State Secretary, Vidar Helgesen, to ask the South African foreign minister for help in preventing this. Colin Powell also called the South Africans. The Kenyan foreign minister, Stephen Kalonzo Musyoka, convened an IGAD ministerial meeting, at Maputo, to galvanize support for continuing the talks under IGAD auspices.[53] These interventions were effective, and the AU in fact endorsed the IGAD process to resolve the Sudan conflict.

Just before its departure from Nakuru, the government delegation presented a series of proposals and amendments to the Draft Framework Agreement, some more restrictive than those they had previously mooted. Attempts to bring the two parties together, either in direct talks or with mediators, failed: they ended up shouting at each other. At the working level the government also tabled conditions for returning to the negotiating table, which included revision of the draft agreement. In Khartoum, Ali Osman Taha had by now succeeded Dr. Ghazi, at the latter's initiative, as chairman of the government's high-level committee for peace.[54] Taha had been following the negotiations very closely, almost day by day.

What Now?

It was now clear that the parties would not reconvene before August. The Americans were beginning to get nervous about finalising an agreement before their October deadline, when a new report on Sudan was due in Congress. A flurry of diplomatic activity was initiated, with General Sumbeiywo and the IGAD envoys visiting the parties and as many other high-level contacts as possible, and asking the heads of state and government in the IGAD region to engage with the parties. General Powell had been on the phone with Ali Osman before the Nakuru round ended, and had asked John Garang to talk to President Bashir. We thought that a meeting of the two leaders might lead to progress in the talks. Some observers of the negotiations were privately speculating about whether the IGAD format had reached a dead end. It had certainly shown signs of fatigue.

Although the framework document had been risky and controversial, events were to show that the strategy behind it worked. Almost a month after Nakuru and shortly after the AU meeting, the Norwegian envoy, on holiday in his hometown, received a call from the *eminence grise* in Norwich, Col Ding, who had been in regular contact with my people and me. Now he said that there had been a meeting in Khartoum about what to do in light of the Nakuru events. Even Abel Alier had been asked for advice. The result was quite stunning: the First Vice President, Ali Osman Taha, would replace Dr. Ghazi as chief negotiator. President Bashir had apparently agreed, although few knew this yet. Ellefsen called Mike Ranneberger immediately. Using a term familiar in tough international negotiations he said, "They blinked!" We knew the whole negotiating process would now change. In what way, however, it was too early to say.

Dr. John remained sceptical. On August 4th in Nairobi I had met him and other key members of the SPLM/A leadership. The Chairman continued to aver that Ali Osman Taha considered the peace talks a threat to his future chances of assuming the Presidency. At the same time, Dr. John was aware of the discussions taking place between Taha and Abel Alier. In a private talk with me he confirmed that Taha had put to Alier a series of proposals, which Col Ding had passed to Garang. These dealt with power-sharing arrangements, the capital, and a political partnership with the SPLM. Garang had not yet responded – he wanted confirmation of President Bashir's endorsement of the demarche and of the proposed discussions between Taha and Garang. He therefore needed to meet Abel Alier for clarification. I stressed the importance of his also calling Bashir directly.

That evening Dr. John rehearsed the SPLM's positions. According to his information, in a recent internal memorandum Dr. Ghazi had reportedly indicated a "status quo plus" settlement, which the SPLM/A would never accept. The Chairman brought up the issue of the capital, and the importance of a secular enclave, not least for the cause of unity. He signalled new proposals in relation to the Nakuru framework document. It was clear to him that the government was under pressure, and that it wanted to avoid taking the difficult decisions needed for the peace process to go forward. At my urging he promised to reflect on concessions the SPLM/A could make that would be meaningful to Khartoum.

A published report from this period, later confirmed by both sides, stated that the Nakuru document was a turning point in Sudanese politics, north and south.[55] Faced with the prospect of entering the final stretch of yearlong negotiations with little political or diplomatic backing, the government suddenly relaxed its repression of the internal political opposition and initiated serious talks with them. The aim seemed to be to trade a commitment to democratization in the post-agreement period for support in the final rounds of talks with the SPLM/A. In their own way, they were trying to start another peace process, from "within". A so-called Peace Forum was inaugurated, and on August 9th – in the first meeting he had ever held with both opposition and pro-government political parties and civil society organizations – the President even pledged to lift restrictions on freedom of the press, assembly, and movement, as well as to free remaining political prisoners. But old habits die hard. The two key Northern parties, the Umma and Democratic Unionists, soon turned their backs, and there was little sign of real change in the government's policies and practices.[56]

Meanwhile Garang made significant inroads of his own, travelling to Cairo to meet Sadiq al-Mahdi, Mohamed Osman al-Mirghani, and the Egyptians. It was clear that the long moribund Joint Egyptian Libyan Initiative was truly dead. The regional and international players supported the IGAD peace process, as did the African Union, South Africa, and Nigeria. He claimed that even Egypt, Libya and the Arab League had now become supportive, focusing mainly on the importance of making unity attractive for the South.[57] I am not sure that the Sudanese government felt cornered, but any debate about abandoning the IGAD process must have concluded that this was no longer feasible.

"Killing" the IGAD initiative without an alternative would have been a foreign-relations disaster for the government. The Americans had continued to press for a settlement. The US envoy, Jack Danforth, had visited Sudan in July. His discussions in Khartoum were candid, and put pressure on the government to re-engage. His meeting with Garang was even tougher. The two of them were never on very good terms: Danforth had in the past stood up to the SPLM/A Chairman, and now he insisted on accelerated progress in the talks and willingness to compromise. I recall Dr. John's ambiguous summary of the discussion: with a sly face he jokingly said, "My memories about that meeting are very poor".

It was in this context that the government had made its strategic decision.

On August 11th the two sides met again, at Nanyuki in Kenya. Bilateral consultations after the opening session were needed to resolve difficult procedural issues, including confusion about which text should be used as the basis for negotiation. But the government had a much softer approach this time, and informally and indirectly expressed regret for their management of the situation at Nakuru. Although they never actually accepted the document as a basis for negotiations, their clear intention was to get the job done. Ways were found for the government to save face and for the talks to proceed without direct reference to the document, and by focusing on the issues separately rather than on the text. In his report to me Vegard Ellefsen said: "It seems that the government has changed strategy entirely and sent the whole delegation on a 'smiling course'." The parties even decided to engage in direct talks, without a mediator or any international participation. This was unprecedented. They went through all the remaining issues and stated their positions. While the SPLM emphasized security issues, the government was most concerned with governance issues and the capital. Still, the head of the SPLM/A delegation, Nhial Deng, and the Troika agreed that a summit would be needed in order to reach agreement. And this was going to happen sooner than any of us expected.

CHAPTER FOUR

From Enemies to Partners in Peace

On August 31st Ali Osman Taha made the call to Oslo, a decisive move in getting high-level negotiations started. As outlined earlier, any of a number of developments, or more likely several of them combined, would seem to have been behind this decision and the timing of the initiative. Darfur was spiralling out of control. The rebellion had dramatically escalated with attacks on El Fasher and Nyala, the capitals of North and South Darfur respectively. While the rebel factions wanted to negotiate, and to take part in the IGAD negotiations, the government did not want to talk at this stage or to involve the Darfur rebels in the negotiations on the South.

Ali Osman Taha had had strong views on many issues throughout the negotiating process. Always considered a hardliner, he was now rumoured to have teamed up with Nafie Ali Nafie, the powerful Islamist "hawk" in the government's intelligence services. The conventional wisdom at the time was that President Bashir and Dr. Ghazi led the "peace camp", and that any serious effort to negotiate an end of the war would have to contend with Taha. In private, however, several observers thought that Taha was a pragmatist. In this view, he could keep the party together while acting as a bridge to the most "militant" hardliners. As foreign minister, he had been the architect of recent approaches to the West. The current foreign minister, Mustafa Osman Ismail, had less credibility with the hardliners. It was a widespread feeling at the time (as reflected in reports from Justice Africa and the International Crisis Group, among others, including the SPLM/A) that Taha was an unreconstructed "hawk". Nevertheless, on the analogy of Nixon in China, it was this reputation that convinced perceptive observers, that only Taha would be able to negotiate peace with the South. Also among prominent Southerners in Khartoum, this was the feeling, although this assessment had a somewhat different basis. [1]

The Strategic Choice

As we have seen, Taha's interest in meeting the SPLM/A Chairman dated to 1990. But it was only in December 2002, when Obasanjo tried to arrange a meeting, that the Movement's leadership discerned serious interest to negotiate. This was reinforced by signals from Taha's London trip in April–May. [2] Ali Osman Taha called on Abel Alier on July 29th, the first time they had met since the Torit incident. The meeting lasted four hours, covering the IGAD

Declaration of Principles, Machakos, and the unresolved issues. Taha wanted to know what the SPLM/A was willing to give up.[3] Although before Torit Alier had met regularly with Taha and the President, he would later comment that this was the first time Taha had voiced an opinion on these key issues. Alier told him that the SPLM/A was ready to make peace, but that the Movement remained very sceptical about Taha's role in the government, and specifically that the regime's attempts to make "peace from within" by suborning Southerners would not succeed.

Now the SPLM/A leadership detected change. The First Vice President told Alier that the government team would start to work out a solution at the next round of talks. To Alier, Taha seemed to acknowledge that the way the government's rejection of the draft negotiation framework at Nakuru had been conveyed, had not been particularly wise. Influenced by the deteriorating situation in Darfur, Taha and the President were fearful of Sudan in the worst case breaking up like Somalia; they needed to act quickly to get a solution. Taha also indicated readiness to give up his position as First Vice President, but it was clear that he did not plan to sit on the sidelines. A deal between the ruling party and the South would shift the political landscape in any case, and elections during the interim period might offer new opportunities. [4]

Encouraged, Dr. John suggested points for further discussion between Alier and the Vice President. During the second week of August Alier had a series of meetings with Taha and the government's negotiating team. Reviewing the Nakuru document, Taha and the delegation made several concrete proposals, and Alier himself suggested compromises. Altogether Alier met the Vice President four times and members of the negotiation team thrice in what amounted to a dialogue between them and the SPLM/A, with Alier as intermediary. We were informed of the discussions. It seemed that Khartoum meant business.[5]

The government team made important proposals to Abel Alier. They would offer the First Vice Presidency to the SPLM and accept two armies during the interim period. Under the 1972 Addis Ababa Agreement the absorption of the rebel Anya-Nya army had failed, and it was clear now that security arrangements had to include provisions for at least temporary maintenance of the SPLA in the South.[6] The government was less amenable to withdrawing its own forces beyond the 13th parallel. The issue of the capital was really about *Sharia*, and had strong symbolic meaning to them. Concerns over wealth sharing were likely to be easily resolved. On the Three Areas, the government remained unwilling to move in any significant way. Taha baulked at including Darfur and the East in the negotiations, and referred to evidence that the SPLM/A was supporting the Sudan Liberation Movement/Army. But the Vice President was very keen on a political partnership with the SPLM/A, an idea the Movement received with mistrust and to which it responded vaguely. Interestingly, in internal discussions with Taha at this point President Bashir and Dr. Ghazi had allegedly expressed more concern about Darfur's breaking out than about the South.[7]

After these discussions Abel Alier went to Nairobi. He handed all his notes to General Sumbeiywo, and on August 17th had a six-hour meeting with Dr. John. Since their last meeting, in July, Dr. John had also received further information from Col Ding. Now Alier urged the Chairman to enter into direct talks with the government. It was our firm view that the process had come to a crossroads: we would either see top-level engagement and a peace agreement, or the whole thing would collapse.

Although he recognized movement on the government side, Dr. John was still reluctant to meet the Vice President, fearing, he said, that to do so would weaken the position of President Bashir. My own discussions with members of the SPLM leadership in Nairobi in early August indicated support for high-level talks, but that they favoured these on the level of Bashir and Garang or Taha and Salva Kiir. But the Movement knew that a continuing stalemate favoured the government by allowing it, through monopoly of oil revenue, to rearm and rebuild its military strength.

Abel Alier's argument that the SPLM/A should signal future political cooperation before a high-level meeting took place was itself problematic. Within the SPLM there had long been mixed feelings about Abel Alier: he had brokered the Addis Ababa Agreement, which had turned out far too weak for the South; there was ambivalence about his subsequent role, both in the South and in Khartoum. Still, he had proven to be a key player. From informed sources within the movement I was told that up to this point Dr. John had not believed that the government was committed to accepting real change for the country and the South. Now he was changing his mind. There was something in the air. On August 20th General Sumbeiywo, having himself realized that the talks would go nowhere without involvement of the highest level, reached Garang by telephone and got what he regarded as a promise to meet Taha.[8]

The Kenyan foreign minister and chairman of the IGAD sub-committee on Sudan, Stephen Kalonzo Musyoka was visiting Cairo at the time, and at Sumbeiywo's request proceeded to Khartoum to see President Bashir. He wanted permission to invite Ali Osman Taha to Nairobi to meet the SPLM Chairman, but while Bashir was positive he did not immediately commit to the Kenyan initiative.[9] Taha was abroad and unaware of these developments.[10] Meanwhile influential members of the ruling party had gone to the President to request Taha's taking over the peace negotiations in succession to Dr. Ghazi. Bashir thereupon agreed to both the meeting and to the change in the delegation's leadership.[11] The Kenyans formally invited the parties to meet on September 2nd.

Given his extensive consultations with Abel Alier and previous attempts to meet the SPLM/A Chairman, Ali Osman Taha must have been pleased with what had transpired in his absence. His constant goal was the stability and sustainability of the National Congress government in Khartoum. Improving relations with the South by achieving a peace agreement was important to realising that goal. It must be assumed that it was this that had animated his many attempts through Col Ding, from the early 1990s onwards, to engage Garang personally into negotiations. Taking the lead as peacemaker on the government's side could also open new political opportunities for him. By stepping in to control the process the First Vice President maximized his chances – as against those of other factions in the regime – to determine the outcome.

Through Norway's ambassador in Nairobi, Abel Alier urged me in late August to call Dr. John to stress the importance of moving forward with the talks by meeting Taha – as Garang hesitated.[12] The Egyptian foreign minister, Ahmed Maher, had appeared on television, in Musyoka's presence, condemning the SPLM/A and its Chairman and calling self-determination a conspiracy, all in Arabic and on behalf of his Kenyan colleague, who one must assume was unaware. But Dr. John was very upset, and called Musyoka to register his dismay. He was not ready to go to any meeting.[13] Before I was able to place the call to Garang, however, I received one myself.

The Call: Taha Makes the Move

As we have seen, this was the now-famous call from Ali Osman Taha about his coming attendance at the funeral of the Kenyan Vice President in Nairobi, and the suggestion that that event might be a convenient moment for a meeting between the two leaders. The Chairman remained uncertain about Bashir's real views, and about the chances for a substantive meeting – as opposed to a mere "photo op" that could be used for propaganda purposes. I stressed to Dr. John that the President was already on record as encouraging direct contact between him and Taha, and I suggested some agenda points for a meeting. I urged him to talk to Bashir on the telephone, but by hesitating even to do this Garang seemed to be stalling.

We continued to raise the pressure. I got in touch with the Americans, who placed calls to Dr. John. Kjell Hødnebø, my Sudan advisor, did the same with Deng Alor, who was in Nairobi with Justin Yak. They were both convinced about the need for high-level talks, and Deng called the Chairman. Col Ding was also on the phone with Dr. John a number of times, trying to convince him to go.[14] We were in continuous contact with the Americans at this point. At Rumbek there were intense discussions among the SPLM/A's key commanders. The majority advised strongly against any meeting with Taha.[15] If Dr. John should meet anyone, it must be the President, not a deputy, and not now but later.[16] Only three members of the leadership advised the Chairman to meet Taha:[17] Pagan Amum, Lual Diing Wol and James Wani;[18] Elijah Majok also expressed support, but was not a formal member.

Resistance to a meeting continued ominously within the government, too. Through our own sources, we heard that two days of heated debate resulted in Taha's having not only support for the meeting but also a mandate to conclude an agreement with Garang on the remaining issues. But a small group of skeptics who were close to President Bashir, including the Defence Minister Bakri Hasan Salih, secretly approached the SPLM/A[19] to suggest that the

Movement should not cut a deal with Ali Osman Taha, and to offer instead direct talks with Bashir. With Taha's distance from the Army, and the competitive environment in the government, this was not surprising. The SPLM/A was worried, however, and rejected these overtures.

The Nairobi funeral forced the issue. Deng Alor and Justin Yak called the Chairman and reported that Ali Osman Taha had now arrived. The Kenyan foreign minister was already complaining that the SPLM/A leader was late for the meeting. Salva Kiir asked whether Garang had made any promises to countries in the region. When the Chairman acknowledged that such signals had been given to the Kenyans, Kiir weighed in to warn that the whole region would be against the SPLM/A if they at this stage refused to meet with Khartoum.[20] The Kenyans allegedly even threatened to expel the SPLM/A from Kenya altogether if they did not turn up for the talks.[21] We learned later that Taha had reinsured himself by approaching Abel Alier too, who he knew would contact Col Ding and tell him he would wait for the SPLM/A Chairman in Nairobi.[22] Col told Dr. John that if he failed to appear by Wednesday, September 3rd Taha would state publicly that the SPLM/A was not interested in peace.[23] Ali Osman duly waited for three days at the Great Rift Valley Lodge, with the Kenyans and a strong delegation of hardcore government representatives.[24] According to Salva Kiir, Dr. John was shocked that Taha had come first.[25] It certainly added to the pressure. But Garang let them wait.[26] The prospect of having Kenya and the IGAD countries criticizing him, and Khartoum attacking the SPLM/A and him personally, finally proved to be decisive. Atlas shrugged. Garang would meet the First Vice President.

But it must be a brief meeting. He did not want to enter into comprehensive negotiations. Abel Alier had transmitted the necessary assurances from Khartoum: President Bashir was behind the initiative; there was no reason to fear that Dr. John would be used in a power struggle between Bashir and Taha. Dr. John flew from Rumbek to Lokichokio and connected to Nairobi.[27] At the airport in Nairobi Dr. John asked Pagan Amum to draft a statement for the press, which he printed then and there. The statement said that the Chairman of the SPLM/A was ready to negotiate with the government and Vice President Ali Osman Taha – to reach a comprehensive peace agreement. Dr. John also sat down with Alier for a briefing about the government's positions.

As these intramural confabulations went on in Nairobi, members of the Khartoum delegation were losing patience at Naivasha. Taha recalls:

> On the third day in the afternoon, we were actually about to leave. It was 1–2 o'clock when my team said to me: "Enough is enough. Let's leave." We packed our bags and put our luggage in the hall. I said: "Let us wait for another two [or] 3 hours, and see. He may come." The Kenyan foreign minister at the time, Stephen Kalonzo Musyoka and General Sumbeiywo were there too, and pleaded with us to be patient and wait.[28]

And suddenly the team got word that the Chairman of SPLM/A was on his way. Dr. John's plane had touched down a little after 4:00 p.m.[29] Garang drove up to Naivasha, and arrived at the lodge at sunset. Taha continued: "I said to my people: 'There you see. Being patient pays off. That makes the difference.' What if I had left at lunch time?"

Taha and Garang were shown into a room, where Foreign Minister Musyoka introduced them, made some introductory remarks, then left them alone. Taha recalls:

> There was silence. Both of us were thinking 'How do I break the ice?' And we talked about this moment later. After some very long seconds, I was just about to reach for the bottle of water on the table and serve Dr. John. But he had thought the same thing, and was quicker than me. He jumped to the bottle and served me a glass of water in a very appreciative way. It was moving. We both laughed, and then we started to talk.[30]

The atmosphere was tense and suspenseful. Taha's previous impression of the SPLM/A Chairman had been very negative: "We both had these images in our heads. This is the bad aspect of war between brothers," he says.[31] Dr. John admitted that most of his entourage had opposed the meeting. When I interviewed him in 2010, Taha politely said that Garang credited Abel Alier and me as instrumental in his decision to show up. The meeting lasted only about twenty minutes but broke the ice.

They met again the next morning at 9:00 for another private discussion, then called in their teams. The discussions then commenced, with the mediators present. The atmosphere at this meeting too was tense. The delegations were sizing each other up. Everyone knew that this would be a ball game completely different from Nakuru. The desire to keep a very low profile limited participation: only Sumbeiywo and IGAD personnel were on site, and no one from the Troika. Foreign Minister Musyoka opened the meeting.[32] On the government side were Nafie Ali Nafie, Idris Abd al-Kader, Mutrif Siddiq, Said al-Khatib, Yahia Babikir and Abd al-Rahman al-Khalifa. Nhial Deng, Deng Alor, Pagan Amum, Yasir Arman, Justin Yak, Samson Kwaje, Cirino Hiteng, Malik Agar and Taban Deng participated for the SPLM/A. This would become the core group, largely remaining the same throughout the negotiations.

It was at this session that Dr. John began a diatribe on the history of the Southern struggle. As Yasir Arman later said, Dr. John believed that one had to examine the patient and diagnose the disease before prescribing the right medicine. So Garang talked all through the first negotiating meeting of some four hours.[33] And for the next meeting or two he just kept talking. The Chairman told me on the phone that he had used the first two days to give Taha a full briefing of the Southern cause, and had asked for an apology for the atrocities committed against Southerners for so many years. "I don't think he knows", Dr. John told me. "Better I tell him now, he needs to understand." During these days in September, Ali Osman allegedly handed over a document – a possible framework for a Comprehensive Peace Agreement.[34] Members of the SPLM/A delegation claim that he wanted a one-week discussion to see if an agreement could be reached, although this has not been confirmed by others. The Chairman of the SPLM/A, referring to the analogy of the patient, had said that a document like this would not solve the problem;[35] a serious disease like malaria needed more time. Sudan needed a paradigm shift – a new dispensation. It was in this context that Dr. John had undertaken what the SPLM/A members would jokingly call his "education" of the government delegates, recounting the history of the South and the background of its claims. But Garang's monologue increased the tension. Taha recalls:

> I kept quiet. You know, that is my nature. I want to assess my counterpart better before I speak. I didn't want to say anything. But members of my team felt the need to ventilate, and there were some heated discussions and accusations. I talked to Dr. John about this later. The communication was genuine and sincere. It was important. I think we discovered that we had something in common. We preferred to speak openly. These first discussions and these days and weeks would be of great help to the process. It was to benefit us much later.[36]

One on One

Neither side had expected the round to last long. But after three or four days they decided to continue. For logistical reasons the secretariat had to move the talks to Simba Lodge at Lake Naivasha. The parties started discussing the agenda, and how to structure the talks. When I checked by telephone the two leaders agreed that the atmosphere in the full sessions had been tense, and they had already begun to meet one-on-one. Garang said that Taha seemed very cautious, a bit stiff and withdrawn at first. Jokes and stories had helped, as they would throughout the negotiations. Ali Osman recalls:

> After a while we felt uneasy about the Secretariat and the presence of a third party. The discussions we had were like a family affair or a family dispute. We felt uneasy about having someone else present. These were things we needed to sort out ourselves, within the family, so to speak. We realized that the presence of the Secretariat could complicate matters more than helping us. That was why we ended up negotiating on our own, without anyone else in the room.[37]

The negotiations alternated between the two leaders alone, and a four-by-four format. No one else was permitted to sit in, not the mediator, nor any of the Troika observers or experts. From now on, the parties took full responsibility for their own decisions. The atmosphere was loosening up.

On the first morning after the move to Simba Lodge, the two leaders delegated Said and Pagan to work separately on the security arrangements. Said, a very prominent member of the National Congress Party, had participated in the talks from the beginning. Pagan Amum had come in after the Machakos agreement, but was no less a figure.[38] A Shilluk from the Upper Nile, Pagan was a very senior Commander and one of Dr. John's closest advisors. The Chairman gave him a lot of flexibility as a negotiator, and at Naivasha he proved to be both a work horse and decision maker, willing to fight and take risks when need be. The two went to work.

On the evening of September 7th, the Norwegian Embassy in Nairobi sent word that Taha and Garang wanted to talk to me. Garang called first. The focus of the negotiations was the most difficult issue of security. The SPLM had outlined a proposal that involved a North–South division of military forces, with integrated units constituting the symbol of national unity and basis for the future national army. The Sudanese Armed Forces would withdraw north of the 13th parallel, and the SPLA below the 12th, with a demilitarized zone between. The government, on the other hand, wanted the SAF to remain in the South, with the SPLA as a kind of home guard. Garang said that this was unacceptable, and that even Taha had admitted privately that the SAF at times were an instrument of Khartoum's islamization and other policies. Regarding the military presence in the Three Areas, the parties were also very far apart. Taha reported the same.

The next day the SPLM tabled its proposal in writing. The government delegation, describing this as a reversal of positions the Movement had intimated the day before, took this badly. I received calls from both sides, all concerned that the Vice President might withdraw from the talks and asking me to persuade him to stay. I talked to Ali Osman that morning. He expressed serious disappointment that his counterpart seemed intent on backtracking from progress they had made in their bilateral discussions. The government's proposal was intended as a compromise, in that integrated forces would be formed on the basis of existing armed units. Taha was particularly unhappy with the SPLM's use of the term "withdrawal", which implied defeat.

Whether incidentally or not, the Vice President also complained about an aspect of the power-sharing issue: he had indicated a willingness to vacate his office for the SPLM/A Chairman, but Garang had proposed that Taha assume a glorified parliamentary presidency until the position of President was available. The Vice President was disappointed and said so. In response I tried to convey the more positive picture that Garang had reported from the negotiations, and his intention to negotiate in good faith and find constructive solutions to the remaining issues. I also went over the SPLM/A positions, explaining and elaborating on them; withdrawal beyond the 13th parallel, for example, might be just a negotiating position.

Having spoken at length with the two principals I realized how far apart they were, not only in their negotiating positions, but also in their worldviews and modes of thought, values and expectations. It was a strange experience. They were two leaders of the same country, but were so far apart. So I started to "translate". I would tell each of them: "I know how you see it, but when you say *this*, your counterpart will hear *that* and understand something other than what you mean." This was particularly useful during the early months of the talks, before they got to know each other. But even then, when confrontations arose on difficult negotiating issues, this kind of "translation" was still very much needed.

Taha Wants to Leave

After lunch on the 8th Garang called me to express concern about not having heard from Taha; they had not met since the 4th. I told him about Ali Osman's reactions, and requested that the SPLM/A drop its insistence on withdrawal of SAF forces beyond the 13th parallel; the 1956 North–South border needed to be respected. I also noted that a term other than "withdrawal" would be useful. When Dr. John wondered why he had received no response to his offer to meet Taha again at any time, I asked him to show willingness not only to meet but also to adjust positions. Later that day the SPLM sent word that a revised proposal would be forthcoming. Despite this, we learned the next day (September 9th) that Taha was threatening to leave: he had never intended to stay so long anyway, and had important things to do in Khartoum. The IGAD chief negotiator and SPLM leaders asked whether I could persuade Taha to stay. The departure of the First Vice President would cause a significant loss of momentum, and I promised to try. The Americans engaged as well. This would become a pretty regular feature of the negotiations.

I called Taha and encouraged him to remain at Naivasha. They had just got started; if he left now, the talks might break down completely. I told him that the SPLM would present new positions on security to accommodate the government. These would involve significant concessions. They would also consider other proposals on power sharing and the presidency if the talks continued. I reminded Taha that Garang had left an important conference of 1,250 SPLA officers at Rumbek and a meeting of his Leadership Council in order to come to Naivasha. It would therefore be impossible for him and international observers to understand Taha's leaving now without very good reason. Ali Osman responded that he was aware of the main elements of the SPLM/A's pending proposal, and agreed that this would lead to a new dynamic in the talks. But he was still concerned about lack of accommodation in important areas; in any case there was now a need to bring military experts into the talks. He had discussed this with the Minister of Defence in the morning. Similar technical advice was needed in the areas of power sharing and wealth sharing. He had commitments in Khartoum. They could return in a week or two to continue the high-level talks.

I was very concerned. Any interruption at this stage would imply a failure of the nascent personal relations between the two leaders. I told Taha that the SPLM was willing to negotiate all remaining issues. If the SPLM/A concessions leaked to the media, Garang would find compromise more difficult. If there was a need for experts' assistance we should bring them to Naivasha. Taha admitted that a break now could complicate matters. The risk of leaks to the press applied to both sides. At the end of our discussion, he undertook to see whether the military experts could come to Naivasha, in which case he was prepared to stay. Later in the day Dr. John approached Taha directly, and offered to drop the word "withdrawal" in favour of "redeployment".[39]

Soon after my conversation with the First Vice President I learned that he would remain at Naivasha after all, and that the Defence Minister and several generals would come from Khartoum to join the negotiations. Direct talks between Taha and Garang resumed. The Sudanese ambassador to Norway, Charles Manyang D'Awol came to convey his government's thanks for Norway's role; the personal relations I had now established with the First Vice President were very important for the talks, and he encouraged me to nurture them. Dr. John called me and said the same: if Taha had left, the SPLM would have withdrawn its security proposals and the negotiations would have collapsed.

The SPLM Chairman was now firm in his decision to continue the talks beyond the security issues that, however, remained his first priority. Taha recalls Dr. John having told him at that time: "If you can give me the key to open the door, then we can make a deal."[40] The key was security. As he told me himself, "When we have completed the security issues, the rest is downhill." He certainly proved to be wrong on that front. The talks would last longer than any of us had ever imagined.

Ups and Downs

Although both leaders remained at Naivasha, the security issues were far from resolved. The arrival of the Minister of Defence, General Bakri Hasan Salih, did not make things easier. The clear impression was of Taha's difficulty in convincing the generals of the SPLM/A's good faith, and that the military wanted to pursue a strategy of fully integrating SPLA forces. Around midnight on September 10th Dr. John called me and said the government delegation was "dragging their feet"; someone was "trying to 'shoot down' Taha", by which he meant people in President Bashir's camp inimical to progress on the security issues. He said that there were questions about Dr. Ghazi's role given his views on security and his removal as chief negotiator.[41] But the Khartoum group who had opposed the Taha–Garang meeting all along were those who were really making difficulties now. I informed Walter Kansteiner about the discussions with Garang and the need for high-level contacts in Khartoum. Secretary of State Powell would, if necessary, call President Bashir.

In any case, Taha now expressed disappointment with the SPLM/A's amended proposal. Dropping its demand for the withdrawal of government forces beyond the 13th parallel was not a concession, he told me. Under terms of the Machakos Protocol the areas at issue were to be regarded as Northern anyway. Taha took issue with the proposed timetable for withdrawal, the post-war size of the respective armies, and the SPLA's suggested redeployment. The government, Taha said, would not give away at the negotiation table that which the SPLM/A would never have achieved militarily.

The same day I had been at an official luncheon hosted by the Norwegian prime minister, Kjell Magne Bondevik, when my mobile rang. I was embarrassed, but at this stage in the Sudan talks I had to be "on call" at all times. It was Dr. John. He was not happy with the government's position on the threshold for armed forces in the South. The talks had come to a complete standstill. I am not a military expert, and new little about troop levels. But I had been sufficiently involved in these discussions to know what we were dealing with. We knew that the SPLM/A never wanted to reveal their true numbers on the military side. Now the issue was the government troop levels. Although the government went too far the other way, there was no reason for the SPLM/A to dig in their heels like this. I told Dr. John that it was time to show flexibility. He argued his case, but in the end, agreed. The talks could proceed. To Ali Osman I explained that the SPLM/A was now willing to show flexibility on the timetable and the size of forces in the South: "Garang's main problem", I explained, was "with the incorporation of the SPLA into the Sudanese Army, with the government having continued control over the major towns in the South, and the SPLA being forced to stay in the bush. This would not be an acceptable situation for a new regional Southern government, and would not fly with the SPLM." I also tried to show that several of the revised SPLM/A positions were in fact concessions. Towards the end of the conversation Ali Osman indicated willingness to try again. The Movement now tabled more flexible alternatives for the composition and deployment of forces in the South.

In response to a request by the government, the SPLM/A delegation also presented positions on the other issues. Several of these positions were close to those of the Nakuru document that IGAD had tabled. The government side reacted – as it had previously – by accusing the SPLM of repeatedly tabling new positions or re-opening settled issues. This time the situation was serious. Taha was upset, and said that it would be difficult for him to defend continued participation in the talks if this maximal and wholly unrealistic proposal remained on the table. Charlie Snyder at the US State Department called me about a conversation Kansteiner had had with Taha that afternoon: the First Vice President had warned of a total collapse of the talks. Taha had told Kansteiner that he had "just a few hours to go" and needed new signals from the SPLM/A now. The Americans had been unable to reach Garang, and asked me whether I could get him on the line.

Learning the 'Art' of Persuasion

Time was short before the American election campaign, and the sooner the talks could be completed, the better. I called Dr. John immediately. He was not in the mood to give way:

> These reactions [he said] are just the government's attempt at diverting attention away from the security issues. The government has asked for our positions on the other remaining issues. Now that they are on the table, they don't want to take them seriously. Our proposal is not an ultimatum, but a basis for negotiation.

I told him how serious the situation was. Both Washington and Oslo were now very worried that the talks might collapse:

> I understand that you have your reasons for handling the situation this way [I said]. Not doing anything now can, however, threaten Taha's position. Should he be forced out of the talks, the whole peace process will suffer. It is critical that you show national responsibility and leadership, and help save the situation with indicating your willingness to show flexibility in key areas.

Garang said he had asked Pagan to contact Said al-Khatib to indicate willingness to discuss the issues. For the Chairman, progress on security was the key to resolving the other issues. I said that direct contact with Taha was now necessary. He countered that the Americans or I could tell Taha he was ready to meet. I therefore advised Snyder to convey the message to Taha as soon as possible.

Later that evening we were informed that Taha had decided to continue the negotiations. After two days of tension Taha and Garang now sat together for seven hours straight, without a break, to discuss the issues. Both leaders later reported discussions that were open, constructive, and inching towards a solution. To ascertain technical soundness, they then brought in two advisors on each side. Further technical discussions took place on Sunday the 14th, a process helped along by General Fulford.

Even when the first hurdles in this initial phase of the security negotiations had been overcome, the most contentious ones remained. These were the size and status of the two armies (national and Southern), withdrawal of government forces from the South, and the line beyond which they should withdraw. That last point was the most difficult: Dr. Ghazi, backed by leading figures in the military establishment, argued against any withdrawal at all, proposing instead a "freeze" of forces in their respective areas during the interim period, while a monitored ceasefire ensured the peace[42].

Garang had also proposed joint integrated units to be deployed in the sensitive areas. Taha was favourably inclined but the Defence Minister, General Bakri, dragged his feet. Joint integrated units had been devised under the Addis Ababa Agreement of 1972, an experience that may have contributed to this resistance – and to SPLM/A insistence. Difficulties after 1972, both in absorbing Southern forces and in continuous skirmishing, did not recommend a similar plan now.[43] In the end the government accepted re-deployment of its forces to the North, but over an extended period and with a large integrated force in the South. There was disagreement too over the size of joint integrated units for the Nuba Mountains and Southern Blue Nile, as well as Khartoum. The presence of SPLA soldiers in the East was the most difficult issue: the government demanded full withdrawal, while the SPLA pushed for a continued presence.

Still more security issues remained. These included how to handle the "other armed groups" – militias and paramilitary groups. A comprehensive ceasefire and financing of the army in the South, as well as national-security institutions, would be dealt with in the final negotiations of the peace agreement. For the SPLM/A a ceasefire could be negotiated only when there was agreement on all other issues. In the interim, the cessation of hostilities was intended to prevent fighting from undermining the negotiations. "Other armed forces" and army withdrawal became very contentious, related as they were to such critical issues as the border and control of oil resources.

The negotiations were tough. The government suspected the SPLM/A of wanting a much larger force in the South than was necessary, in preparation for independence or in case of renewed war; the SPLM/A was as naturally concerned that the government was using the negotiations to reduce the Movement's military power as much as possible. The mutual mistrust was profound. Each side separately conveyed its concerns to me, explaining the other's ulterior motives. Overcoming these suspicions was quite a task.

I recall talking to both of them from Afghanistan on September 17th on a crackly phone line from a hotel full of holes from mortar shells. Since the cessation of hostilities agreement would expire on the 30th, I wanted the two sides to sign an extension as soon as possible. They told me not to worry: they would do it soon. Ali Osman was quite relaxed on the phone, and said he was "cautiously optimistic": issues remained, and it might be necessary to call on me for help. Dr. John said the talks were moving well, and that he, too, was optimistic: he had given so many concessions on security that it should not be difficult to find solutions to the other issues.

Agreement on Security

But it was too early to celebrate. A flurry of activity, by now typical, engaged the various negotiators, the observers, and their respective governments. Colin Powell called President Bashir, urging the importance of finalizing the talks; the President complained that the SPLM constantly tabled new proposals. An informal group from both sides tried to resolve the most difficult issues. Abel Alier was called upon at a few junctures. The cessation of hostilities agreement was extended for another two months. The highest hurdles were troop levels and government withdrawal. Khartoum would not under any circum-

stance accept withdrawal beyond the 13th parallel, and wanted any withdrawal to take longer. They also wanted to limit severely the SPLA's post-war
size. The SPLM/A continued to advocate a speedy time frame for withdrawal
and significant SPLA troop levels. I had been back and forth between the two
sides on the phone. Privately they mooted possible trade-offs involving other
issues. My Sudan advisor, Kjell Hødnebø, was at this time the only observer
from the Troika. He reported developments to me every day, and was also
important behind the scenes. We had facilitated Abel Alier's presence at the
talks, together with colleagues from the United Sudan African Parties led by
Joseph Ukel. Alier, Hødnebø and the USAP people had daily meetings, and
coordinated pressure from the Southern Sudanese side, as well as from the
Troika.

One of the final issues discussed on 22–23 September was the size of the
Joint Integrated Units. The US view was that the natural compromise for the
latter would be 10,500, implying a government reduction relatively greater
than an SPLA increase. We thought 12,000 would strike a better balance. Col
had come up with that number after communicating with both parties. Kjell
Hødnebø also proposed 12,000 as the natural compromise, and ensured that
Alier, Oslo, and Washington ultimately supported the same figure. But neither
side would give in yet. The government threatened to walk out. Alier, his
USAP colleagues, Col Ding, Kjell and the IGAD Secretariat now took
concerted action.[44]

In a brief but intense discussion, I told Dr. John that the most sensible thing
now was to accept less than he had wanted. Dispute over the size of the Joint
Integrated Units in the South must not be allowed to block an agreement:
12,000 troops on each side would do. Reluctantly Garang said he would drop
his objections. I did not know then just how dramatic the scene at Naivasha
had become. That morning, the defence minister and generals had left the
talks. The rest of the Khartoum delegation had packed their bags and were
ready to go. General Sumbeiwo and Fink Haysom went to the parties and
formally tabled the proposal of 12,000 troops for each side. But they rejected
it. Three hours later, after additional calls, the mediators came back and both
parties accepted the proposal.[45] Whether a reinforcing message had come in
from the Southern Sudanese leaders between the first and second meeting, I
am not sure. What is clear is that agreement resulted from a coordinated effort
of influential stakeholders on all sides, with Col Ding and Abel Alier playing
instrumental roles in pushing for compromise[46], as well as the mediators and
the Troika. The message was the same from all of us, and it was this united
front that made the difference.

The deal was done on security. I called Ali Osman and John Garang to
congratulate them. Both were tired, but relieved. They confirmed that three
weeks of personal negotiation had worked really well, and that they had developed a good rapport. Taha also said that he had been in contact with President
Bashir, who was familiar with the final text, gave his full support, and was
looking forward to implementation.

It had been risky of Taha to bring the military leadership into the talks. It was a tactic he would often use when he sensed resistance in Khartoum. Rather than act as a messenger, he wanted stakeholders themselves to sit with the SPLM/A and see what it would take to reach a compromise. This was particularly important with the military leaders. After initial tension, and a sense of backtracking, any compromise would be much more sustainable. Ali Osman did the same with religious leaders later, in relation to *Sharia* law and the capital, and in other areas. Dr. John started bringing in stakeholders too: women's groups, military commanders, local leaders, chiefs from Abyei, and so forth.

The Protocol on Security Arrangements was signed on 25 September 2003. The major compromise in it was the SPLA's continued existence as a separate army during the interim period. The reduction of forces to agreed levels would start at the commencement of the interim period. Government forces would withdraw to north of the 12th parallel, SPLA forces to the south. Joint Integrated Units would in total comprise thirty-nine thousand officers and men, drawn equally from the SPLA and Sudanese Armed Forces; if the referendum opted for unity, these units would form the nucleus of a national army. More than a symbol, however, they were designed to address security in the Nuba Mountains and Southern Blue Nile: six thousand soldiers would be deployed in each of the two areas, which meant that the SPLM would keep three thousand there. In Khartoum would be a contingent of three thousand soldiers, 1500 from each side.[47] A Joint Defence Board would be established, comprising the commanders-in-chief, chiefs of staff, and defence ministers of both sides. General Bakri also gave the SPLM/A a verbal commitment to withdraw government troops from the Nuba Mountains and Southern Blue Nile.

Recalling the breakthrough at the talks Taha recently said:

> The withdrawal of the SAF forces from the South would not have happened without the commitment of the President. I have told my brothers in the South this many times. No civilians would have been able to do this [i.e. convince the Army to redeploy]. If they had tried, there would have been a coup. The agreement on the withdrawal was only possible because of President Bashir.[48]

Taha emphasized the role of the President in implementing the agreement, the more so because Dr. Ghazi continued to raise objections to any withdrawal from the South. In Ghazi's view, such a security agreement would practically split the country in two. Consensual unity was not given a chance. In his consultations there had been some interest from several quarters in his proposal of a "freeze"[49] including from Danforth and the Kenyans, but they dropped the idea immediately after a categorical rejection from Garang.[50] Denied support for his strategy, Dr. Ghazi offered his resignation as Peace Advisor to the President. The resignation was not accepted, lest the government's internal divisions come to light.[51] Dr. Ghazi remained part of the process for a few more months, before leaving the government altogether. But the security arrangements continued to stir up controversy within the government and the ruling party at the highest levels.

There had been no such disagreement on the Southern side. Abel Alier had told Ali Osman: "Let us call a spade a spade. The problem between you and us in the South is that you believe you can manage us by using the army."[52] In Taha's own opinion, a settlement without redeployment of the Sudanese Armed Forces to the North would have failed, as inevitable incidents would have spun out of control.[53] Dr. John was adamant. According to his close advisors he would often say: "I have been 'absorbed' once, and I shall never allow myself to go through the experience again in my life."[54] Although "freeze" was not the same as absorption, it seemed clear that nothing but withdrawal would give the Southerners the assurances they needed.

In the Security Protocol these included an internationally monitored cease-fire, with the help of IGAD and the UN. Details about these arrangements would be subject to negotiation later, after the completion of a comprehensive peace agreement. As an essential part of the Security Protocol, "other armed groups" (i.e. militias) would have to be integrated into the SPLA, the government army, or some civilian agency. Critically for the SPLM/A, the National Security organs would be restructured, with internal and external branches administered under a Ministry of National Security responsible directly to the Presidency. That this provision had not been subject to detailed negotiations would later have consequences for the implementation of the overall peace agreement.

A New Modus Operandi

With the signing of the Security Protocol the two leaders had taken full ownership of the negotiating process. They now preferred to conduct the talks themselves, order the agenda, and set the deadlines. It was at this juncture that their relationship really took off: "We spent hours and hours talking, about philosophy, the Creation, about God, Sudanese life, and personal experiences," Taha explains.[55] Dr. John gave a Bible to Ali Osman, who reciprocated with a Koran, each encouraging the other to read. In their long private sessions they would often talk about topics completely unrelated to the issues at hand, such as philosophy and religion. "It was not only a personal relationship but an intellectual affinity," Yahia Husein Babikir observed.[56] Others grumbled about the amount of time they spent together talking about "nothing".

The role of the Chief Mediator and IGAD secretariat had thus diminished to that of facilitator, arranging technical meetings and the briefings of international experts. When needed, the mediation team would provide advice and text proposals to the parties, for example on wealth sharing and power sharing. General Sumbeiywo would still assist in relation to the timelines for the completion of talks on various topics, and hold the parties to their agreed roadmap; he was an effective "watchdog". But the parties themselves took care of the talks from now on.

As for the international observers, apart from me Walter Kansteiner had been most active on the phone. We coordinated updates and messages to the parties. Jack Danforth was less engaged. Colin Powell stepped in when needed or asked, and President Bush was ready to do the same. The Secretary of State's calls were intended to give the parties an extra push or remind them that the United States was following the talks very closely. This was different from the more personal role I had begun to play, which had become more and more important. When it came to substantive issues in the negotiations, I used to tell them that they seemed not to come from the same place, but from two different planets. They both laughed when I jokingly blamed the British for putting them together in one country.

The security negotiations had shown a need for third party representatives to help each of them "read" the proposals tabled by the other side, to recognize concessions, to discern nuances and facilitate "soft landings". As the negotiations proceeded, this became a regular feature. There was no one else in the room, and since they disclosed the deliberations to very few people, our telephone conversations became quite important. When they were "stuck" or really irritated they would call me to complain. I normally talked to both, and tried to explain why a certain comment was made or a position was taken, where a solution might lie. Col Ding and Abel Alier performed similar duty, the former with Garang, and the latter in relation to both.

Both Ali Osman and John Garang were greeted by huge rallies when they returned home. They praised the leaders who had managed to reach agreement on one of the most critical issues. People could see that peace now really could be a possibility. Taha received a lot of praise for his efforts. At Rumbek Dr. John was received by hordes of people. Southerners had walked for days to get there. For the first time, Sudanese state television followed President Bashir's earlier shift in terminology, and started to use the term "SPLM Chairman Dr. John Garang", instead of "rebel leader" when they covered the rallies. They also broadcast an interview with him. I recall Dr. John's describing this to me as quite a breakthrough.

After the Breakthrough

The parties had agreed to resume high-level discussions in mid-October that would last until the beginning of Ramadan about ten days later or, if progress warranted, could continue until the Eid at the end of that month. Meanwhile much preparation went on behind the scenes. The Americans held discussions on the implications of the Security Protocol. General Fulford visited Khartoum and Nairobi in the period 4–8 October, where he found both sides eager to discuss implementation issues such as timetables for withdrawal and the integration of "other armed groups". The meetings with John Garang went well, and those with President Bashir extraordinarily so. At the same time, Fulford and the Americans were concerned that the respective military leaderships interpreted the Protocol differently. According to the government, the agreement involved at least partial subordination of the SPLA to the Sudanese Armed Forces, not two armies on an equal footing and under a joint leadership structure, as the SPLM/A saw things. We brought in military experts from the Troika to help in technical discussions. General Sumbeiywo, on his side, was worried that the Americans were trying to take over the peace process in order to meet artificial deadlines for domestic political reasons.

Meanwhile the United Nations issued a Presidential statement from the Security Council in support of the IGAD process and the Security Protocol. Jack Danforth had been instrumental in making this happen. This meant international recognition of the Security Protocol, which would be useful during the implementation phase and provided a basis on which the planning process for peacekeeping operations could start. There was agreement to maintain the various monitoring arrangements until such an operation began. At the UN, however, attention had turned to the situation in Darfur. The number of internally displaced people had risen to 500,000, and 70,000 had fled to Chad. Pressure to do something was mounting in the US and Europe. I conveyed our concerns about the situation to both Garang and Taha.

Disaffection in Darfur highlighted the narrow base of our Southern peace process. We needed to prevent the exclusion of various political groupings from upsetting that process. With Dr. John I repeatedly raised the issue of integrating the "other armed groups" (or militias); with the government I stressed the importance of Northern support for the process, but they did not want broader participation at the negotiation table.

Dr. John was also concerned about this, and had used the break in the negotiations to meet leaders of the National Democratic Alliance. On October 15 at Rumbek an Alliance delegation led by its Deputy Chairman, Abd al-Rahman Sa'id, endorsed the agreements reached so far between the government and SPLM/A. But they were concerned that they – and the issues dear to them, including the capital and reforms in the North – might be sacrificed for the sake of a deal between the SPLM and the ruling party in Khartoum. The meeting approved participation of Alliance members in the special committees during the interim period and so-called pre-interim period, but the issue remained.

Before the Vice President and the Chairman returned to Naivasha, technical discussions had gone on for some time in three committees: power sharing, wealth sharing and the Three Areas. The talks proceeded on the basis of the Nakuru document, although never explicitly. On wealth sharing, technical experts from the international financial institutions and Troika helped to clarify and demystify the issues, leading to less politicised discussions, but the real negotiations were still pending.

The atmosphere at Naivasha was relaxed. A seasoned Norwegian expert on Sudan had tried to prepare me for this. Sudanese – Northern and Southern alike – will always be friendly, always cordial. Getting them to negotiate seriously was another matter. While the two delegations normally used separate parts of the restaurant for meals, they chatted amiably during breaks or during the long hours when their Principals were negotiating without them. At one stage the delegations intermingled so much that fear arose of informal deals, and Dr. John was asked by one of his own to intervene and put a damper on the socializing. During the negotiations, the hotel was almost full of delegates, observers from the Troika and IGAD countries, technical advisors sent from observer countries, and others. It was sometimes easy to forget that the Sudanese government and SPLM/A had been at war for twenty years.

The preliminary technical talks and easy atmosphere belied near-stalemate over the major issues. As Said al-Khatib on the government side put it: "'The specter of signing something looks a bit distant, because for the past two weeks we have met without any progress on the wealth sharing issues we have been discussing.'"[57] Secretary of State Powell went to Nairobi and Naivasha on 21–22 October and met the parties; hopes in the US for a partial deal coinciding with Powell's visit proved overly optimistic. Since their own arrivals the previous week, Taha and Garang had had only one twenty-minute meeting. Differences persisted in interpretations of the Security Protocol. SPLM pressure to accommodate the National Democratic Alliance and other opposition parties, which Taha resisted, also contributed to delay. US attempts to "talk up the talks" – and Powell's urging completion of the talks by the parties' own declared deadline of 31 December – revived General Sumbeiywo's concern about an American "takeover".

At this time, major military operations in Iraq had ended in apparent military victory for the US, and an international donors' conference was held in Madrid. There I exchanged a few words on Sudan with Secretary Powell, who had just come from Naivasha, where I was heading. Powell gave a positive assessment, although he was beginning to get impatient. "Now, they have to finish this", he said. "They have been dragging this on for too long already." From Madrid I went to the IGAD Summit in Kampala on 24–25 October. As Co-Chair of the Sudan Committee in the IGAD Partners' Forum, I had a good opportunity for one-on-one discussions with relevant heads of state and government. With President Bashir I discussed a range of questions, but without going into detail on the talks proper. In meetings with President Museveni of Uganda and the Ethiopian Prime Minister, Meles Zenawi, the need for regional pressure in support of completing the peace talks was discussed. I attended other, confidential meetings on Sudan. President Kibaki of Kenya, who was now Chairman of the Sudan portfolio in IGAD, was still recovering from a serious road accident, and it was clear that active leadership on Sudan must come from elsewhere. As a result General Sumbeiywo, who had had close personal relations with President Moi, had lost some political clout. Elements in Khartoum wanted Kibaki to replace him. Kibaki confirmed him instead, but the doubts about his position had been unsettling.

New Hurdles

This round of negotiations had begun with wealth sharing arrangements and the Three Areas. On the phone Taha had been particularly worried about the lack of progress on the latter issue. History was clearly on the government's side in relation to Abyei, he explained; Garang's problem was that the Ngok Dinka were strongly represented in the SPLM/A and his delegation. I asked whether he would have a similar problem with Misiriya Baggara on his side. He admitted the similarity, but said the differences were more compelling, and the longer this process dragged on, the harder it would be to find a solution.

When I arrived at Naivasha, the parties had not budged. The government continued to reject a separate administrative arrangement for Abyei, and was dead against a referendum in the other two areas. The SPLM held rigidly to its position on self-determination for the Three Areas. The government accused the SPLM/A of backtracking on points already sorted out in the Machakos Protocol; further concessions would lead to "endless claims" from Darfur and other areas of the North.

Regarding wealth sharing the government was also upset over SPLM/A demands for a separate currency and central bank in the South, and allocation of oil resources remained unresolved.

Beginning where Powell had left off, I shuttled between Taha and Garang, trying to identify possible solutions to the outstanding issues, and urging them to compromise.

But this exercise revealed new positions. Dr. John was convinced that the Abyei issue was all about oil, while Ali Osman said the issues were unrelated. After much discussion Taha signalled some flexibility. It later became clear that this was premature and that Abyei would haunt the parties long after the signing of the peace agreement.

Colin Powell's visit to Naivasha and the emphasis the Americans put on the Sudan negotiations attracted a great deal of international attention to the talks. Foreign dignitaries appeared, unannounced. Countries without any role in the talks sent envoys and observers, seeming to position themselves for a role after a peace agreement. Many Sudanese stakeholders and prominent individuals also came. All of this disturbed the negotiations, wasted time, and distracted the leaders from the task at hand. Garang and Taha both complained about this and the large media presence. On a few occasions General Sumbeiywo instructed the parties to retire from view, and finally he rightly restricted access altogether.

There was some irony in the leaders' complaints. The continued presence of Dr. Ghazi (still the Presidential Advisor for Peace) was not without tension. The arrival of a National Congress Party delegation of fifty people, including Mubarak al-Fadl, complicated matters, and allegedly led to attempts at brokering side deals with the SPLM/A. Some delegates felt that this undermined Taha. The Vice President, however, preferred to have people on the team or present at Naivasha. This was consistent with his overall strategy, but Troika observers remained concerned, and the Americans took up the point with Khartoum.

Much of the eventual progress on wealth sharing was owed to the tireless work of the technical team. World Bank and IMF experts cleared the air, transforming politically sensitive issues into simple technical matters. Dr. Endre Stiansen had begun as one of the Norwegian observers, but joined the IGAD Secretariat as a resource person responsible for coordinating the wealth sharing working group. Resource persons from the World Bank, IMF and other bodies contributed at different stages. Norway funded this part of the work, and also sent experts to advise on oil and gas reserves. Conclusion of the wealth sharing talks was delayed only as a tactic, in case trade-offs were needed later over other issues. Although Ali Osman complained about stalling, both sides wanted a comprehensive "package deal". Garang's theory was that it would be easier for the government to sell an overall agreement than to defend itself in Khartoum one issue at a time. Ali Osman told me much the same thing: a "package deal" would allow each party to claim victory on important issues.

Stalemate

In practice, however, hesitation to compromise led to stalemate. Just as the government accused the SPLM/A of backtracking, so the government appeared willing to consider positions close to the SPLM/A's, at times only to abandon them later. I in turn referred to proposals tabled by each side that were reversals of previous ones, and said we expected responsible leadership in moving the negotiations forward. Neither leader expressed irritation with the other, but nothing happened.

During the Ramadan break I talked to both parties on the telephone. They continued to express confidence that the talks could be finalized by the end of the year, perhaps even by December 15th. Discussions on the technical level would continue throughout the recess; the principals were scheduled to resume negotiations on December 4th. By then there had been changes in the Troika team. In the UK Hilary Benn had succeeded Valerie Amos. British foreign secretaries had had little involvement in the peace process, which was now largely managed by the UK Special Representative for the Sudan, Alan Goulty. The lack of high-level UK engagement was unfortunate.

Others also disappeared from the scene. On the American side Walter Kansteiner told me in October that he was leaving his position. By November 1st he was out, and no one replaced him for seven months. In the interim Charlie Snyder was Acting Assistant Secretary for Africa. He was an old hand on Sudan whom we all knew quite well, and was able to act as an interlocutor within the Administration. Views varied widely among the State Department, the National Security Council, the Special Envoy on Sudan, the White House

Staff, USAID and, not least, in Congress. This made life difficult for international partners. At this juncture, however, American engagement had one common denominator – the need to complete the negotiations. And at the highest levels there was close engagement. We worked with Charlie and sometimes Jack Danforth to get the necessary calls made by Richard Armitage, the powerful Deputy Secretary of State, General Powell, National Security Advisor Condoleezza Rice and, if necessary, by President Bush. On November 29th, Dr. Ghazi left the government's negotiating team and his mission as Advisor for Peace Affairs for President Bashir was terminated.

The negotiations resumed on December 1st, and the expectation was that they would finish by the end of the year. The American President asked for completion of a Framework agreement by December 19th. Members of the government delegation felt such deadlines were of little help, and neither the British nor we or General Sumbeiywo thought that this one was realistic. But the sense of urgency nevertheless led to a flurry of calls from the technical experts, the Special Envoys of the Troika and the Secretary General of the UN, Kofi Annan. The deadline also made it easier for us to keep out visitors.

Darfur: Full Fire

During the latter half of 2003 the government went on the offensive in Darfur. What ensued has been well documented.[58] Witness accounts, and evidence collected by the UN International Commission of Inquiry on Darfur (ICID) and later the International Criminal Court are detailed and probative: [59] According to these reports, the *janjawid* were unleashed in full force, with government troops and aircraft deployed in numbers. Darfur was being bombed, burnt and looted, and Darfurians killed and maimed or forced to flee for safety. Hundreds of thousands were displaced; the numbers were uncertain because access to and travel in Darfur were severely restricted. Under these conditions no independent monitoring could take place.

When Ali Osman Taha initiated the high-level negotiations with the SPLM in September 2003, Darfur was on the radar screens of only the most knowledgeable international observers. We were aware that attacks were taking place, with consequent displacement, but none of us really saw signs of a conflict of the nature and severity we had seen in the South. We thought we could support political negotiations that could bring the situation under control, preferably before the IGAD talks on the South were completed. We were wrong, and realized it too late. The efforts of the Chadians in repeated negotiations on humanitarian ceasefires with the Sudan Liberation Movement/Army were supported by the UN Special Envoy for humanitarian affairs, Tom Vraalsen, a Norwegian senior diplomat, together with colleagues in the AU, as well as other international observers. Tom was frequently in Oslo and briefed us. We followed the negotiating process closely. But we still underestimated the dimensions of the conflict.

During this period the government started to accuse Garang and the SPLM/A of supporting the rebels in Darfur. Ali Osman Taha raised this with me several times, saying there was clear evidence. When I expressed concern, the SPLM Chairman said: "No, this is not true". It was not difficult to guess what had been going on. It was an obvious step for the SPLM/A to support resistance not only in the Three Areas and the East, but also in the West, in Darfur. Before the Taha–Garang negotiations began in September 2003, it is clear that the SPLM/A was following parallel tracks, negotiating for peace and using military action to strengthen its hand. Dr. John's approach was "fight and talk".[60] This was an explicit strategy on the part of the Movement, as evident in the attack on Torit. Garang also made full use of international diplomacy. He would arrange the timing and use all his tools, in a way that he thought would maximize impact. [61]

And although the government rejected such a strategy,[62] its tactics seemed quite similar. Even as talks were under way they undertook significant military movements, and they were engaged in proxy operations through supplying and supporting militias in other parts of the country.[63] They imported weapons and armaments on a large scale, partly in connection with the Darfur conflict. Like the SPLM/A, the government was negotiating for peace, but ensuring that it was ready for war, and using military tactics to achieve its goals in the interim to ensure that it could negotiate from a position of strength. It is important to remember that during the period that preceded the high-level talks between Garang and Taha, before September 2003, it was not clear whether the IGAD talks would go anywhere.

In the Troika, we discussed the problems of Darfur repeatedly. Clearly, we could have pushed harder for participation of the Darfur rebels in the talks. My experience in pressing for inclusion of the National Democratic Alliance – which the government rejected outright – gave me no hope of success. When I raised the issue with Ali Osman Taha, there was no movement whatsoever. The government's strategy was obviously to enter into a partnership with the South that would strengthen its hand nationally. Opening the talks to the Northern opposition, and thereby risking an alliance at the negotiating table between the Southerners and the opposition parties or the Darfur rebel movements, would to them be suicidal. Nor did Dr. John, who after all now spoke alone for the NDA, push the issue too hard. He had little to gain from sharing the stage, and much to lose if expanded talks collapsed. The negotiating parties ultimately decided whom to negotiate with. We could not force them.

The SPLM Visits Khartoum

Following agreement between Ali Osman Taha and John Garang, a high-level SPLM delegation visited Khartoum for the first time on 5 December 2003. They travelled via Tripoli in a Libyan aircraft and with Libyan Security assisting the SPLM, since no security guarantees could be provided in the capital. The delegation consisted of Pagan Amum, Yasir Arman, Samson Kwaje, Edward Lino, Abd al-Aziz Adam al-Hilu, Seif al-Balula, Anne Itto, Awot Deng and Grace Datrio. This was historic. Lino, the head of the SPLA's security service, was among those overcome with emotion. The delegation held a series of meetings with government representatives and leaders from the Nuba Mountains, the opposition National Democratic Alliance, and a number of civil society organizations. The delegation was very well received, officially and by the public. Both parties considered the visit a major political breakthrough; in the words of Ali Osman Taha, "a political partnership was in the making". The visit made a difference also at Naivasha, by providing momentum for the negotiations.

The Vice President and the Chairman headed for Naivasha again in the first week of December. When I talked to them soon after their arrival, they had been briefed in joint sessions by the two technical teams headed by Nhial Deng on the SPLM side and Idris Abd al-Kader for the government. The briefings and updates, primarily on wealth sharing and the Three Areas, took a couple of days. As for the timetable, both men appreciated the urgency of the situation, thought they could manage in time, but also stated that deadlines ultimately were up to them.

A word here about the UN role may be appropriate, for it was at this point that Kofi Annan, the Secretary General, called the parties.[64] He had been engaged in the Sudan process for a while. The UN had observer status at the negotiations, but was seldom present in the initial phase, and then with Ambassador Mohamed Sahnoun. Much later, when there was a need for engagement related to a possible peace keeping operation, Taye-Brook Zerihoun or Chris Coleman would be there. The UN had been frequently updated about the negotiations, but the engagement was very limited. At the political level, I had kept Kieran Prendergast, Head of that department, informed regularly. and from time to time Kofi Annan called me to check on the latest developments. We could certainly use the authority of the Secretary General at a critical point in the negotiations. And during the implementation negotiations, the UN provided important support, both in the security talks and in other areas.

The Foreign Minister of Sudan, Mustafa Osman Ismail, had been a friend since my first visit to Khartoum in 1998. Now he called me from Brussels for an update. I briefed him about my discussions with Garang and Kofi Annan, and about a telephone conference I was about to have with the First Vice President. Interestingly, Mustafa wanted me to call him after I had talked to Taha. I was not usually a channel of communication within the government of Sudan, but people in Khartoum sometimes felt they did not know what was going on. I used the opportunity to express once again our deep concern over the Darfur situation and referred to the visit of the Special Envoy Tom Vraalsen. The foreign minister was quite defensive, and characterized international interest in Darfur as an attempt to divide the country.

Despite the promising start, the wealth sharing negotiations in the end proved far from easy. Several key issues remained unresolved. These were the allocation of oil revenues, non-oil revenues, land rights, the currency issue and Central Bank, and the system of reallocation of resources to the States. The main controversy was over oil. Given the location of most of the oil fields, there was a strong feeling among Southerners that the oil was theirs. The SPLM's point of departure was therefore that the oil was in the South, and that any agreement should reflect that. The government, on the other hand, held that natural resources were *national* resources. The Sudanese government had engaged foreign companies to explore for oil, and had invested in infrastructure. It should benefit from this investment through revenues.

The Deal on Oil

A lot was at stake. Both parties knew they were negotiating over what would be a permanent division of resources in the event of Southern secession after the interim period. The income generated from oil clearly made such negotiations difficult. At the same time, Dr. John wanted a proper allocation of non-oil revenues. To the government, Southerners' expectations of a significant share of oil income and non-oil revenues were unrealistic, even greedy. The government saw the wealth sharing negotiations largely from the perspective of damage control, an effort to keep as much as possible. The negotiations also had direct budgetary implications for them. Garang however, saw the wealth sharing negotiations as part of the larger goal of making unity attractive for the South. The lack of trust between the parties also played its part in these negotiations, with transparency around oil production, licensing arrangements, and income becoming a major issue.

Initially the SPLM wanted 90 percent of the region's resource revenue to go to the Government of Southern Sudan. They also demanded a share of non-oil revenues from the North. The SPLM requested two Petroleum Commissions, one in the North and one in the South, and full transparency of all previous oil contracts and production permits. But for Khartoum, with a huge debt problem, the oil income was a matter of economic survival. Regarding currency, a lot of political symbolism adhered to the *dinar*, which had been introduced by the current government in 1992 to replace the Sudanese pound. Disliking the Islamic connotations of the *dinar*, the SPLM/A wanted either a return to the old currency or a separate currency in the South, with two central banks. They had already started preparations to print their own fiat money disassociated from the Islamic banking system, a decision that created strong reactions on the government side. The government supported the status quo, with minimal changes in wealth sharing arrangements. Both parties had clearly started from "maximal" positions on these issues. Although several concerns were settled after the technical experts' intervention, the most controversial political ones remained.

1 Signing of the Machakos Protocol, 20 July 2002: Ghazi Salahuddin, Presidential Advisor for Peace (L) and Salva Kiir Mayardit, Deputy Chairman SPLM/A (R) with President Daniel Arap Moi, Kenya (photo: Antony Njunguna, Reuters/Scanpix).

2 In Naivasha, January 2004: Ali Osman Taha (L), Chief Mediator General Lazarus Sumbeiywo and Dr. John Garang (R) (photo: Philip Dhail).

3 Naivasha, 7 January 2004: Dr. John Garang (L) and Ali Osman Taha (R), Foreign Minister of Kenya, Stephen K. Musyoka (far L) and Said al-Khateeb (far R) (photo: Philip Dhail).

4 Naivasha, May 2004: Ali Osman Taha, Dr. John Garang and their respective families (photo: Philip Dhail).

5 Nairobi, October 2004: Ali Osman Taha, Dr. John Garang, Nhial Deng, SPLM/A (L), and Mutrif Siddiq, the Government of Sudan (R) (photo: Philip Dhail).

6 Nairobi, 12 October 2004: First joint meeting of the two Sudanese leaders with a foreign head of government; from left, the author, Nafie Ali Nafie, Ali Osman Taha, Norwegian Prime Minister Kjell Magne Bondevik, John Garang, Nhial Deng and Special Envoy Tom Vraalsen (photo: Philip Dhail).

7   The U.N. Security Council meeting, Nairobi, November 19 2004: the author (R), Ali Osman Taha (L) who salutes Dr. John Garang (outside the frame) (photo: Antony Njunguna, Reuters/Scanpix).

8   Nairobi, 9 January 2005: The two leaders before the signing of the Comprehensive Peace Agreement (CPA) (photo: Antony Njunguna, Reuters/Scanpix).

9 Nairobi's Nyayo Stadium, 9 January 2005: US Secretary of State Colin Powell (L) and the author (R) witnessing the signing of the CPA (photo: Sayyid Azim, AP/Scanpix).

10 Nairobi's Nyayo Stadium, 9 January 2005: Some of the Heads of State and government dignitaries present at the signing, the Foreign Minister of Kenya, Chirau Ali Mwakwere (L), Ali Osman Taha, President Omar Hasan al-Bashir, President Mwai Kibaki, President Yoweri Museveni and Dr. John Garang (photo: Philip Dhail).

11 Oslo, 10 April 2005: The first meeting of women's organizations from the whole of Sudan took place before the Sudan Donors' Conference, with the two leaders present (photo: Philip Dhail).

12 Khartoum, 9 July 2005: The crowd on the day of the inauguration of Dr. John Garang as First Vice President of Sudan (photo: Philip Dhail).

13 Juba, 6 August 2005: The funeral of Dr. John Garang de Mabior, the pallbearers are the Sudan Armed Forces. In the background: Salva Kiir (L), former President Moi and Kenyan President Mwai Kibaki (R) (photo: Philip Dhail).

14 Close to Kauda, Southern Kordofan February 2007: Internally displaced migrating home from Khartoum (photo: Fred Noy, UNMIS).

15 Abyei town in the state of Southern Kordofan, May 2008: the town was burnt down. Abyei remains the worst of many "hotspots" in Sudan (photo: Tim McKulka, UNMIS).

16 Agok, 21 May 2008: Displaced women and children from Abyei waiting for humanitarian aid (photo: Tim McKulka, UNMIS).

17 July 2008:
Soldiers of the
Sudan People's
Libaration Army
redeploys from
Manyang south
of the River Kiir
to positions
south of Agok
(photo: Tim
McKulka,
UNMIS).

18 Oil
production
site in Upper
Nile State, one
of the areas
subject to
violence and a
"mix" of
ethnicity, poli-
tics, arms and
cash (photo:
Tim McKulka,
UNMIS).

19 Garbo (close
to Juba, regional
capital of Southern
Sudan), October
2006: Residents
are mourning the
loss of a relative
due to militia
attacks (photo: Tim
McKulka, UNMIS).

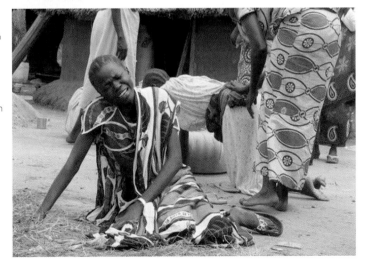

20 Duk Padiet, State of Jonglei, September 2009: Troubled atmosphere in the wake of a serious militia attack which allegedly claimed 100 lives (photo: Tim McKulka, UNMIS).

21 Town of Malakal, November 2006: A child collecting water and a discarded bomb shortly after clashes between the SPLA and the militia of Gabriel Tanginye (photo: Tim McKulka, UNMIS).

22 Girls skip rope at a UNICEF-supported Khorbou Centre Basic School in Juba (photo: Georgina Cranston, UNICEF).

During previous rounds, the SPLM had lowered its demand from a share of 90 to 70 percent. A week or so into the December negotiations, progress was very limited. The government wanted a 75/25 split in its favour. It was dead against any non-oil revenues going to the South, but held open the possibility of all non-oil revenues from the South going to the central government. As the talks proceeded, they raised the issue of a sequential split, with more resources being transferred to the South during the second and third years after the signing of a peace agreement. Under this model, in the last year the South would get a share of nearly 40 percent. This proposal was intended to address the challenge of loss of income for the Sudanese state, and the need to find ways either to compensate for the losses or to adapt budgets gradually to a different financial situation. As the haggling proceeded, the SPLM reduced its demands, from 65 to 60 percent. Of non-oil revenues they asked initially for 5, then 4, then 3 percent. The government offered nothing. In discussion with me Ali Osman referred to the mediators' proposal of a nearly 50/50-arrangement, as reflected in the Nakuru document, and said that the SPLM should just accept that proposal. Any provision of non-oil revenues, however, was completely out of the question.

During this most intense period, my calls were so frequent that I knew the prayer times of Ali Osman and his delegation better than I knew my own schedule. I similarly got to know Dr. John's habits. He was a "night person", like me, and easy to get on the line after most people had gone to bed. "Gate keepers" got used to the voices of my assistant and me, calling at the oddest times. Kenyan cell phone connections were poor, and we would often have to call numerous times to complete a conversation.

Towards the end of December we were all getting concerned. The main wealth sharing issues had still not been sorted out, nor had much progress been made on the Three Areas. During a Troika telephone conference the Americans proposed that the Troika should present a document with solutions for the remaining issues. Mike Ranneberger, already on the Sudan-team, and appointed Senior Representative on Sudan, stated that it was important to have a framework agreement capturing the main principles before January 20th – the date of President Bush's State of the Union address. The parties were promised a Rose Garden ceremony. Colin Powell weighed in with the two sides as well. Although the UK and Norwegians were equally concerned, they hesitated to use external pressure in this way, and in the end the idea was shelved.

I remained in touch with both parties. On New Year's Eve I had several lengthy telephone conversations with both Garang and Taha. Although they had not been able to complete this round of talks in accordance with their own timeline, both were optimistic. After pressure from many of us the SPLM had seen the writing on the wall on oil-revenue allocation, dropped almost the whole claim on non-oil revenues, and was open to a 50/50 solution, wherein half of the income from oil produced in the South would go to the Southerners. They were also withdrawing their request for a Petroleum Commission in the

South, instead negotiating for a stronger position in the National Petroleum Commission, its chairmanship, and a share of positions in the Ministry of Energy and Mining. They maintained their claim for a new currency and separate Central Bank. The government also moved on resource allocation. When I discussed the issues with Ali Osman on the phone he referred to an earlier telephone conversation between Powell and President Bashir, in which the Secretary of State had suggested a 55–45 percent arrangement, with Khartoum getting the lower number.[65] Now, however, both parties seemed to be moving towards a 50/50 deal.

By the end of December there was agreement on almost all wealth sharing issues. Now, however, Ali Osman threatened to leave the negotiations unless there was progress also on two of the Three Areas, the Nuba Mountains and Southern Blue Nile. We encouraged international partners to man the phones to prevent Taha's premature departure. He remained. Taha and Garang continued the talks on the Three Areas simultaneously, but still there was little progress.

New Deadlines

Three major issues remained in regard to the Nuba Mountains and Southern Blue Nile: popular consultation; the role of *Sharia* in state legislation; and land, about which the SPLM requested a Commission to deal with disputes over ownership. On Abyei, the third Area, the parties were very far apart. I encouraged Dr. John to contact Abel Alier on the Abyei issue. Taha reiterated the view that the *Sharia* issue had been settled in the Machakos negotiations, so the issue regarding its role in the Nuba Mountains and Blue Nile did not arise. He was also very uncertain about what the SPLM meant by "popular consultations".[66] When we discussed *Sharia* and the marginalized areas Taha could get really animated. He would never show anger or shout, but his tone became insistent, and I could sense I was touching a nerve. Now for the first time I raised the possibility that popular consultation could be conducted indirectly, through parliamentary authority: an alternative to direct consultation through a referendum. This would depend, of course, on the legitimacy of a state parliament in the eyes of the people.

Still the talks dragged on. On wealth sharing, two issues remained: currency, and sharing of oil resources.[67] Regarding the latter, the government maintained that the state was the owner of all natural resources, while the SPLM claimed that the resources belonged to the local community. They agreed on a process whereby resources above the surface would be subject to a national process applying both communal tradition and legislation. A National Land Commission would be established, with an equivalent for Southern Sudan. As for resources below the surface of the earth, the question was much more complicated. It was likely that the parties would never agree, so they had chosen not to deal with it at all. They concentrated instead on agreeing to divide the income from the oil, and on process and governance arrangements for the exploitation and production of oil.

In the end, both sides gave way on the key issues. The SPLM accepted the 50/50 deal on oil revenues, and nothing on non-oil revenues. The government formally accepted abandonment of the *dinar*, while the SPLM/A accepted one National Central Bank, that would have a strong Southern Branch, called the Bank of Southern Sudan. On January 7th the wealth sharing protocol was signed. I travelled to Nairobi and Naivasha for the occasion. This was made into a major event, with speeches from both sides, and by General Sumbeiywo and me – on behalf of the IGAD Partners' Forum – and a lot of national and international media present. Dr. Ghazi was not there. He later publicly acknowledged dissatisfaction with the new negotiating format, and the setting of priorities in the talks. The Foreign Minister, Mustafa Osman Ismail, commented on these tensions in public, and confirmed that there had been differences of opinion, but that these issues now had been overcome. Years later Ghazi told me that the difference between him and Ali Osman Taha was over security arrangements, not much else.[68]

What none of us mentioned in any of the speeches on this occasion – or later – were the issues not subject to negotiation. First, no provision had been made for oil contracts that would come into effect only when a final peace agreement was signed. This provided a loophole that the government could use to sign contracts that were in the pipeline and would not be subject to the wealth sharing agreement. Secondly, the parties ended up negotiating an agreement on revenue sharing but not resource sharing. This was a deliberate choice made early in the negotiations,[69] and was in turn the indirect cause of the difficulties surrounding the Abyei issue and the demarcation of the North–South border.

A third omission was any reference to water. Given the controversy surrounding water resources, and in particular the Jonglei Canal in the South, this may be surprising. On the other hand, these are to a large degree international questions linked to all nine countries of the Nile basin. This omission was therefore deliberate. It was also one that would prevent an already uneasy neighbour, Egypt, from becoming even more nervous about the outcome of the peace process.

I did not discuss any of these issues with the parties. They had had enough trouble reaching agreement on the issues at hand. But my presence at Naivasha gave me another opportunity to sit down with each leader for several hours to review the remaining negotiating issues. Significant problems still had to be sorted out, not least the Three Areas. Because of mounting international pressure, strong American interest, and the desire from both sides to get the issues over and done with, the two leaders were uncertain whether they could afford a break right now. I managed to convince them to continue negotiations immediately after the signing ceremony. The Americans still wanted a framework agreement to be signed by January 20th in Washington, DC.

At the same time the situation in Darfur was becoming more acute, and

pressure increased for further negotiations between the rebels and the government. After a third round of talks chaired by Chad had broken down in
mid-December, President Bashir declared, "'Our top priority will be the anni-
hilation of the rebellion and any outlaw who carries arms against the state'".
He described the Darfur rebels as "hirelings, traitors, agents and renegades
whom the enemies of the Sudan employed for carrying out their plots against
the country." Moreover, he said, they were a small group, "not representing
the people of Darfur in any way and are pursuing personal ambitions of seizing
power, not only in Darfur, but also in Kordofan and even in Khartoum."[70]
This was a signal and a tone that boded for more military action and not
wasting time on talks.

CHAPTER FIVE

Inching Forward

There was no time to lose. Both for the Southern peace process itself and for Darfur, completion of a comprehensive agreement was now imperative. I urged Dr. John and Ali Osman to continue the negotiations immediately, without even a day's break. They did. On the day after the signing ceremony the two leaders negotiated non-stop for ten hours on the Three Areas. But that issue had complicated the wealth sharing negotiations, and now threatened to undermine the whole peace process.

As the discussions proceeded, some progress was made. Dr. John confirmed that of a list of twelve outstanding issues the parties had prepared, six were now resolved and, in his view, five were soluble. The sticking point was Abyei. The SPLM/A insisted that the Abyei area really belonged to the Bahr al-Ghazal and should be transferred to the South by an administrative order. This was based on what they claimed were historical facts relating to the settlement of the nine Ngok Dinka "chieftainships" in the Abyei area. They wanted such an order imbedded in the peace agreement, settling the arrangements until a Southern referendum could take place. The government, on the other hand, basing its claim too in part on historical rights, was happy with the status quo, in which Abyei was part of Kordofan and thus of the North.

Prior to the direct negotiations between Ali Osman and Garang, the parties had gone through largely unproductive discussions on the Three Areas led by General Sumbeiywo. In the first round nine days had been spent discussing the agenda, which showed the level of posturing and delay. Three subcommittees, one for each Area, were set up for separate talks to address the root causes of the problems and table proposals for dealing with them. But the Nuba Mountains subcommittee failed to get beyond "root causes", and the Abyei subcommittee was never even officially convened because of a dispute over the chairmanship and representation. The Southern Blue Nile committee made it as far as discussing proposals.

This format did not work and by the end of the round there had been little progress. A brief consultation at the end of May 2003 failed. Both parties were able to show their constituencies that they were standing firm. In July the issue was considered as part of the discussions on the draft framework agreement; as we have seen, it was partly in protest against the inclusion of the Three Areas in the draft peace agreement that the government delegation withdrew from the negotiations. The government objected both in principle and to the content of the proposals.

It was only when the two leaders started direct negotiations that there was any progress on the Three Areas. The issues were touched upon during talks on security arrangements, but not really dealt with before the almost parallel negotiations on wealth sharing and Three Areas in the autumn of 2003.

The Three Areas and the Two Sudans

The Three Areas were like microcosms of the whole Sudan, and they crystallized two completely opposite visions for the country. For the SPLM the fate of the Three Areas – and of Darfur and the East for that matter – was the rationale for participating in the negotiations: the movement, and Garang in particular, wanted to transform the country. Striking a deal for the South only, at the expense of other marginalized peoples and of their allies in the Three Areas, was out of the question. Peace depended on justice. Only through devolving power and resources to the marginalized areas would Sudan be able to achieve peace and avoid fragmentation.

Khartoum argued that devolution could lead to "balkanization". They were particularly worried about self-determination. The government might accept limited autonomy, but giving the Three Areas a referendum could tear the country apart. Besides, Khartoum saw the Three Areas as part of the Northern Sudan, and their view was that the Machakos Protocol confirmed this through its reference to the 1956 borders. On this, however, there was disagreement, which came to the fore in connection with the discussions on the status of the capital much later. Abyei was admittedly somewhat different from the other two Areas, but here too the government stood firm.

There were very strong political constituencies behind each position, the government's and the SPLM/A's. These in turn had allies at the very top of the leadership on each side. The ruling party in Khartoum had close links to the Misiriya Baggara, whose leaders were extremely vocal about their own rights in Abyei. For the SPLM/A, the situation was even more difficult: key members of the leadership came from the Three Areas. Several prominent commanders were Ngok Dinka from Abyei. Abandoning the Three Areas for a "South only" solution would seem to betray them and their people, and cost the Movement support elsewhere. Standing firm for the Three Areas and other marginalized regions was what made the SPLM a *national* movement.

In several phone conversations with Ali Osman and Dr. John about the Three Areas in October 2003 I encountered a red line. Taha said: "Self determination for all three areas? What then about the East and about Darfur? Where will it end? It will lead to a full fragmentation of the state." Later that month, in a private conversation at Naivasha (as my notes from this discussion indicate) he told me that the government ultimately "would not be opposed to the area [Abyei] being left as part of Bahr al-Ghazal". He had mentioned the same thing to Garang. But these views were never voiced in the talks proper, and the government's stated position on Abyei hardened very soon.

After completion of the wealth sharing protocol in January 2004 things started to move. At Naivasha I had a long chat with Abel Alier, who had an important proposal I later discussed with both parties and my Troika colleagues. Given the competing versions of Abyei's history, an arbitration commission could be appointed, whose conclusions would be binding. The discussion then, said Abel, would focus on who should be on the commission, what its mandate would be, and so forth. The key issue would be the referendum – what question it would pose, when it would take place, and how the area would be governed until the referendum. The referendum, in his view, should simply pose a choice between autonomy in the North and incorporation in the South. I saw this as a plausible way out, although it would be a hard sell. Garang was open to the idea of a commission, but had serious concerns about other elements of Alier's proposal.

I had lengthy discussions with Ali Osman Taha. He cautioned against any expectation of agreement soon on the Three Areas. He identified the same issues as Dr. John, but highlighted the differences instead of the common ground. Otherwise he reiterated the government's positions. Taha stated that the very word "referendum" was "inflammable". He pointed out, however, that Alier had some good ideas on the way forward, and encouraged further discussion.

Meanwhile Abel Alier had, on his own initiative, started writing a paper in which he identified two phases of an Abyei solution, one of stabilization, resettlement of refugees, and autonomy, the second of consultation about future status.[1] For the SPLM to accept this approach I knew that it must include a referendum on whether to belong to the North or South. Ali Osman read the paper and expressed interest.[2] Garang's reaction was very negative: the proposal was too similar to the one that had failed under the Addis Ababa Agreement;[3] the timing of consultation was wrong, for if an Abyei referendum were scheduled for after the exercise of Southern self-determination there was no way to guarantee that it would take place at all.

Playing to the Danforth Gallery

Special Envoy Danforth visited Naivasha on 14 January 2004. While he clearly wanted to give the negotiations a final push Dr. John told me that "each side" was "playing to the Danforth Gallery" with hardline positions. Andrew Natsios, the Administrator of USAID, was in the delegation, and had come via Darfur and Khartoum. Darfur had made a great impact. Natsios was fuming with anger, not only at what he had seen there, but also at the government strategy he saw unfolding in Darfur. While Danforth was at Naivasha, key members of the government's negotiating team had gone to Khartoum to brief Bashir, who was preparing to visit Cairo. Garang's assessment was that a week had been lost: "A telephone call would have been enough". At the same time, it was clear that Danforth's visit was important in placing Darfur at the top of the agenda for both parties. I had stressed the situation with Taha the week before, as I would do later, worried that the whole peace process could be compromised, but American concerns had more impact.

After Danforth had left, Taha and Garang got back to business, sitting for hours discussing Abyei. Taha wanted an administrative arrangement with autonomy, headed by Ngok Dinkas, but no referendum. He tried to sweeten this position by proposing Commander Deng Alor as Governor. This was an indication of what the SPLM interpreted as clear attempts at creating divisions within the Movement. As negotiations dragged on, fear arose that what had been gained through the Machakos Protocol and the other Naivasha proto- cols could now be lost over the Three Areas. After all, many Southerners paid only lip service to the notion of New Sudan. But among those who did not were Deng Alor and Edward Lino from Abyei, Abd al-Aziz Adam from the Nuba Mountains, and Malik Agar from Southern Blue Nile. For them change in the North was essential.

The Abyei sub-committee had by this time looked through the historical claims and possible options for a way forward. In this context, Alier's idea of an independent commission was tabled. Its efficacy was enhanced by new discussions I had with the two principals over the telephone. Ali Osman wanted me to press the SPLM: its proposal for an Administrative Order would never work, and a referendum was unacceptable. I told him that my ability to influence the Movement's position was very limited. Given the historical complexity of this issue, we also needed to consult experts on history and international law.

There was more in the wind than Abyei. The government delegation started to reschedule meetings or cancel them without any explanation. Taha told Dr. John that he had to go back to Khartoum again for personal reasons, after which he planned to make the pilgrimage to Mecca.[4] We failed to dissuade him, and he left abruptly, in the middle of negotiations, confounding both the SPLM and international observers. The parties scheduled the next round for February 17th, and Garang and Taha agreed to keep in touch by telephone. It would later become apparent why the government seemed to have chosen delaying tactics at this particular time. It was immediately after this that the crisis in Darfur really exploded.

Ali Osman told me and others that he was going on the *hajj* to Mecca. At the same time I was aware of growing criticism of Taha in Khartoum for giving too much away in the talks. This continued to focus on the security arrange- ments; Majzoub al-Khalifa Ahmed, former governor of Khartoum and a powerhouse in the ruling party, Dr. Ghazi, and some leading army officers remained critical.[5] I was later told that Taha had gone to Khartoum so suddenly to mollify them, before proceeding on his pilgrimage. This may well have been his personal reasons.[6] In any case, upon Taha's return from the *hajj*, a new situation had arisen in Darfur.

Firestorm in Darfur

The violence in Darfur was at its highest level during this period. After an intense campaign President Bashir announced victory and an end to military operations on 9 February, and outlined formal proposals for resolving the Darfur conflict. Although the signals were rather vague, until then the government had deflected any suggestion of a political settlement. At the same time, however, his claim that the government had recaptured all rebel-held territory and had full control of the region proved wildly inaccurate, as would soon become clear. The escalation of January and February drew widespread international attention and condemnation.

The results of this major military operation and other attacks in Darfur are reflected in the report of the UN's International Commission of Inquiry on Darfur, published in 2005. The commission established that "the Government of the Sudan and the Janjaweed are responsible for serious violations of international human rights and humanitarian law amounting to crimes under international law."[7] It further reported that government forces and militias had

> conducted indiscriminate attacks, including killing of civilians, torture, enforced disappearances, destruction of villages, rape and other forms of sexual violence, pillaging and forced displacement, throughout Darfur. These acts were conducted on a widespread and systematic basis, and therefore may amount to crimes against humanity.[8]

Some have described these events as genocide, others as ethnic cleansing, war crimes, and crimes against humanity, that last being the core of the International Criminal Court's indictment of President Bashir. A second arrest warrant, for genocide, was issued on 12 July 2010, as this book went to press. In any case, the facts were that almost one million were now internally displaced and 200,000 refugees across the border in Chad. The number of deaths from war-related causes reached about 150,000.[9] A huge humanitarian operation was mounted, but it was impeded. Media access was also hampered. Still, witnesses were numerous.

When the high-level talks with Taha were about to start in July 2003, John Garang had briefly mentioned the possibility of including Darfur and the East in the negotiations. Abel Alier was the intermediary, and this was one point of many in a confidential exchange. Taha said no, referring to the support of the SPLM/A for the rebel groups. That the SPLM Chairman blocked any such attempts,[10] is therefore not correct. But Dr. John never insisted, and it may be that he wanted simply to be able to claim that he had tried. A specific request to include Darfur in the talks had indeed been rejected earlier, at Machakos in 2002, when both parties had referred to the IGAD mandate. Whenever I raised this issue later, with both Taha and Garang, the answer was always the same: "No" from the First Vice President, and "It will not work" from the Chairman.

Before the high-level talks started, Garang's strategy was to negotiate seriously for peace and a peaceful transformation, while working for regime change with the National Democratic Alliance and supporting the rebel movements in Darfur. Members of the SPLM/A leadership have confirmed that military training was provided in the 1990s. Much later, before Machakos, rebel leader Abd al-Wahid Mohamed al-Nur contacted the Movement for political assistance. He has since been quoted as acknowledging military support for the Darfur Liberation Front later Sudan Liberation Movement and Army.[11] Other credible sources close to the SPLM/A leadership confirm the same.[12]

Many Southerners thought that Khartoum was "too deformed to be reformed".[13] The SPLM therefore had two possible courses, pursuit of a New Sudan, or regime change. Garang seemed to want to have both options available. The question was: for how long? When I was made aware of the accusations against the SPLM/A, we didn't know whether they really were true. Nevertheless, I privately raised the issue of military support with Dr. John and said that such support – if it were going on – would have serious implications for the credibility of the SPLM/A at the negotiating table. What has not been clear to me since was how long Dr. John and the SPLA had engaged in support of the rebel groups, and whether they were still doing so during the first half of 2004, when the Naivasha talks seemed likely to reach an agreement. That the SPLA mounted a mission to evacuate Abd al-Wahid from Wadi Salih in February 2004 does indicate a continuing relationship between the Sudan Liberation Movement/Army and the SPLM/A quite late in the talks.[14]

Apart from repeatedly discussing Darfur, I also raised with Ali Osman Taha our concerns over government support for militias, whether in Upper Nile or in Eastern Equatoria. In both cases such support was not conducive to a negotiated peace, especially at the phase of the talks we were in now. Thus the government side too seemed to be running parallel tracks, with Ali Osman Taha engaging in peace talks while elements in National Security and Military intelligence, with or without the consent of the top leadership, were seemingly trying to undermine the peace process. The significant militia attacks in 2003 and 2004 were a clear indication of this. But just as Dr. John denied military support for the Darfur rebels, so Ali Osman denied government support for the militias.

With the help of the UN and African Union, some progress was made in the talks on Darfur. The violence continued, however, despite a ceasefire. At the same time, the rebel groups began to splinter. Early on, the National Movement for Reform and Development had broken away from the Justice and Equality Movement. Now factions in the Sudan Liberation Movement/Army were attacking each other. Further fragmentation ensued. This did not improve the likelihood of reaching a negotiated end to the Darfur violence.

Both the SPLM/A and the international community seem to have misjudged the situation in Darfur in two important ways. We all predicted that negotiations for a comprehensive peace agreement in the South would end much sooner than they did. Secondly, we all assumed that the intensity of the conflict in Darfur would continue at the relatively low level of other Sudanese rebellions. This implied that there was time to get a deal done on the South and then to address the Darfur issue and the situation in the East, which was also tense. On both accounts we were wrong. At every juncture in the negotiations, new hurdles prevented progress. Delaying tactics were also used, including in January 2004 just before the massive government campaign in Darfur was launched.

The government knew full well that completion of the Naivasha process would focus all international attention on Darfur. But now the scale of the operations in Darfur was such that action could not wait for the negotiating process to run its course. But the continuing negotiations did in fact lead to a certain paralysis of the international community. Darfur seemed to have become hostage to the talks. Behind the scenes, therefore, I started to sound out the possibility of a separate political process after Naivasha, based on the parties already at the table. I was planning to pursue this actively later. This could for example be a "fast-track" negotiation involving the two key negotiators and the Darfur rebel groups, after completion of the last protocols.

Whether Taha supported the military campaign in the Western region, or merely acquiesced in it, is unknown; we hardly have any facts with which to judge, and Ali Osman's decision, that year, to absent himself from the country for the *hajj*, may well be relevant. In any case, the military option Khartoum was willing to give up in relation to the South, it had now grasped with both hands in Darfur.

The Americans Wave Sticks

As Darfur exploded in conflict, the US Congress and Administration were irritated with the lack of progress in the talks and the way the Sudanese government had handled the last round. Congress was also beginning to look at measures that could be taken to put additional pressure on Khartoum. In a letter to President Bush, two Congressmen, Donald M. Payne and Thomas Tancredo, requested an investigation of twelve Sudanese officials' involvement in support of terrorism over the past decade, including an attempt to assassinate President Mubarak of Egypt. A list of names was circulated in Congress. Taha's name was on it. There were rumours of substantial evidence against him. While calling attention to Darfur, this was mainly an attempt by some in Congress to keep the focus on the Southern peace agreement.[15] Publicizing the questionable past of several key players in Khartoum empowered the Administration to wave a few "sticks", intended to increase the pressure on Ali Osman personally. Hearings in Congress were originally planned for February 10th, and were later delayed until late February when the Sudan Peace Act was up for renewal.

When Ali Osman returned from Mecca, I telephoned to congratulate him on having performed the *hajj* and offered my interpretation of what was going on in the US Congress. This included both the questions being asked about him personally and the punitive measures under consideration. Those seen as the "hardliners" in Congress seemed to be increasing the pressure. He was probably aware of the planned hearings, but I still gave him an analysis based on my own sources. I also conveyed the SPLM's concerns about the way the last round had ended. There was a clear need for him to prove them all wrong, re-engage with Dr. John, and continue the negotiating partnership. For me it was critical to use this information to try to turn things around, making Ali Osman understand that the sure way to counter these developments was to move quickly on the negotiating front and show renewed commitment in the talks.

I pushed for ceasefire negotiations on Darfur, and for him to engage personally in changing the government's policies in the Western region. Taha did not commit – as yet. On the negotiations he reiterated his commitment and reassured me that they would return for the next round on February 17th.

I had a teleconference with the First Vice President on February 13th. By then President Bashir had made his Darfur declaration and outlined the political steps that would be taken. These included a general amnesty, control of arms to the region, corridors for humanitarian aid and return of refugees and internally displaced people, and facilitation of development assistance. I commended these steps, but emphasized that they had to be complemented with an urgent political process that included direct talks with the rebel groups. I advised Taha to take advantage of the presence in Khartoum just then of officials from both the US and the UN, to discuss the Darfur crisis.

The fact that he was now targeted personally in Washington for involvement in terrorist activities, showed the seriousness of the situation and the need to move on both the IGAD talks and a political process for Darfur. Ali Osman controlled his temper. But on the phone I could hear how indignant he was. With great intensity he said he had nothing to be ashamed of. He referred to Charlie Snyder and the US Administration and said, "The way they are approaching this part of the world is not acceptable. If they will insist on this type of behaviour, they will not succeed. I will not be intimidated, not by the US Congress, nor anyone else." They could take him to Guantanamo if they wanted, he said.

I did not know then that this had been a reference to an earlier conversation with Dr. John. When the two of them decided that there would be no Rose Garden ceremony by January 20th, Dr. John had joked: "I don't know what they will do to me, but I know exactly what they will do to you: they will send you to Guantanamo."[16] Both of them had laughed at the time.

A Relationship at Risk

With the talks due to reconvene again soon, I tried to prepare the ground with long discussions on the phone with both Ali Osman and Dr. John. In their opinion, a tentative agreement on major issues related to the Nuba Mountains and Southern Blue Nile had been reached before the last round had broken up; remaining differences over a few issues, such as the geographical definition of the Nuba Mountains, could have been sorted out. No progress had been made on Abyei, and the prevailing view was still that the government had just walked out of the talks.

Privately Dr. John conveyed his concern that Khartoum was intent on stalling. The situation of "No war, no peace" would benefit the government: it continued to generate income from the oilfields, and would be able to tap more before a peace agreement was a reality. After a deal they would have to share 50 percent of the resources with the South, so there was actually a financial disincentive to settling soon. The government might have a strong interest in dragging out the talks at Naivasha to deflect attention from military operations in the West. Ali Osman rejected outright any such speculation about the government's commitment, and was crystal clear that they wanted an agreement without further delay.

Ali Osman informed me at this juncture that he was "taking the heat" in Khartoum over the security arrangements, wealth sharing, and the Three Areas.[17] He had no personal interest at all in delaying the negotiations. But managing and accommodating popular psychology in Khartoum was a challenge, he said. On Darfur, Ali Osman gave new signals. He wanted a political solution. This could be accomplished through an All-Darfur conference and security guarantees. Roger Winter and Charlie Snyder were at this time pursuing links with the rebel leaders, and Ali Osman indicated that he would be willing to work with them. In fact the Americans had talked to him that morning, and we compared notes.

As Ali Osman tried to defuse the situation in Khartoum, Dr. John had to navigate tricky waters in the National Democratic Alliance. Mohamed Osman al-Mirghani and Taha had planned to open negotiations to implement the Jeddah Protocol of 4 December 2003 between the ruling party and Democratic Unionists. This would effectively split the opposition alliance, which was not in the SPLM's interest. Mirghani had asked the SPLM/A and the government for Alliance representation in the next round of discussions on power sharing. By the time Garang went to Asmara to calm the waters, the Alliance was on the verge of collapse. Garang insisted that the SPLM/A remained fully committed to the Alliance, which would be part of any power sharing arrangements in the North. Mirghani, wanting Dr. John out of the way, organized farewells for him in Asmara, knowing that he had to catch a flight in time for the talks on February 17. But Garang smelled a rat, stayed on, and chartered a plane just in time for arrival in Naivasha. By then the situation was under control. The Alliance had agreed to the broad principle of the Jeddah Protocol – power sharing among the Sudanese parties – but revised the content substantially. The Sudan Liberation Movement/Army, the Darfur rebel movement, had been brought into the Alliance. New negotiating committees were established for a planned round of talks, as soon as agreement had been reached between the Government and the SPLM/A, now expected in March.

The Go-Between

Dr. John could usually sense when Ali Osman Taha was on the verge of walking out of the negotiations, a frequent tactic of his. Ali Osman would become evasive, less engaged. That was when Dr. John would call me and say, "I think Ali is going to leave. You have to make him stay." Or Ali Osman himself would convey to me a certain sense of unease, impatience and exhaustion: "Now I am going back to Khartoum for a while. It is enough. If they cannot move on this issue, or if you cannot make John adjust his position, it is enough. I am not sure I am coming back."

The threats did not always work. Dr. John was a counterpart with staying power, who was always ready to continue the talks, or to wait for the next round – starting exactly from where they had left off. From a negotiating perspective, any loss of time was unhelpful, so I would usually agree with Dr. John that an interruption would not help move things along. I would either convince Taha myself, or mobilize support from Troika partners. Sometimes we succeeded, other times not, as in late January 2004. The combination of Ali Osman's "departure" tactics and Dr. John's tendency to take his time, and wait out his opposite number, and their mutual stamina, ultimately dragged out the talks for much longer than expected. In the end, this was the responsibility of both parties.

At this juncture, upon their return in February, other factors and constituencies also influenced the negotiations. Pressure on Dr. John from key members of his delegation was significant. He had to negotiate very hard on the Three Areas. At the same time, the SPLM/A knew that they could also benefit from "pounding" these issues at a time when international pressure was mounting on the government as a consequence of the war in Darfur. That pressure might help them reach an acceptable solution for the Three Areas. Darfur played out in a different way on the government side. Anxiety over the Three Areas had only increased as a consequence of the Darfur crisis. The government side feared that they might be forced to accept a deal for all the marginalized areas, and potentially also for Darfur and the East, that would lead to a break-up of the country. This made their position on the Three Areas even more entrenched than before.

Despite these challenges, both Ali Osman and Dr. John were committed to finishing the negotiations, and to doing so personally. After so many months they were able to sense each other's moods, which shifted obviously with the negotiations. When they got stuck, they could both be quite cranky. Each had good intelligence on the other side. I would get a good sense of this through our numerous phone calls. Most of my interactions with the parties were by phone. During my visits to Naivasha[18] I went back and forth between the two of them, on a one-on-one basis. Except at the very beginning of a meeting, I was not accompanied by the Norwegian Special Envoy, our staff, any of our observers or mediators. To have done so would have made the leaders more reticent and therefore made the meeting less effective. By this stage I had developed a level of confidence with both Dr. John and Ali Osman that involved a very high degree of transparency. But the two were also aware of the close coordination and information sharing among the Troika. In some cases proposals for possible solutions were best done in full confidentiality, however, as with the discussions on Darfur, which I never shared with anyone at this juncture.

It was during these private discussions that I really got to know the two leaders. After an initial briefing and update from my team, I would often go to the SPLM Chairman first to get his perspective on the status of particular issues. I was normally well informed in advance by our own people in the negotiations, my own frequent phone calls, as well as from informants on both sides. (One of the best-informed people, who continuously updated us with surprisingly accurate intelligence, was Col Ding. He had amazingly good information from the government side and was at the same time very close to the SPLM leadership.) I would usually get an update from Dr. John on the most recent developments, and then relate the results of my latest discussions with Ali Osman. I then discussed possible solutions with him before proceeding to his counterpart. The First Vice President would sometimes have his staff or members of his delegation with him for the first half hour or so of our meetings. Afterwards, however, it was time for business. We often carried on for two or three hours. After several rounds at Naivasha I had become a trusted go-between.

At this later stage, the two leaders knew each other extremely well. They joked that they had probably spent more time together than with their wives and families. They had developed a sense of fellowship and sympathy. Every time there had been a long break in the negotiations, however, Dr. John told me that they had to "warm up" the relationship again. Often a day or two or three went by before they got down to real business. Then, though, they concentrated on getting the negotiations done. During these more intense periods I was a sounding board, a "wall of lamentation" (when the other party was "unreasonable"), facilitator, and sometimes an informal mediator. I would often have a proposal or two on how to move forward when the two of them were stuck, or a potential solution to one of the tricky issues. In some cases I would agree with Ali Osman that the SPLM/A had gone too far and had to adjust their position. I would then put pressure on the Chairman. In other cases it was the other way around. The government and Ali Osman knew where I stood. I wanted a just peace for Sudan. At the same time, I strived to

be an honest broker. They knew where I was coming from and what my
agenda was. I did not play any games. The reason for the government's
engagement with me, and Ali Osman's in particular, was of course that I could
put pressure on the SPLM. Very few people were in a position to do that in
an effective way. At the same time, I was not a tool they could use for their
own purposes. I had my own opinions about where a just solution would lie,
and would tell them. Nor was I blind in relation to Dr. John and the SPLM.
At times I could be among their toughest critics. I ended up as perhaps the
best-informed participant in the negotiations and, to my surprise, was often
far better informed than those present in the formal talks. On several occasions I had to brief General Sumbeiywo, and even our own observer, about
the status of affairs.

In an e-mail message from this period I advised against high-level deployment to the negotiations from the Troika, saying:

> I have experienced repeatedly that I have been better informed about the
> negotiations than any of the troika-representatives in Naivasha . . . The
> two guys, Ali and John, keep their cards to themselves, and you often
> need to be briefed by them personally to know what is going on. This is
> often easier on the phone than on site. To some extent not even members
> of the negotiation delegations are fully aware of what's going on.[19]

I mentioned how I had had to cross check – with the two leaders themselves – information and reports from the observer team, and that they were
not always correct. This is another example of how closed and personal the
negotiations were. The two leaders did much of the job themselves. At the
same time, they were briefing their own teams about what was going on and
setting them to work. Both Ali Osman and Dr. John had regular, often daily,
briefings with their closest advisers and negotiators to ensure that they were
informed.

Make or Break

Although Ali Osman made no concessions at Naivasha without backing from
the President and the party leadership,[20] there was still no doubt that he was
in control of the process, and had indeed invested his political career in it. Dr.
John was aware of the tension in that relationship, and he jokingly referred
to the partnership the two of them would develop once a peace agreement was
signed, and even about the time limit of President Bashir's tenure. Many
people's perceived Dr. John as a would-be kingmaker.[21] Others noted that the
agreement under negotiation was tailored to continue their partnership after
it was implemented – a scenario in which the two had key roles.

The talks proceeded over Abyei and popular consultations in the other
two areas. I urged Ali Osman and Garang to set firm deadlines for complet-

ing of these talks. After I discussed this with Charlie Snyder and Sumbeiywo, the end of the round was set at March 16th. Congressional hearings on the Sudan were scheduled for the 11th. The two leaders followed a strict schedule. The Abyei committee had been reconvened, and worked through various options, one of which the SPLM/A received positively but the government side, after consulting Khartoum, rejected. Similarly, while Ali Osman touted Alier's paper as the basis for agreement, Dr. John found it unacceptable. According to him, the government now seemed more interested in a future political partnership with the SPLM than with solving the immediate issues at hand.

After more than a week of fruitless talks on Abyei, it was clear that there had been no movement. My notes on calls with Dr. John and Ali Osman read: "No progress", and "Getting very concerned". Three options were under consideration. The first was the SPLM/A's proposal for an administrative order, whereby the area would be annexed to Bahr al-Ghazal and hence to the South; a commission would settle border issues. Under the second proposal, a truncated Abyei would have a special status under the Presidency in a package deal on oil resources. The third option, included in the Nakuru document but never formally tabled, proposed a referendum in Abyei and an international commission to determine the border. In February and early March, none of the parties really wanted that last course.

From afar I looked at trade-offs between the Abyei issue and others. From Ali Osman's perspective, a commitment on political partnership between the National Congress Party and the SPLM/A could balance concessions on Abyei. I responded that movement on Abyei had to come first. I also predicted that a referendum was bound to be proposed unless the government came up with an alternative the SPLM could accept: "There is no deal without this", I said to Ali Osman, referring to Abyei. "You can forget it. Hell will break loose." We all threatened and cajoled; nothing worked. The constituencies on both sides were far too strong.

Both Ali Osman and Dr. John asked me to come to the negotiations and see what I could do to help. External help certainly seemed necessary. In my last telephone conversation with Ali Osman before I went to Naivasha I said: "This is not the deal breaker. No one will understand that the fate of thirty million people will depend on an area of 100,000 Dinkas and some cows and camels herded by a few Misiriya families. This is not possible!" But of course we all knew that the issue was about oil as much as history and customary rights. I insisted on an agreement before March 16th, and warned that without any progress by the 11th, it was not unlikely that the Americans could consider coercive measures.

Abyei – the Ultimate Test

Despite the many hours spent travelling, I was always happy to go to Naivasha. With my own background in East Africa, chatting with the Kenyans in Swahili, enjoying the familiar sounds, smells, the fresh air, I felt like I was coming home. The two-hour drive from Nairobi was beautiful. The Rift Valley is one of the wonders of Africa, with panoramic and breathtaking views. I thought: I will never get tired of this. But the drive was not without worries. The Sudan negotiations had come to the one issue that seemed a complete red line for both sides.

Upon arrival at the lodge, I was pleased to see a number of old friends, the hippos that spent their leisure time there. Bored, they would come up on the green lawn, walk about, have a look at what was going on, and chew on whatever they got hold of. I guess they were more used to the foreign tourists in shorts and safari hats than to these tall Dinkas and the others in white turbans and *jallabiyyas*. At this juncture, the negotiating circus had been going on for eight months, and they should have been used to it. But I was always happy to see them.

On 6–7 March I spent hours discussing the Three Areas with Dr. John and Ali Osman, had several meetings with General Sumbeiywo, and sat down with Abel Alier to discuss the Abyei stalemate. I tried to get some indication from Ali Osman what he wanted in return for concessions on Abyei. Partnership with the SPLM/A was critical for the political elite in Khartoum, who needed allies and legitimacy to retain their hold on power. Garang was very wary of marrying the National Congress Party, given its history and agenda and the resulting duopoly's exclusion of other political forces. This was a difficult bargain. Was there any alternative?

Superficially the government's argument over Abyei was attractive and persuasive. In line with the Machakos Protocol and African practice, any agreement should honour the colonial boundary, in this case between North and South at independence on 1 January 1956. Abyei was thereby part of the North. But everyone knew that the oil was what mattered. Nor were the historical records clear about the borders, which had changed before and since independence. The SPLM had tabled proposals on oil sharing, but the government would not discuss them, as it was their position that it was entitled to 100 percent. The government was willing to consider a commission to advise on the future status of Abyei, which could be defined following their report. Until then the area would be under direct administration of the Presidency. IGAD's negotiating team and the Troika were actively supporting a referendum, which seemed the obvious compromise. With Taha I also discussed Darfur, which continued to deepen Khartoum's anxiety about the Three Areas: recognition of self-determination in Abyei risked engendering demands for it everywhere else.

At this point Ali Osman made a quick trip to Khartoum for consultations.

Upon his return, presumably with a renewed mandate, the government tabled (March 15th) a "package-solution" on all remaining issues. This accommodated the SPLM on quite a number of points, but not Abyei. It was rejected by the SPLM. Interestingly, the package deal also omitted reference to the capital.

Now Garang told me privately that someone else, preferably from the outside – a "referee", as he put it – was needed to solve the Abyei problem. I agreed. So did Ali Osman, who used the word "arbitrator".[22] In the Troika we had seen this coming, and I had already talked to the Americans about the possibility of their brokering the agreement directly. They had enough clout to get the job done. At the same time they were increasingly frustrated and irritated, and the rest of us were worried that they would start to lose interest. Engaging them over Abyei might be the best way to retain American focus while achieving a solution acceptable to both parties.

Consulting the People

As the Americans worked on Abyei, I was asked to help in another area. Dr. John was worried about the two other areas, the Nuba Mountains and Southern Blue Nile. While he upheld the SPLM position on self-determination, he understood by now that the government would never agree. Abyei was difficult enough. I had been through this issue numerous times with Ali Osman, and he was adamant, so I tended to agree with Garang's reading. It was as if one were hitting a brick wall. At the same time, Dr. John was under significant pressure from within the Movement. I had tabled the idea of using the state legislatures, after democratic elections, as the means of popular consultation – instead of holding referenda. Fink Haysom had come up with the same idea. In discussion with the SPLM/A delegation he had cited the case of East Timor, where the term "popular consultations" had been applied. It was an ambiguous term, as the consultations in East Timor in actual fact were a referendum.[23]

During my visit to Naivasha, Dr. John asked me to talk individually to Abd al-Aziz and Malik Agar about the impossibility of the Nuba Mountains and Southern Blue Nile exercising self-determination by referendum along the same lines as the South as a whole. It was quite clear that it would not "fly" with Khartoum. He had failed to convince them. Garang wanted me to convey our collective understanding that indirect consultation was reasonable, with the precondition that credible elections had ensured a legitimate state legislature. I sat down with them separately, gave them my reading of the negotiations, and explained Khartoum's fear of "balkanization". From this perspective popular consultations could not include a referendum. They would, however, provide the opportunity for the people to state their opinion about the solution imbedded in the CPA, through a newly elected state legislature. In theory it was possible that a majority of the state legislature could reject the provisions in the CPA for their area, and call for a referendum. In such a scenario, this would have to lead to a whole new process during the interim period, and subsequently be handled by the Government of National Unity. The CPA itself, however, could not include such provisions, given the situation in the negotiations. I promised the support of the international community, both in making sure that elections were free and fair, and in providing assistance to their people.

The SPLM/A in those two areas was also very concerned about the application of *Sharia*, and what they called "Islamization" of the education system. Following elections, I explained, this issue could be dealt with in state legislatures. With the SPLM/A in the central government, the regional status quo would not be an option. The issue of peace dividends was also important. Recalling my previous visits to the Nuba Mountains, I knew how marginalized and intimidated people felt. I made a personal pledge on my country's behalf: whatever the government, Norway would stand firm and support them. The two commanders ended up agreeing to the proposed text we had worked on. Dr. John was very pleased. This text formed the basis for the Protocols on the two areas.

None of the promises I made was kept. The international community and donors forgot entirely about these marginalized areas, and no peace dividend was paid them. I was later to regret deeply my role in persuading Abd al-Aziz and Malik. Elected politicians' long-term commitments on their own or their successors' behalf can be illusory, as these turned out to be. What I did just added to the betrayal the people of those areas have since felt at the hands of the Khartoum elite and the international community. That betrayal is deeply felt and needs to be borne in mind when future scenarios for Sudan are considered. Recent interviews with the government's negotiators confirmed that self-determination with an option of secession for the Nuba Mountains and Southern Blue Nile had indeed been a "red line".[24]

After months of negotiations and my intervention at the final stage, agreement was reached on most of the content of the protocols for the two areas. These included administrative arrangements, autonomy, and popular consultations on the status of the two areas through the state legislatures after elections had been held. A Land Commission would be drawn from both parties and the areas themselves. Power-sharing arrangements remained undetermined. In Washington the Congressional hearings had been held, with no substantial implications for the talks or measures targeting the Sudanese government. The next deadline, March 16th, also passed without an agreement.

I was in touch with the Americans over Abyei. As usual, they were in interagency discussions involving the Special Envoy, the State Department, the National Security Council, the White House and USAID. That last was important, as the Administrator, Andrew Natsios, and two members of his team, Roger Winter and Brian da Silva, had strong links to the SPLM. Intramural US negotiations could be as tough as international ones. A draft proposal for

Abyei was emerging from the parties, historians, and experts on the area and on international law. Jeff Millington was central in this process and in drafting the language. The Americans did not include the UK and Norway in their deliberations. I was a bit nervous; my experience with the Americans was mixed when their positions were subject to inter-agency negotiation. It was a risky business, not least because once the position was finally decided it would be virtually impossible to change. Those with most knowledge were not necessarily the most influential in the process. And the longer it took, the greater was my anxiety.

Decision Time

The plan was for Jack Danforth to come to Naivasha to present the American proposal as an established fact. We asked to see it in advance. On March 19th a high-powered delegation arrived, including Danforth; Andrew Natsios, the USAID Administrator; Roger Winter, Natsios's Assistant Administrator; Charlie Snyder, the Acting Assistant Secretary of State for Africa; Ambassador Mike Ranneberger, Jeff Millington, Kate Almquist, and Brian da Silva, all of them old Sudan hands. The presence of several SPLM/A sympathizers mitigated some of the doubts the Movement had with Danforth.

I called Charlie upon their arrival in Nairobi, a few hours before they were to meet the parties. He told me the substance of the proposal. I was quite shocked. It contained much the same framework we had discussed: an independent commission to review the history of Abyei and reach a binding decision on its borders, a referendum for the Abyei area, and intermediate administrative arrangements with a special status under the Presidency. But the timing of the referendum was the problem. It would take place six months *after* the referendum for Southern Sudan. I knew that this was a "red flag" for the SPLM/A. The Abyei referendum was not guaranteed, and would be seen as "Addis Ababa" all over again. I immediately told the Americans that if that were the case, the SPLM would reject the whole proposal and likely walk out. I recommended the proposal be changed. I was later informed that Roger Winter also objected on the same point in a meeting with Danforth and the delegation upon arrival in Nairobi.[25] Hectic redrafting ensued. The proposal was adjusted so that an Abyei referendum would be simultaneous with the referendum in the South.[26]

Confident now of approval, I called both Ali Osman and Dr. John and, without divulging the details, urged them to consider the American proposal very seriously. It should, I said, be a compromise acceptable to both sides, and be seen as part of a larger "package" with room for adjustment.

Danforth presented the proposal to both parties that afternoon. Under its terms, Abyei would have a special status under the Presidency during the six-year interim period. An international Abyei Boundary Commission would consider the historical record and determine the borders of the Area. The

Ngok Dinka would vote in a referendum on whether the Area belonged to the North or South, simultaneously with the referendum for the South granted in the Machakos Protocol. Implementation of the agreement would be internationally monitored. Oil revenues were meanwhile to be allotted on an 8–42–50 basis to the local authority, regional government, and central government respectively.

The presentation went well. Both sides got a couple of hours to review the proposal and come back. The SPLM responded that the proposal was not SPLM/A-policy, but that the Movement would accept it "in the interest of peace".[27] On the government side, despite some grumbling, there was also a generally constructive attitude. They asked for more time. Nafie Ali Nafie and Al-Dirdiri Mohamed Ahmed went to Khartoum the next day to discuss the proposal with President Bashir. They returned on the 22nd to declare that the proposal was accepted "as a basis for an agreement". President Bush had by then called the two leaders and they had formally conveyed the same positive message. The Americans later thanked Norway for intervening, stating that the adjustments and phone calls before the meeting had helped save the initiative. On my part, I was relieved that the most contentious problem had been solved – at least for now.

In subsequent bilateral discussions, Taha told Garang that Abyei needed to be part of an overall package, and that it was in this context that the government had accepted the proposal. He stressed that the decision on Abyei remained subject to trade-offs with other issues. The SPLM/A had hoped to "pocket" Abyei for free, Taha said, based on the intervention of the American "referee". This was not the case. There was therefore some nervousness in the SPLM/A delegation as discussion of the remaining issues started. But although some adjustments were made, in the end the American proposal survived in the protocol the parties completed in May.

After the agreement on Abyei, only the power sharing arrangements remained to be completed. The cessation of hostilities agreement was extended for another month, implying a deadline of 30 April. Although there had been useful discussions on the issue under the auspices of General Sumbeiywo, and parameters had been devised in connection with the Machakos Protocol, much had been left undone. At this stage, the IGAD secretariat took a more active role. They listed sixteen outstanding differences between the parties, mostly related to power sharing. Now was the time for bargaining and trade-offs. The negotiations continued at two levels, the two Principals and a committee of the two parties.

The committee consisted of Idris Mohamed Abd al-Kader, Mutrif Siddiq, Al-Dirdiri Mohamed Ahmad, and Said al-Khatib on the government side, and Nhial Deng, Deng Alor, Justin Yak and Pagan Amum for the SPLM/A. I proposed areas where I thought the SPLM/A might table compromise proposals. In conversation Taha told me that three or four of the questions were easy – he and Garang could immediately "tick them off". The most difficult were the Capital, the Presidency and political leadership positions, election arrangements, the proportion of Southern participation in central government organs, the extent of decentralization to the states, reform of the security organs, and the nature of the partnership between the SPLM and the National Congress Party. Both he and Dr. John confirmed on the phone with me that they were willing to undertake some serious "horse trading" on these remaining issues.

Not for the first time we began to hear rumours that hardliners in Khartoum were complaining that Taha had given too much away in the negotiations. Now they wanted to prevent a full agreement. They would do this by planting calumnies about each leader that were bound to be reported to the other, and so preclude further cooperation. It was alleged that this could be one reason the negotiations had shown little recent progress. I never got this confirmed.

The Politics of Khartoum

Abel Alier suggests that the National Congress Party's initial rationale for engaging in the negotiations was to forge a partnership with the SPLM/A that could help it survive politically and provide a degree of international legitimacy.[28] That was worth some concessions. Although achieving peace certainly was important in itself, this was the likely motive also behind Ali Osman Taha's personal engagement. As the negotiations proceeded, he must have realized not only the greater complexity of the job at hand but also the reasons for some of the positions of his counterpart. My personal opinion is that Ali Osman broadened his focus from his own and his colleagues' mere political survival to encompass the achievement of a peace agreement both sustainable and attractive enough for unity to prevail in Sudan. That in turn implied more sharing of wealth and power than he had anticipated – and that had ever before been allowed by Sudan's political elites.

Views about this in Khartoum varied. From time to time the President would make provocative statements about the negotiating issues, and we heard reports of unease within the party elite. Taha told me of tough negotiations with his colleagues. Although some hardliners, such as Nafie Ali Nafie, were in the delegation at Naivasha, others in Khartoum had ample scope as potential spoilers. Despite the backing of the President and key members of the Cabinet on all negotiating decisions,[29] complaints in Khartoum about those concessions that had already been made had grown louder.[30] I could sense that the pressure on Taha was mounting. He needed a good agreement on power sharing.

As we have seen, bringing stakeholders from Khartoum into the talks was one of his strategies to broaden responsibility for the agreement. These included the Misiriya tribal shaykhs, religious figures, leaders of the ruling party, and others. Most of them duly met Garang and discussed the issues with him. It is likely that this was part of an agreed strategy. The meeting with

Muslim leaders was particularly successful. Expecting an enemy of Islam, they were deeply sceptical. Dr. John spent a whole day with them, made it clear that the South was not against Islam, and told them about Southern concerns and his commitment to freedom of religion. He of course spoke fluent Arabic, demonstrated knowledge of Islam as well as of Sudanese history and culture, and promised that mosques would be protected in the South. Garang made a very strong impression. The meeting ended with the Islamic leaders inviting the SPLM/A Chairman to Khartoum as a national leader.

In the Machakos Protocol, the two parties had already committed to "establish a democratic system of governance". With no objective measure of popular support for either the government or SPLM, the negotiations on power sharing were about political control. The risk of total exclusion of other parties from the putative Government of National Unity in Khartoum and the post-war Government of Southern Sudan was a major concern to the Troika. Since inclusion of these parties in the negotiations had been blocked by Khartoum, and they were not therefore party to the deal, there was a risk that they would become spoilers and undermine the agreement.

Lack of representation in government institutions immediately after the peace agreement could increase that danger. This had been the reason during previous rounds for the Troika and other international partners to push for early elections that would legitimize the government. Understanding that some kind of elections would have to be held, Taha repeatedly appealed to the SPLM to commit to a more formal and longer-term political partnership. Simply put, but not explicitly communicated, he wanted a partnership that would help them both win the elections and remain in power. This came up repeatedly, and Ali Osman asked me several times to intervene with the SPLM. I discussed this with Dr. John and SPLM leaders, but they were very cautious.

The Real Issue: Sharing Power

At this point the status on the outstanding issues was as follows. The agreement on Abyei was ready to be finalized, but the government was making its signature conditional on other issues. The same was the case with the Presidency, but in this case it was the SPLM that made finalization conditional on an overall agreement. On the Nuba Mountains and Southern Blue Nile, popular consultation and governance arrangements remained incomplete. The issue of the capital was particularly contentious, and really amounted to whether *Sharia* law should apply or not.

The talks got off to a slow start. According to Garang, Ali Osman might be ready to bolt again. On March 30th the Troika met on the status of the negotiations and the strategy for the final phase. Ambassador Alan Goulty went on the offensive and criticized the recent role of the Americans at Naivasha. General Sumbeiywo complained, again, that the US was about to take over the talks. The two negotiating parties and the IGAD secretariat were frustrated and asked Ambassador Ranneberger to explain the instructions he had received from Washington. The US was trying to keep up the momentum, after the breakthrough on Abyei, towards a "package deal" on the remaining issues. In light of the government's compromises over Abyei, the Americans argued, it was now the SPLM's turn to deliver on power sharing. Ranneberger mentioned that the Americans might table their own proposals on that subject, too.

The UK and Norway were not entirely happy with this. Ambassador Goulty feared that the American behaviour could drive the negotiations off track. The UK asked for a more modest US profile, and to let the parties take charge of the talks together with Sumbeiywo, whose leadership should be respected. On the Norwegian side we did not want great pressure from the outside at this stage; there was a danger of total collapse or for an agreement that was not "owned" by the parties and therefore unsustainable. In our view, there was still movement in the process, and we needed to let the parties themselves arrive at a balanced "package", with trade-offs over the various issues. Ambassador Ellefsen referred to recent reports from our Embassy in Khartoum about rumours of tension surrounding the negotiations and even of potential coup attempts. The US doubted these rumours and regarded Taha as pretty safe, without much opposition.

At this juncture there was also impatience in the government delegation in Naivasha: they felt that the SPLM/A was holding things up.[31] At the beginning of April, however, things started moving, and by April 5th there was agreement on several of the remaining issues. On the Presidency, the SPLM/A repeated its longstanding acceptance of the First Vice President position, with the National Congress Party taking a subordinate Vice Presidency instead of the premiership. This was to accommodate Taha, and ensure that he had a powerful position in the new government; Garang would "take care" of the South, and Taha the North – that is in terms of ensuring implementation of the agreement. The two sides undertook to try to arrive at consensus rather than majority decisions in the Presidency. A solution was also found on the reform of the security organs. Regarding SPLM representation in central political institutions, they agreed that the SPLM/A would have one-third of the positions, the National Congress a majority, and other political forces the rest. The parties also continued to negotiate the power-sharing arrangements for the two other Areas and the issue of the capital. On April 7th Charlie Snyder visited the negotiations, and the parties promised an agreement at Easter. His visit was used tactically by each side to complain of the other's inflexibility.

I remained in touch with both leaders during this period, but I needed a break. I went to France for a week at Easter, expecting Ali Osman and Garang to move on the key issues on their own initiative. After only a couple of days, however, my mobile phone started ringing. It was Dr. John, informing me that they had encountered significant hurdles on the capital and the percentages of representation in the two Areas. I ended up on the phone with both Ali Osman and Dr. John for almost three days. There was hardly anyone left at Naivasha:

from our side only Endre Stiansen was there in his capacity as resource person to the IGAD secretariat.

The Status of the Capital

The Capital issue had been on the table at Nakuru. That session had ended in a complete stalemate, and the government walked out. Now it was up to Ali Osman and Dr. John to resolve this difficult question, in one of the most intense negotiating periods in the power-sharing talks. Nothing had changed. The SPLM claimed that a national capital was a capital not only for the North, but also for regions where Islam had few adherents; the capital needed to be inclusive, reflect the diversity of the country, and privilege no single religion. But the Machakos Protocol had accepted that the North was subject to *Sharia* law; as far as the government was concerned there was no issue at all, and no need to re-open the discussion.

One of their negotiators, Amin Hasan Omar, was so adamant that he acquired the nickname of "Not an inch" from the SPLM/A delegation. [32] From the Troika side we had discussed the issue many times and worked on various, increasingly tortured schemes involving a religiously neutral "enclave", the freezing of *Sharia* during the interim period, and exempting Southerners altogether from *Sharia* law, with safeguards for non-Muslims, as Abel Alier had proposed.

Neither Garang nor Taha was willing to move on his position. Nor did either have any new alternative to propose on the subject. The situation became very tense. At one point Garang even called on the Egyptian government to intervene with Khartoum. Taha likewise dug in his heels;[33] I had seldom, if ever, heard him like this.[34] The only hint of daylight was Dr. John's explicit remark that the issue should not become a deal breaker.

Ali Osman was a lawyer. In his view, existing legislation could be retained, for it already distinguished between non-Muslims and Muslims. *Sharia* law did not apply to the former, but only to the latter. This distinction could be further strengthened, both in legislation and in its application. In the end Dr. John had to admit that he had a point: it could be possible to develop a legal framework respecting differences of religious background, and in a sense apply two different systems of law in the capital.

The practical problem with this was implementation. Were the law enforcement agencies to ask individuals which religion they belonged to before knowing which law would apply? Would this constitute a robust enough protection of non-Muslims? After failing to convince Taha on the issue of a secular capital, a secular enclave, and freeze options for the interim period, Garang finally decided to search for several elements that together could constitute a sturdy framework of protection and safeguards for non-Muslims in the capital. This was in line with Alier's proposals. The elements included broad representation of Southerners in law enforcement agencies, training of staff and officers, a robust appeals process, and a Presidential Commission to monitor application of the laws. The latter was critical. Southerners would be protected against the so-called *hudud* punishments under *Sharia*. If this protection failed, the Commission would have the power to take the issue back to the Presidency. This mechanism was very important as a way out for the SPLM, should experience show that non-Muslims were being dragged to court for violations of *Sharia* law. The Commission would allow the possibility of re-opening the issue of the capital during the interim period. The solution was conditional on practice and application.

In the end, it was a solution along these lines they finally agreed upon. On Good Friday, after realizing that they would reach agreement, Ali Osman presented Garang with an Easter egg. After thanking him, Dr. John jokingly replied: "I delivered the Capital, now you have to deliver on the two Areas." They both laughed. They had reached a breakthrough. Although Garang had fought for a different solution, this issue proved not to be a red line for him in the way it clearly was for the government and ruling party.[35]

The discussions then continued over the issue of the governorships of the two Areas. Both sides wanted the governorship in both the Nuba Mountains and Southern Blue Nile. After a tug of war, they ended up with the most sensible solution, sharing the top positions in both areas. The Governor of Southern Kordofan (the Nuba Mountains) would come from the National Congress, and the Deputy Governor from the SPLM. The opposite would be the case in Southern Blue Nile, with a change mid-way in the interim period.[36]

An important remaining issue was representation in the legislatures of the two Areas. It seemed clear that this should be part of an overall package on party representation in the national legislature, the Southern parliament and in the state legislatures. The Nakuru proposal gave the Southerners 30 percent, and Garang assumed they could end up with 33 percent. Before much progress could be made, Ali Osman Taha left for Khartoum on April 18th to beat back a challenge to his Islamic leadership position by Dr. Ghazi. This was not the first time they had competed for the leadership position, and it would not be the last.[37] He survived and, more importantly for the peace negotiations, his hand was actually strengthened. While Taha was in Khartoum, Garang took the opportunity to confer with the National Democratic Alliance in Asmara.

The Trade-Offs

When Taha and Garang returned after a week, it was clear that the break had been useful.[38] Two issues remained in the power-sharing arrangements: the percentage of Southern representation in the National Parliament, and the level of representation for the other parties in both the South and the North.

Both sides felt that they were very close to agreement on both the power-sharing arrangements and the Three Areas, but each accused the other of holding back. In discussing this period recently the key negotiators on the government side said that it was the SPLM that were dragging their feet.[39] Garang, on the other hand, claimed that the government wanted to complete its offensive in Darfur before the rainy season. We observers also thought that the government might be delaying the talks while dealing with the crisis in the West. In any case, by now, early May, Darfur totally dominated the news. Colin Powell called to give the parties a final push to sort out the last issues. The *New York Times* was filled with reports of atrocities and the problems with humanitarian access. The extraordinary level of public attention put pressure on the American government to do something. Special Envoy Vraalsen was briefing the Security Council on his last visit to Darfur. A Presidential Statement of the Security Council was under discussion.

On May 13th each party presented its proposals for overall resolution of the Abyei issue. The compromise tabled by the Americans for resolving the most contentious issues was included in both papers. They differed, however, over Abyei's formal position and the rights of the Misiriya and the Ngok Dinka. Despite differences of opinion, neither side saw the issue as insurmountable. Given what they had achieved on the capital, there was a sense of implicit trade-off over Abyei.

But even as we seemed to be reaching an end, I was concerned that the credibility of the whole process could be called into question by the international community; all eyes were on Darfur. It was only a matter of time before Darfur became a separate agenda item in the Security Council. While Dr. John said he would use "all his energy and strength to engage with the parties and find a solution to the Darfur conflict", he stressed that an agreement at Naivasha was a necessary basis for a resolution of Darfur. I replied that no further delays could be accepted. Time was up.

Ali Osman agreed. His mind was already on the nature of a signing ceremony, and he encouraged me to talk to colleagues about attending. I promised to do so, but used the opportunity to raise the credibility problem we were facing as events unfolded in Darfur. I expressed our grave concern about the situation, and called for an end to the attacks on civilians and access for humanitarian workers. I said the situation in Darfur would now overshadow the peace process entirely unless the parties immediately concluded the talks.

A Very Long Day

For once, Dr. John and Ali Osman met their own deadline. The parties had been sitting together without interruption from 16 February until May 25. They were done.

The ceremony was scheduled for May 26th. We had been invited by General Sumbeiywo to observe the signing of the two protocols. The foreign minister of Kenya, Stephen Kalonzo Musyoka was there, and two of the Troika countries were represented at the political level, by Andrew Natsios and Charlie Snyder from the US, and me. We sat outside on the lawn at

Naivasha, waiting for the parties to come out with the agreements in hand, about one thousand people in all: I was sure that my old friends, the hippos on the premises, had never seen such a crowd. The ceremony was expected to start at 1:00 p.m.

Nothing happened. We were told that there was just one last little problem that had not been resolved. Sumbeiywo came and asked us to step into the lodge. The SPLM/A had rejected the numbers for representation in the Nuba Mountains and Southern Blue Nile that we thought had been agreed, a 45/55 percent split in each state. They wanted equal representation in both areas and called for a reduction in National Congress representation in the South from 20 to 15 percent. The Government, for its part, had re-opened the agreed text on the Three Areas, rejecting the term "autonomous" and asking to change the name of the Nuba Mountains to "Southern Kordofan". All this required new talks at the highest level, even as all the dignitaries were waiting outside on the lawn.

Sumbeiywo asked us to talk to both parties. Foreign Minister Musyoka, Andrew Natsios, Charlie Snyder and I agreed, pressing first Dr. John and then Taha to stick to the previously agreed text. Abel Alier also intervened. The bigger problem was the SPLM/A. Garang would not budge. I assumed that he was under pressure from his people in the Nuba Mountains and Southern Blue Nile. We agreed that I would meet Garang alone, and in a separate room I told him that it was time for him to back down. Finally, he conceded. I went to Ali Osman with the news, and stressed the need for no changes in the text.

By then, people had been waiting outside for hours. But we were not done yet. The government delegation complained about the terminology in several places. These issues too were eventually sorted out. The Protocols on power sharing and the Three Areas were finally signed at 10 p.m. Amid whoops of joy and prayers of thanks, Sudan's government and the SPLM/A had signed accords paving the way to ending Africa's longest-running civil war. The two leaders gave speeches, as did Sumbeiywo and Musyoka. I spoke as well, on behalf of the IGAD Partners' Forum. With these two protocols, and the two previous ones, the Comprehensive Peace Agreement was almost a reality.

"Things will not and can never be the same again," John Garang declared at the signing ceremony, drawing cries of joy from Southern Sudanese women. "We have reached the crest of the last hill in our tortuous ascent to the heights of peace": the road ahead was flat; the Protocols marked a paradigm shift. He also suggested that the deal could give fresh impetus to peace efforts in Darfur. It was an impressive performance, and showed the qualities of a potential national leader.

Ali Osman Taha spoke generously of the agreement as the beginning of a New Sudan, a term normally used by the SPLM/A.[40] I pinched myself. Taha stressed that cooperation of all political forces was now critical. He spoke in Arabic, directly to the television audience at home. "We thank God Almighty who led us to this great achievement," he said, adding that he hoped the deal would advance peace efforts throughout the country. It was gratifying to hear both leaders express public appreciation for the role I had played, and to ask for my continuing help in finalizing the overall agreement.

I had five meetings with both Garang and Taha at Naivasha during this visit, shuttling back and forth between them, trying to sort out the last issues and, after the signing, emphasizing the need to "sell" the agreement and ensure the inclusion of other political parties in the relevant commissions and governmental institutions. There were reports about resistance in the North to some of the concessions, and it was now critical to reach out and broaden the ownership of the peace agreement. They committed to do so. I also encouraged them to put all the protocols now signed into one Framework agreement. This would emphasize the end of substantive negotiations, the imminence of a comprehensive agreement, and readiness to prepare for the post-conflict phase: a Security Council resolution to mandate a peace-keeping mission, establishment of the Multilateral Donor Trust Fund, and other relevant processes. To this suggestion there was general agreement – even Nafie Ali Nafie, the hardest of hardliners, was enthusiastic. This became the basis for the Nairobi Declaration of June 5th, acknowledging completion of all the Protocols that would constitute the Comprehensive Peace Agreement for Sudan.

As Rebecca Garang put it recently, quoting her husband: "The international community was holding a baton, and the baton would descend on whoever is seen as obstacle to peace."[41] That President Bush made about ten phone calls to President Bashir during the course of the negotiations is an indication of this.[42] Garang felt the pressure. Speaking on the Voice of America on May 30th, Dr. John said the following: "This peace agreement was reached, not necessarily because the parties wanted to, but because both parties were forced to," and continued: "We negotiated an agreement, because we were forced to by a lot of pressures. The cost of continuing the war was felt by both sides to be much higher than the cost of stopping the war. So, we stopped the war."

But the two leaders would not have been able to get to this point without a very strong personal commitment. The talks had taken on their own dynamics, as had the partnership between the two.

CHAPTER SIX

Sealing the Deal

With the completion of the Naivasha Protocols and signing of the Nairobi Declaration, most of the job was done. Several security issues, which included funding of the SPLA, demobilization, and the status of "other armed groups", remained. Implementation modalities and timelines for the various provisions of the protocols also needed to be agreed upon. Pressure to complete the talks was intense, and fatigue was setting in. But the mediators insisted on an Implementation Protocol,[1] which in turn involved important political issues such as ceasefire arrangements, the timing of elections, and the post-war political partnership of the two sides. Plans for cooperation in the "pre-interim period" and deployment of transition teams from both sides were also on the table. Dr. John and Ali Osman soon discovered that their agenda was once again full.

The SPLM Chairman proved indefatigable, never ready to give up without a result he could defend to his own people. This often led to tension even with allies, domestic and foreign, including sympathizers within the US government, and it was particularly notable during the talks on the Three Areas. In order to create stronger ownership of the agreement, Garang ensured that leaders of various factions signed the protocols on behalf of the Movement.

The First Vice President also had to cater for important constituencies in Khartoum.[2] In some cases Taha left the negotiations because the resistance in Khartoum was real, and he had to bring his colleagues on board.[3] Still, his opponents were growing stronger, and threatened to undermine him. He told me that the negotiations at home at times were as hard as those with the SPLM/A. Some resistance related to concrete issues, such as the security arrangements and the position of the Misiriya in Abyei. Other tensions grew out of political power struggles in Khartoum, where rivals seemed to begrudge Taha an easy victory that might enhance his personal prestige.

On the evening of May 26th, after the whole "circus" was over, Dr. John was in very good spirits, and as I opened the bottle of champagne I had brought with me, he joked about the impact of Southerners arriving in Khartoum. "I am really looking forward to it", he said. "You know, we will open clubs, people will dance, women will dress the way they want, and young girls will have bare stomachs." The latter was what Southerners now jokingly called "separation of state and religion." Southerners could not, in his view, be harassed and persecuted by the religious police after this. He believed that a Southern presence in the government would have a transformative effect on Khartoum. "You will be surprised with the people who will come to us for a glass or two!" There was of course a more serious side to the issue. In speeches after the signing, the SPLM Chairman said that the agreements "contain all the objectives we have fought for". This may have been true. Yet critical trade-offs had been made. The key to making marginalized peoples feel like equal citizens had been the inapplicability of *Sharia* law. The SPLM/A had got assur-ances for Khartoum, but the impression was thereby strengthened that the New Sudan was "new" for the South (and potentially for Abyei) but less so for the rest of the country. For this the SPLM/A was heavily criticized by other parties in the National Democratic Alliance. In the Nuba Mountains, Southern Blue Nile and, for that matter, Darfur and the East, implementation of various commitments in the Protocols would depend on the willingness for change at the centre, the strength of the South to fight for their cause, and the power of reformist political forces in the country.

The National Congress government had won its most important point, *Sharia* law, which would formally remain the basis of national legislation and continue to be enforced on Muslims in the capital. Referenda had been avoided in the Nuba Mountains and Southern Blue Nile. They also had reason to hope that the SPLM would help it to win the elections during the interim period, and thus to secure their hold on the government. Abyei had been a bitter pill, made easier to swallow by the fact that the issue would go to a Commission. Both parties therefore had reason to be satisfied with the outcome of the talks. However, there were clouds on the horizon, casting long shadows over their achievement and with a potential of undermining what they had just signed. Darfur was most important. But also other potential spoilers were at play.

Darfur at Naivasha

At Naivasha in late May, I spent a lot of time discussing Darfur with both Dr. John and Ali Osman, emphasising that the international community could not be expected to support the implementation of a peace agreement if Darfur was still on fire. The issue was credibility. Up to March 2004 the primary focus of foreign governments was on humanitarian rather than political issues. Our colleagues in the US, Andrew Natsios and Roger Winter, then Assistant Administrator of USAID, were in the forefront. On our side, the Deputy Foreign Minister, Vidar Helgesen, was most closely involved. In April this changed, as international media coverage increased, and access to refugees in Chad revealed the true horror of what had been going on. Mukesh Kapila, the UN's own humanitarian coordinator for Sudan, made headlines around the world by using the word "genocide". "The only difference between Rwanda and Darfur now'", he said, "'is the numbers involved. [The slaughter in Darfur] is more than just a conflict, it is an organized attempt to do away with a group of people.'"[4] Kapila did not last long in his job, but the alarm had been sounded.

It was during the past months that I had increased my own engagement on Darfur, discussing the crisis with Taha a number of times, insisting that any delay in tackling the situation would have huge implications. The sustainability of the peace agreement was at risk, to say nothing of the Donors' Conference for Sudan we would host in Oslo, and the feasibility of resolving Sudan's debt problems. Sure enough, on May 26th, a strong Presidential statement on Darfur was approved in the Security Council. It called for action on a number of fronts, including disarming of the *janjawid* and a complete halt to all military activities in accordance with the ceasefire agreement. The statement urged a speedy implementation of the monitoring mechanisms in support of the African Union and its efforts.

I was deeply concerned about the situation and said so to both leaders. Khartoum had constantly resisted negotiation. But in our private discussions Ali Osman was more open-minded.[5] How much influence he had on government policy on Darfur was uncertain. It was more urgent than ever to complete the talks in Naivasha, so all attention could be turned to Darfur. President Mwai Kibaki of Kenya had invited the North–South parties to a high-level ceremony in Nairobi on June 5th. For me, this was another opportunity to discuss the situation in the Western region with Ali Osman and Dr. John.

I wanted a solution for Darfur either before, or at the same time as, the signing of the comprehensive peace agreement. Both leaders agreed, but agreement without responsibility was easy: while willing to help, Dr. John said Darfur was a problem mainly for the government and the National Congress Party; Ali Osman conveyed deep concern and promised to give the situation his highest priority. Before leaving Naivasha I listed some urgent points that had to be addressed by the two of them, the first of which was Darfur; I would come back to this repeatedly during the next few months. The subsequent allegation that the IGAD negotiators and observer countries, including the Troika, completely ignored the Darfur crisis is incorrect.

The Sudanese military and security apparatus seemed to control the operations in Darfur, the Darfur file being in the "hands of Security".[6] At the time some observers questioned whether Ali Osman Taha had had any role.[7] Taha himself denies any connection.[8] He goes further, disclaiming any links to the "Arab Gathering" and Musa Hilal's or other militias in Darfur. Khartoum insiders have described his relations with the Sudanese armed forces as strained. Multiple sources attest to his characteristic *modus operandi* of remaining behind the scenes, denying that he had any direct involvement.[9] Taha also claims that he warned against using ethnically based militias early on and had argued internally for a political process to resolve the crisis, unsuccessfully.[10] Now, during the final stage of the Naivasha process there was little doubt that the latter had become quite urgent, also to him.

Signing Amid the Fighting

While it was therefore clear that the peace agreement so meticulously negotiated at Naivasha was at risk if Darfur was not addressed, there were other threats to its implementation. In late May and early June a series of provocative militia attacks took place at Akobo and Bor. The SPLM/A was in the process of negotiating separate deals with various militias, but had not yet won them all over. Conducted by renegade elements probably supported from within military intelligence in Khartoum, the attacks were clearly intended to forestall the signing of the final agreement. The orders allegedly came from the top.[11]

The SPLM/A threatened to boycott the signing ceremony in Nairobi, and agreed to meet the government delegation at Naivasha on June 3rd only if a set of preconditions were met. They wanted a full discussion of the attacks, which constituted serious violations of the agreement on cessation of hostilities; assurances that the attacks would cease; and an end to propaganda against the SPLM/A in Khartoum. They also asked for Darfur to be included in the text of the planned Nairobi Declaration, a summary of the protocols. The SPLM/A expected trouble in winning agreement to these demands, but the government undertook, in measured language, to try to stop the militia activities and the negative media accounts. The parties duly met at Naivasha to draft the Nairobi Declaration, constituting what diplomats call a *chapeau* or summary of the four protocols. The SPLM pressed the government to include a commitment to resolve the conflict in Darfur, as well as statements relating to democracy and civil rights. The government delegation resisted. The SPLM/A was also unhappy with its failure to get a stronger text on political inclusion. They complained to me, but went ahead.

The signing ceremony in Nairobi on June 5th was intended to "cement" the peace agreement and ensure its ownership by the parties and the countries in the region. The "Nairobi Declaration" made it possible to proceed with important international processes, including a substantial monitoring operation and a UN peacekeeping mission. The night before the ceremony Taha told me he was committed to carrying the process to the end, and claimed that the government was not behind the militia activity in the South. He also committed, in public, to solving the Darfur conflict. I urged him and Garang to speed up the process for the implementation talks, and to use this interim period to make progress on Darfur, possibly with "fast track" negotiations involving both leaders. We agreed to keep in touch on both issues. Negotiations on the Implementation Protocol would commence on June 21st.

Within the Troika there had been a concern that a condemnatory Security Council resolution on Darfur could jeopardize both the Comprehensive Peace Agreement and attempts behind the scenes to get a Darfur process under way. If the outrages in Darfur continued, however, such a resolution was unavoidable. The Security Council, and particularly the US and UK, could not allow

Darfur to be held hostage any longer to the IGAD negotiations. Secretary of State Powell called Taha at the beginning of June, adding to the pressure. We hoped and expected that Garang and Taha would take action together, starting a political process that would combine a Darfur settlement with the final Sudan peace agreement. Just a week later, on June 11th, the first Security Council resolution on Sudan was adopted. Several Presidential statements had been issued previously, and a number of debates on Sudan and Darfur had taken place. This resolution, however, anchored the Naivasha agreement firmly in the international framework and obliged the international community to support the peace process and implementation of the agreement.

The resolution also mandated appointment of a Special Representative of the Secretary General for Sudan (SRSG), to take charge of a major peace keeping operation. There had been much preparatory discussion among the Troika, the IGAD Partners' Forum, and the UN Peacekeeping headquarters. We advocated a "light-footed" operation like that of the Joint Military Commission in the Nuba Mountains, of limited numbers but a rapid response capability, including significant airlift capacity. According to one account, the JMC monitoring the 2002 Nuba ceasefire "not only kept the peace for three years, but also helped calm potential flashpoints for inter-communal violence, disarm combatants, support the provision of humanitarian aid, and facilitate conflict resolution and the free movement of civilians and goods."[12] The JMC model also built confidence between the two sides. But the UN was not ready to adopt this model, which was quite different from its traditional peace keeping operations.

In our view, larger deployments were warranted only in the Three Areas, and some other "hot spots" in the South (for example areas of oil-exploration and of previous unrest). Darfur was a different matter altogether. Deploying thousands of troops in the South was a waste of money. The need for boots on the ground would be greatest in areas of contention in the South, on the border, around the oil fields, and in the areas where militias had been active, not where the SPLM/A would have control after withdrawal had taken place. The Sudanese government agreed,[13] and communicated this to the UN. But the UN's Department of Peace Keeping Operations was adamant. They insisted on their usual deployment model, and were uninterested in a dialogue about modalities with us or with the parties. Our concerns would later prove justifiable, when there was very limited capacity and flexibility to prevent violence or to protect civilians in Abyei, Upper Nile, Jonglei and Equatoria during the interim period.

In the Nuba Mountains it was possible to compare the two missions' effectiveness. In its report of December 2006, the Overseas Development Institute attributed growing insecurity to "the inability of UNMIS [United Nations Mission in Sudan] to monitor the situation on the ground with equal effectiveness". The report referred to

the lack of disarmament of militia, particularly of former PDF fighters . . .

> Another persistent complaint was the lack of patrolling by UNMIS, both
> on foot and by helicopter . . . The area in which communities feel the
> handover from the JMC to UNMIS has left the greatest vacuum is local
> level reconciliation work.[14]

It also complicated matters that Egyptians were deployed in the Nuba
Mountains, where memories of nineteenth-century misrule lived on.

Much discussion took place over the position of Special Representative.
The Troika supported Norway's candidate, Tom Vraalsen. The Dutch nominated Jan Pronk. Other names circulated, and a lot of lobbying took place.
The Secretary General appointed Pronk, virtually without consultation. John
Garang was upset with the way this was handled. When the Secretary General
had called, Garang felt "ambushed": only after expressing his preference for
another candidate did Garang learn that Pronk was in the room with the
Secretary General and that the call was on speakerphone. Kofi Annan had
made his decision.

Jan Pronk and I had been colleagues as ministers, and I told him of the
SPLM's concerns, and of the need to take them seriously. But early missteps
were to hamper his relations with the South for a long time. Pronk simply
spent too little time with the SPLM/A leadership and with Southerners generally. In signing a Separation of Forces Agreement with the government side
alone, despite its planned deployment to the South, UNMIS seemingly ignored
the Security Protocol. (UNMIS later rectified the error.) Pronk ended up
spending most of his time on the crisis in Darfur, despite a mandate inadequate for the purpose, and despite the CPA being of critical importance for
overall peace in the country. On Darfur, however, he became a famously
strong advocate, to the point where, much later, the Government asked him
to leave the country.

Risks and Dangers at 'Home'

Because of the South's experience of the 1972 Addis Ababa Agreement the
SPLM/A wanted to anchor implementation of the pending comprehensive
agreement with an array of international guarantees, including Security
Council resolutions, peace-keeping forces, international observers of elections, a credible Assessment and Evaluation Commission, and so forth.
Internationalising the agreement was a way to hold the government to
account. The SPLM also wanted time-bound procedures of implementation,
as advocated by the mediators and by us on the Norwegian side. These would
be negotiated and signed in a separate Implementation Protocol. It was this
negotiation, with particular focus on ceasefire issues, which took place during
the summer. In the early autumn of 2004 the talks on the UN mission took
place, and following that the rest of the implementation issues, in an elabo-
rate matrix prepared by the IGAD secretariat.

The two leaders, Taha and Garang, decided to leave these talks to their officials, and then come in towards the end to resolve any remaining issues. The first topic, beginning on June 28th, was conclusion of a permanent cease-fire. At the same time Ali Osman Taha and John Garang were busy on their respective home fronts where, after long absence, their presence was urgently required.

Garang had been negotiating for so long that concern had arisen about the effects on the strength and agility of the Movement and Army. There was also a need to sell the agreement to Southern constituencies. Dr. John embarked on a highly successful three-week tour. The Chairman addressed huge rallies of people who had walked for days to hear him. Southern Sudan had never seen anything like it. I talked to him a couple of times on the satellite phone during this period, and it was a very relieved and enthusiastic leader who told me about the sweeping support for the Naivasha protocols and the enthusiasm among his people.

In Khartoum, Ali Osman also needed to catch up. He told me that he used this time with core constituencies, explaining key points of the various protocols, alleviating concerns and responding to questions. He held numerous meetings, ensuring that the National Congress Party and its supporters were thoroughly briefed. I knew that Taha faced criticism from some hardliners for the commitments he had made. On the phone, he spoke openly about some of the challenges he was facing, but he also expressed confidence that none of this would weaken his or the government's commitment. At this time the situation in Darfur seemed out of control; the alarm was ringing globally, and a stream of high-level foreign delegations flew in to Khartoum to talk to the government and visit Darfur. Ali Osman and his colleagues were busy receiving all these dignitaries, including Kofi Annan and Colin Powell, both scheduled for the beginning of July.

Delaying Tactics

Another challenge had already been posed by differing interpretations of the agreements. General Fulford visited Sudan during this period and talked to military leaders on both sides. He was particularly concerned about the lack of knowledge of the agreement and the provisions in the Security protocols, as a result of which the parties' military forces seemed to have very different interpretations of what those provisions meant. The general could see many difficulties down the road. Both the Americans and I asked Garang and Taha to clarify the issues when they reconvened and make sure there was a common understanding of how the agreement should be implemented. We were also worried about the apparent mobilization of military forces, not only in relation to Darfur, but also in other areas. Through the movement of significant military equipment and people, the government and the South Sudan Defence Force seemed to be strengthening their positions around oil-producing areas and in the South generally. New unrest flared in Upper Nile. This had happened many times in the past, and during the talks, and was another reminder that agreements were not guarantees for peace.

Meanwhile the teams were working on the implementation issues at Naivasha, without much success. The most difficult questions included security arrangements, terms of troop withdrawal, demobilization, establishment of a Joint Integrated Unit in Eastern Sudan, and funding of the Southern Army. There were issues also related to the Three Areas and militias. Troika efforts were uncoordinated during these negotiations, and technical advisers were very few. At the political level I heard little from the Americans, who focused increasingly on Darfur; the British and others were beginning to lose patience with the protracted Naivasha negotiations.

There was much speculation that Khartoum used delaying tactics during the last phase at Naivasha, and throughout the implementation talks, to deflect international attention from Darfur. Fear of wrecking the North–South agreement was thus a factor in the Darfur crisis, and precluded resort to the toughest measures in international diplomacy and in bilateral relations. This approach, giving precedence to completion of the Naivasha negotiations, allowed in many observers' views the atrocities in Darfur to go on longer than would otherwise have been the case. Despite sharing this opinion, Dr. John had no choice but to press for quick completion of the talks. Bringing the Darfur issue to Naivasha had been rejected and to insist would have led to collapse of the talks, which may have been just what one could expect that some of the hardliners in Khartoum may have wanted.

Both Taha and Garang told me of their intention to use the Naivasha agreement as the basis for resolving the Darfur conflict. I talked to them before leaving Naivasha in June, and urged establishment of a mechanism during their "break". Just before leaving for Nairobi in early June they discussed assigning someone from each side to contact the Darfur rebels, and Nhial Deng from the SPLM/A and Said al-Khatib or Yahia Husein Babikir were mentioned. In the argot of the time, Taha favoured a "Nuba plus" arrangement for Darfur, while Garang privately preferred a "South minus" arrangement, but they did not enter into detailed discussions.

I contacted the Darfur rebel groups myself to try to prepare the ground. In June and July Abd al-Wahid Mohamed al-Nur and I were on the line a number of times, and followed up with others, including Sharif Harir, the anthropologist who had been a researcher at Bergen University. I raised the possibility of "fast track" negotiations on Darfur with Abd al-Wahid, and an alternative of informal Naivasha-style negotiations conducted for example by the Centre for Humanitarian Dialogue or a similar body. He was quite receptive. He continued to call me, wanting active engagement, even after he had moved to Paris and was given up by many international stakeholders.[15]

Fast Track on Darfur?

The clock was ticking on Darfur. At an UNCTAD conference on Trade and Development in Sao Paulo in mid-June, I met the Sudanese Minister of Finance, the Minister for International Trade, and the Sudanese Ambassador,[16] who briefed me on the government's most recent steps on Darfur. The ambassador had been involved in arranging preliminary consultations with the rebel groups, and laying the groundwork for a possible negotiating process. Three government envoys were in Geneva awaiting representatives from the two main rebel groups. The ambassador confirmed that a "non-meeting" had already taken place on June 3rd, and expressed the view that the Naivasha accords could be a model for Darfur with regard to autonomy, power sharing and wealth sharing. Since those who knew that agreement well were best positioned to negotiate a solution, he called for direct Norwegian engagement.

I responded that it was essential that a firm decision was now made by his government to proceed with substantive Darfur negotiations. They were urgently needed. I wanted to know whose views the ambassador and his colleagues represented and what mandate they had. They responded that President Bashir and Vice President Taha had given them the green light. The ambassador said that an intermediary such as the Centre for Humanitarian Dialogue was unnecessary: it was better to take a "shortcut". He wanted me to engage directly in the talks, either personally, or in the context of IGAD.

Not knowing how serious this initiative was, I was non-committal. I said I was certainly willing to help, but that in my opinion the negotiating parties themselves had the best background to engage directly in this way. This implied the additional involvement of Dr. John, who had the confidence of the rebel groups.[17] I indicated that this would be an even better "fast track" arrangement. The group was receptive to this proposal. It was interesting to hear their praise of Garang and the SPLM/A: they considered him much easier to deal with than the Darfur rebels were. I was pleasantly surprised by this conversation. The Naivasha negotiations had clearly changed attitudes.

A meeting I had with the UN Secretary General was most important at this stage. I had briefed him and his senior colleagues regularly over the last year or so of negotiations. From time to time he had called me for an update, and to ask what he could do to help. I had the deepest respect for Kofi Annan; his authority was an asset we could use at critical junctures. The Secretary General was scheduled to make a high-profile visit to Sudan in early July, in connection with the crisis in Darfur. It was very important for me to make sure that he was fully briefed. Towards the end of the meeting I asked the staff to leave the room, and shared with him the private discussions I had had on the crisis, including the idea of "fast-track" negotiations facilitated by Ali Osman Taha and John Garang – information I had kept to myself. We needed to avoid any initiatives that could undermine such a process.

During this period, I also had telephone discussions with Ali Osman.[18] The situation in the West – not Naivasha – now fully occupied him and the rest of the government. I enquired whether he had had time to discuss with his colleagues the fast-track approach. Taha continued to favour that approach over the current talks hosted by Chad and the more international options being discussed. Taha had asked Said al-Khatib to advise the government's Darfur team, and later to join them in preparing for negotiations.[19] This had not happened, however, and no one had – as yet – taken up the idea of joint SPLM/A-government outreach to the rebel groups. It seemed essential to avoid negotiations with a lot of public attention – and the attendant distractions of international observers, the temptation to "play to the gallery", and the obligation to report to a sponsoring body. There was no time for this now. I told Taha that we would support such informal negotiations with a small team. Taha said that such an initiative would need the approval of the President and Cabinet. He seemed unsure of getting that support, but he promised to pursue the initiative with the President and his colleagues. Khartoum clearly still saw in Darfur primarily a security issue, a view that stemmed from the conviction that Hasan al-Turabi had fomented the rebellion. The Darfur file was therefore still in the hands of National Security.[20]

Meanwhile our intelligence sources confirmed that the government was getting ready for another military offensive. An almost unprecedented humanitarian crisis was unfolding. Relief agencies could not get access. Dr. John offered an entry point through SPLA-controlled areas. This option was discussed at a high-level meeting in the US in late June (the so-called Tidewater meeting on Cape Cod). Andrew Natsios and Hilary Benn were among the participants. In a letter to me in mid-June, reporting on a visit to Darfur a few days earlier, Benn had written: "This is the most serious humanitarian emergency in the world today and the international community must take urgent action if we are to avert a catastrophe." I agreed. He urged me to take all possible action. Our deliberations at the Tidewater meeting were tinged with despair. I could not even share our hopes for a fast-track negotiation process for Darfur.

A Missed Opportunity

After leaving the Tidewater meeting I reached Dr. John by satellite phone amid his tour of the South already mentioned. I had hardly ever heard him prouder. The crowds were beyond any expectation. The people yearned for peace. We discussed Darfur, and he reconfirmed his willingness to engage in a fast-track process with the Vice President. I tried to call Ali Osman but was unable to reach him. When I finally got hold of him, after trying – I believe – for three days, I learned that the Chadians had asked Libya to take over the Darfur negotiations. I knew that his would be unacceptable to both Khartoum and the rebels, given Libya's record in such negotiations and its strategic interests.

Taha had just come from an emergency cabinet meeting, which had agreed to ask the African Union to take responsibility for the Darfur negotiations. I knew that the battle was lost. Still I told Taha how little confidence I had in this approach, which risked degenerating into a "big circus"; the "fast-track" option was much better, even with the risks involved. Ali Osman said that he agreed, but that they had to shut out the Libyans.

I have reflected on this several times, and asked myself: What if I had reached Ali Osman a few hours earlier? Would that have made any difference? The answer depends on whether Khartoum really was ready for political negotiations on Darfur, and whether the Justice and Equality Movement could have been brought on board. Taha told me that he had raised the issue with the key figures in the government and ruling party. According to him, when he had argued earlier for political negotiations,[21] the response had been negative. He had now discussed the "fast-track" proposal with the core leadership of the party, but there had not been enough support. The party leaders argued that Dr. John and Ali Osman already had their hands full, that the situation in Darfur was anyway very different from the South, and that any link to a negotiation framework redolent of "self determination" could lead the rebel groups of Darfur in a similar direction.[22] Besides, they did not really trust Dr. John who, after all, had supported the rebels.

Reasonable as these objections seemed, handing the negotiations to the AU could also be a convenient solution for a government wanting to appear willing to negotiate but preferring delay. There was no expectation that AU-sponsored talks would succeed, at least not within the time frame we hoped for. Khartoum anyway regarded Darfur as its own business, and Garang's meddling, even in partnership with Taha, seemed to hold little attraction. Garang's success in such a venture would also hold its own risks, of strengthening his and the SPLM/A's influence in the West.

I still felt a sense of desperation at this missed opportunity. I was acutely aware that the Naivasha talks had contributed to slowing down a solution to the Darfur crisis, and that a fast-track negotiation process was urgently needed. My strategy had been to get a credible Darfur process started – and even completed – before the signing of the overall comprehensive peace agreement. I had failed. Disappointed, I reported this to Kofi Annan directly while he was en route to Sudan.

During his visit the Secretary General and Sudanese government issued a Joint Communiqué in which the government pledged to disarm the militias in Darfur, prosecute the perpetrators of human rights abuses, and remove obstacles to humanitarian access.[23] Although the government denied complicity in the militia attacks, Annan stated that its failure to act could lead to action in the Security Council. Colin Powell visited Darfur that same week, and added to the pressure. By that time, Jack Danforth had left his position as Special Envoy, and (on 1 July 2004) became US Ambassador to the United Nations. One of the first things he did in that new post was to propose a Security Council resolution on Sudan.[24]

The government had accepted political negotiations to resolve the Darfur crisis, but with the African Union at the helm. On July 15th the AU held its first meeting on the subject, in Addis Ababa, with Sam Ibok in charge. Both of the main Darfur rebel groups were expected to attend. As I had feared, a host of observers asked to be present, among them the EU, France, the US, the UN, and the Centre for Humanitarian Dialogue. Neither of the rebel groups turned up. Despite their factional differences, they shared a lack of confidence in the African Union, a fact confirmed when I spoke to their leaders, Abd al-Wahid al-Nur and Dr. Khalil Ibrahim.

The first round finally commenced in August in Abuja, followed by four more, first under Sam Ibok and later under Salim Salim, the veteran Tanzanian diplomat. Procedural issues and angry exchanges dominated the discussions. It was only during the fifth and final round that any movement occurred. The talks lacked commitment. Nor had the AU made enough effort to build confidence and trust; discussions I had with the rebel leaders in late 2004 and early 2005 revealed even greater animosity towards the AU than before the talks. Unfortunately, virtually all my concerns about this negotiation framework and format were proven right.

In July 2004 the Sudanese Minister of the Interior, General Abd al-Rahim Mohamed Husein, announced a new plan for settling the internally displaced of Darfur, now numbering more than one million in eighteen different locations. For those familiar with the so-called "peace villages" – places of utter poverty and violent abuse – in the Nuba Mountains, the plan sounded very ominous. There, after villages had been burnt and all their property looted or destroyed, civilians had been corralled in heavily guarded camps little different from detention centres. Fortunately, the government did not go ahead with this plan for Darfur. But it showed a pattern of thought in Khartoum and a failure to learn the lessons of the past. That other voices had prevailed was promising.

Putting the Brakes on Naivasha

During this period (mid-2004) there was no contact between Garang and Taha. Darfur was occupying all of the First Vice President's time. For two weeks in July Garang was unable to reach him by telephone, and concluded that the government had "shelved Naivasha". He wanted to finish the Naivasha process, then deal with Darfur; the Government seemed to want the reverse – to resolve the Darfur problem, one way or another, then return to Naivasha. They questioned Garang's motives: they claimed again to have evidence of SPLM/A support for the rebel groups; Garang made a public statement that "genocide" was unfolding in Darfur.[25] Because of Darfur, the climate of confidence between the parties, and between the two leaders, was rapidly deteriorating.

The thirty-day deadline for progress in Darfur included in the last Security

Council resolution was fast approaching. Ali Osman was therefore fully engaged over Darfur matters and would not come to Naivasha to complete the talks. When General Sumbeiywo and the former foreign minister of Kenya, Stephen K. Musyoka, came to Khartoum they were only reluctantly received at all. From other sources I later heard that Taha was again under attack, particularly from Turabi and his network, but also by others in the government and the party, and needed to remain in the capital to control the situation.[26] Dr. John, on the other hand, was now convinced that it was only through the Naivasha agreement that the Darfur situation could be solved. Once a new coalition government was installed in Khartoum, it could lay the foundation for solving the problems of Darfur and the other marginalized areas.

The Chairman informed me that he had had several discussions with the leaders of the Darfur rebel groups, and had told them that they had a moral duty to negotiate. They had replied that it was difficult to negotiate with a government that bombed and killed innocent civilians on a daily basis. The temperature was very high, and Garang doubted whether the parties would get anywhere at the negotiating table. He thought it would be helpful if completion of the Naivasha talks could be included in the Security Council's next resolution on Darfur. This would make explicit the linkage between Darfur and the other marginalized areas of the country. Garang thought that Khartoum might be willing to get back to business after the Secretary General's report to the Security Council. This implied early September. He wanted my help to bring this about.

At the same time, more militia attacks had taken place, mostly in Western Upper Nile. On the day of our conversation, the Chairman had received word of a major attack on civilians in this area. Later we learned that more than 70,000 people had been forced to flee. I was deeply concerned, but also used the opportunity to press Dr. John on the need to start the dialogue called for in the accords. He agreed that such talks were a priority, and that the militia were welcome to join the SPLM/A. But he pointed out that the quickest way to bring their activities to an end would be for Khartoum to stop supporting them.

The strategy of spoiler elements to sabotage the Naivasha process was well known.[27] Attacks in Upper Nile were orchestrated by the National Security apparatus and Military Intelligence, and allegedly also condoned at the very top of the government.[28] These attacks led to a humanitarian crisis, and attracted attention in the media, the international community and, later in the month, the Security Council. A plan was uncovered to launch an attack on Torit,[29] using forces of the notorious Lord's Resistance Army. Some of us recalled that fighting at Torit had upset the negotiations once before, in 2002, and we feared it could happen again. But events on the ground in the South led in a quite opposite direction, a major Ugandan offensive against the LRA.

In Darfur, the situation continued to be extremely serious. The African Union, mandated to monitor the ceasefire of April 8th, was very slow to deploy. The AU was considering a second phase, with a force of two thousand and an expanded mandate to protect civilians. The Sudanese government adamantly opposed expansion of the mandate. The civilian population in Darfur was still without protection, and international agencies had been unable to provide adequate assistance. It was an unacceptable situation.

Trouble in Khartoum

As events unfolded in Darfur, with no improvement in sight, we continued to push for return of the principals to Naivasha. Although Ali Osman had hinted to me that he would be back on August 18th, there was no sign of a government delegation's preparing to leave Khartoum. I talked to Ali Osman again on August 24th, urging him to get back to the negotiating table, even if only to start off the talks. Our prime minister, Kjell Magne Bondevik, called President Bashir, mainly to impress upon him the need to implement all aspects of Security Council resolution 1556 on Darfur of July 30, not least the disarming of the *janjawid*. He also made the case for solving the Darfur crisis within the framework of the Naivasha agreement. Bashir was non-committal. Without clarity about when Khartoum would resume the talks at Naivasha, Dr. John decided to go on an international tour in early September. He visited Washington, DC to mobilize American support for the final stage of the negotiations and the post-conflict phase. He also visited several other capitals, including The Hague. When the same message was repeated a week later from the Norwegian side, by the State Secretary for Foreign Affairs, Vidar Helgesen, in Khartoum, Taha stated that he could not return to Naivasha now. If he did, and the focus was on Darfur, he feared that the talks would collapse.

By mid-September Dr. John and Ali Osman had still not met. Taha indicated willingness to restart the talks at the technical level, with any remaining issues to be resolved as a package by the principals at the end. He did not wish to spend several months in Kenya again. Garang wanted the opposite, first a top-level meeting mandating the technical talks, then keeping track of the negotiations, making sure they could resolve remaining issues towards the end. General Sumbeiywo too requested a meeting of the two leaders. I decided to try to move the process forward, and on 10–13 September I had several telephone discussions with Taha and Garang. I urged Taha to respond positively to Sumbeiywo's invitation and set a firm date for his return to the negotiations. The Vice President said he had already told Sumbeiywo of his willingness to meet.

We spent a long time discussing the situation in Darfur. I referred to our attempts to establish a "fast-track" on Darfur, and noted that what we had feared at the time seemed to have become a reality: Abuja was looking more and more like a "circus" – with very limited results. I doubted that the talks there would succeed. Taha blamed American pressure on his government for the lack of progress in Abuja. According to my notes he said: "It now seemed that the Americans have a different agenda on Sudan, the same one as Turabi's Popular Congress, and maybe Garang, as well?" Turabi's agenda, he said, was "Guns against the Government!" Ali Osman also told me that he was very unhappy with statements Dr. John had made on Darfur, using terms such as "genocide". Ali Osman said that he had been subject to severe criticism within the government because of this.[30] In his opinion, a discussion on Darfur with Garang now would lead nowhere, and he needed to speak openly with his counterpart about all this before the Naivasha talks could resume.

Taha explained his decision to refrain from meeting during the past two-three months by reference to the difficult atmosphere in Khartoum and the internal pressure he had been under.[31] I took note of the Vice President's complaints about Garang and his doubts about the SPLM's willingness to pursue a partnership and would convey his concerns. I also emphasized, however, that Dr. John had his own complaints, not least about militia activities in the South, which seemed to be supported by elements of the government. It was imperative that they got all these concerns on the table, and were able to speak openly. Given the time that had elapsed, it might be useful to speak on the phone to sort out any misunderstandings and clarify the agenda for the talks. Taha was open to this. I repeated that the main thing now was to give a firm date to General Sumbeiywo. He mentioned two options, and stressed that he did not want a lengthy meeting, but to "clear the air" and kick start the negotiations.

That Taha was under significant pressure we had picked up from several quarters. When President Bashir's political advisor, Qutbi al-Mahdi, visited Oslo he had spoken of the severe criticism of the First Vice President within the government because of the compromises he had accepted. I referred to this in my discussion with Ali Osman, and said that it was always difficult to explain compromises to those who have not been party to negotiations. I told him that Garang also had a lot of explaining to do to his constituencies. It was essential that the two of them protect their partnership. Ali Osman agreed: "That is also how I see it". Everyone must avoid behaving like a man and woman fighting over a child. Like a child, the peace agreement could not be divided up without destroying it. I liked the analogy. The two leaders needed to meet urgently, and we would be willing to reschedule Garang's coming visit to Norway to facilitate an early return to Naivasha.

After this, I talked to the Chairman of the SPLM/A. Dr. John wanted to return to Naivasha immediately. Norwegian flexibility would make it possible to reconvene on September 23rd. He was open to talk to Taha on the phone. Since he had tried so many times to call him in July, he would leave it to Taha now to initiate the contact. Dr. John was pleased with Taha's intention to protect the "baby" they had negotiated. He also mentioned recent rumours that the SPLA allegedly had 3,000 men in Darfur: "I don't have one single one there!" Whether this was entirely correct I do not know.

Back to the Talks

As the lack of progress in Naivasha became apparent, the impatience of the international community reached new heights. The Security Council's resolution of September 18th instructed the Secretary-General to "report to the Council on the progress or lack thereof by the Government of Sudan in complying with the Council's demands in this resolution and the effort by the Government of Sudan and the Sudan People's Liberation Movement to conclude a comprehensive peace accord on an urgent basis".

It was at about this time that the now Permanent Representative of the US to the UN, Jack Danforth called me. Knowing the need for deadlines in the negotiations, he proposed that the Security Council, for the first time, meet in Nairobi. His intention was to put pressure on the parties and set a firm deadline for completion of the negotiations. Taha and Garang would be invited to attend, as would I, to speak on behalf of the Partners' Forum. I immediately supported this idea, and promised to do what I could to ensure that both leaders would respond positively.

Yet another week or two would pass before the two leaders reconvened. In Nairobi on October 7th they finally met at a hotel to discuss implementation arrangements. They began with the ceasefire and related security issues. The ceasefire agreement was indeed challenging, but the legwork had largely been done with the agreement on cessation of hostilities. This was not the case with the size and demobilization of the two armies, and the financing of the SPLA. On the latter issue, the SPLA claimed to need 200,000 men; observers estimated its current strength at between thirty thousand and forty thousand. On the government side, a lack of transparency on the size of the Army was similarly troublesome. Challenging discussions also took place in relation to Eastern Sudan: the SPLM insisted that Joint Integrated Units should be deployed in Kassala. The government strongly opposed this, partly because of unease with the idea of giving the Southerners any military role in Northern Sudan. Although the SPLA had deployed at least a battalion in the area, the government wanted them out as soon as possible. On the issue of "other armed forces" the SPLM/A insisted on full integration of the militias, either into the government army or the SPLA. They would not accept the existence of any third force. The government wished to delay integration for as long as possible.

When I visited Nairobi on October 9th, Taha and Garang were relaxed and the atmosphere was good. Having been able to sort out their personal issues, they gave no indication of any animosity. Three days later, the Norwegian prime minister arrived and met separately with each, and had a historic joint meeting at which I was present. In these discussions it became clear that the financing of the SPLA was a very difficult issue. The government's position was that the Southern Army should be funded from the resources allocated to it. According to the SPLM/A, the Security Protocol defined the two armies as parts of one national army, which should therefore be funded equally from the national defence budget. The parties continued the discussions on East Sudan. Garang expressed a fear that withdrawal of the SPLA unit could lead to a complete "blow-up", and a potential new Darfur, unless a Joint Integrated Unit was established. Both sides claimed to see the issue of "other armed groups" as relatively easy to resolve. The issue was, nevertheless, not exactly what it seemed, but fundamentally about control of the oil-producing areas in Upper Nile, and hence an issue of high priority for the government.

Again we expressed serious concern about the situation in Darfur and the need to follow up on the Security Council resolutions and protect civilians. Taha responded that the government was committed to abide by every paragraph of the resolution, and was also open to increasing the numbers of observers on the ground and expanding the mandate of the African Union's observer force. Garang made an interesting observation which he shared with me. While counter-insurgency units were normally based on individual recruitment,[32] the government had taken the process one step further in Darfur and made an ethnically based operation, and the instrument was the *janjawid*.

The prime minister encouraged the two leaders to make progress, in order that a positive report might be tabled at the IGAD Summit in Nairobi on 14–16 October. I participated in the summit in connection with the inauguration of the new Somali president. The report was positive, but the parties could not yet announce completion of the talks. They had decided to take a break, beginning October 16th, for the month of Ramadan. Garang insisted that the overall ceasefire agreement, replacing the previous cessation of hostilities accords, should be finalized in its entirety before further negotiations on the other remaining issues took place. In my view this condition was unreasonable. I went back and forth between him and Ali Osman on the phone and in person before their final meeting at 11:00 a.m. on the 16th. I should have been en route to Addis Ababa by then, but delayed my departure to help break the stalemate. Garang gave up his position in the end, and Taha returned to Khartoum. The two leaders agreed to come back and complete the talks on November 16th. General Sumbeiywo told me afterwards that the talks would have been in a very difficult spot had I not delayed my departure and intervened.

Dr. John and Ali Osman had appointed a technical committee consisting of one team from each side to negotiate during Ramadan. Their main focus would be issues of funding of the armed forces and the time and manner in which numerous militia groups would be integrated into structures of the Sudanese army and the SPLA.

During the October negotiating round there had been new speculation about who was using delaying tactics, and why. The atmosphere had been quite different from that of Naivasha, with little energy, even less external attention, and the sense of an unnecessarily prolonged process. Ambassador Tom Vraalsen, who had replaced Vegard Ellefsen as Special Envoy for

Norway, and Endre Stiansen were present at the negotiations. I continued calling the parties and I planned to visit the talks again in connection with the Security Council meeting in November. But the round had concluded without any concrete agreement on the outstanding issues. Meanwhile the Abuja negotiations on Darfur continued, with a new round scheduled to start around October 20th. Discussions between the government and National Democratic Alliance were still under way in Cairo. The two leaders had enough on their plates.

There was more to come. It was during this period that tensions within the SPLM/A came to the fore. There had long been reputed misgivings related to Garang's leadership style from some quarters. Now his next in command, Salva Kiir, was reported to be increasingly frustrated. He was dissatisfied with the lack of consultation during the Naivasha talks, and felt sidelined. Some sources say that Salva also was worried about being shunted aside in favour of Nhial Deng. Tension was building up, and there were even stories going around of a potential coup. I heard the rumours but did not take them seriously at the time.

History at the Security Council

The Chairman and the Vice President were scheduled to return to Nairobi on November 19th, primarily for the meeting of the Security Council. Prior to this, the Troika was asked to brief the Security Council on the status of the IGAD peace process and the situation in the country. Ambassador and Special Envoy Tom Vraalsen conducted this briefing. The situation in Darfur had deteriorated even further. On the rebel side, new splinter groups had been formed, making the situation on the ground and at the negotiation table even more complicated. Rebel groups and government-sponsored militias alike were violating the ceasefire agreement. The fighting was spreading to new areas, with new groups becoming involved in the havoc. In addition to deteriorating security, there had been forced relocations of displaced people by the government, without any protection and in contravention of agreed procedures. Humanitarian access and conditions for humanitarian workers were also worsening. Disturbing developments were taking place in relation to other conflicts in the country, both in the East and in parts of the South, where the situation in Western Upper Nile continued to be very serious. There was a fear of new "Darfurs" in other parts of the country – unless the peace agreement was completed.

At the Security Council we stressed the urgency of addressing the short-term issues in Darfur. At the same time, the conflict had to be seen in a national context. Only a comprehensive peace agreement could provide the basis for a sustainable solution to the problems of all the marginalized areas in the country. We urged the Council to put its full weight behind such an agreement and ask for its speedy completion, at the latest by the end of the year. At the same time we stressed the importance of coherence among the various processes, the AU negotiations on Darfur, the IGAD talks, and even the opposition talks in Cairo.

On November 18th John Garang and Ali Osman Taha returned to Nairobi for the Security Council meeting. I had meetings with both of them, first with Ali Osman, in which he expressed the government's commitment to finalize the negotiations before the end of the year, and to "finish Darfur" as soon as possible. But on the latter, the question was how to get there. At this juncture I was urgently calling for the IGAD negotiations to be completed on time. The IGAD secretariat had arranged for the final round of talks to start only on December 11th. I thought this was too late, given the need to get the agreement done by the end of the year. I urged Taha to make use of their presence in Nairobi to meet his counterpart and sort out some of the important issues, and to agree on an earlier return than scheduled. It was now time to put all tactics behind, and focus on how the last issues could be resolved.

The Vice President agreed with this, but added: "there are still some doubts and suspicion between us. If we could trust each other it would be possible to delay some of the issues, and in particular some of the details, for the interim period". He was frustrated with the number of questions that the SPLM/A had raised about the implementation modalities: "Some questions are logical, and we need to agree on them, others seem unnecessary to raise now". I responded that what seemed like trivia to one party could be very important for the other side. It was critical that they decide which issues really needed resolution now, and which could be dealt with later. I inquired what these might be for Taha, and he responded that the time lines for integration of "other armed groups" into the new Army were very important. The timing of the establishment of the Government of Southern Sudan and the question related to the Central Bank also needed to be resolved now. As for the latter, he thought it could easily be resolved by having two windows in the National Bank, one for the central bank and one for Southern Sudan. Funding the SPLA beyond the integrated units, however, was a clear-cut issue: it had to be funded by the government of the South. On this issue there was no way the government would give in. There had been additional discussions in the Cabinet on this issue lately, and the conclusion was clear. There was no wriggle room.

I inquired about the transfer of oil revenue, and whether payments would be in US dollars or local currency. Taha responded that this issue would be clarified when the SPLM/A was represented in the governing bodies of the National Bank and the rules and regulations were set. He then gave a longer technical explanation that indicated that the transfers would be in local currency. I knew this would be a problem.

The SPLM Chairman agreed that it would be wise to spend an extra day with Taha to try to sort out some of the issues, and not least to arrange a comprehensive instruction for the delegations and their technical negotiations. Dr. John wanted me to convey this to Taha. I referred to my discussions with Ali Osman, and what seemed to be the key issues for the government. Dr. John responded that speedy integration of the militias was a sign of seriousness in the peace process. Smaller groups in the South needed to be included in the process too, and the opposition groups based in Asmara. But the funding issue was on the top of the agenda for the SPLM/A Chairman. When I referred to this as a "red line" issue for the government, Garang said: "It is also for us". The currency question with regard to oil-income was in his view a political and not a technical issue, and needed to be resolved now. When it came to returning earlier than December 11th he had a problem. He had already arranged a trip in Southern Sudan, including to Equatoria and Bahr al-Ghazal, where the SPLM Leadership Council would be convened. Because of the situation in the movement, he had to stick to the plan. I was concerned, and stated that it would not be possible to break a promise that was given to the Security Council. Garang understood and said that they would stick to their commitment to finish before the end of the year. This would also be a reward to Colin Powell for his engagement for peace in Sudan. As he was due to leave office, he deserved this.

The meeting of the Security Council in Nairobi the next day was chaired by Ambassador Danforth. It was one of the few times a Security Council meeting had taken place in Africa, and it now gave the IGAD process its full attention. This was also one of the few times in history that a representative of a so-called "non-state actor", a rebel leader, directly addressed a formal meeting of the Council. Speaking in his national capacity, Danforth said pessimists might be tempted to dismiss the meeting as "just a photo opportunity or another memorandum", as atrocities continued. He told the Sudan's Vice-President and SPLM/A leader that it was up to them to prove the doubters wrong by delivering on their word. Danforth said that once the North–South peace agreement was in place, the flow of support would increase, on the understanding that the parties were fulfilling their commitments.

In addressing the Council Ali Osman Mohamed Taha said that the imminent peace had not been "achieved through manoeuvres and posturing", but was "a result of digging by bare hands". The Naivasha peace process gave the best possible chance for peace in Sudan. The Sudanese government was committed to implementing the Protocols. In his address, John Garang said that the Resolution would anchor the process and create momentum for peace, rather than war, and its message of greater unity was a good one for southern Sudan and the whole world. He commented that failure to reach a political settlement by 31 December would have serious consequences, more serious perhaps than sanctions and, therefore, he pledged full commitment by the SPLM/A. Both leaders raised Darfur as an issue of critical importance, with Garang stressing that the only way to avert further tragedy there was "to install a broad-based coalition government of national unity."

Speaking on behalf of donors, and anticipating the International Donors' Conference on Sudan in Oslo, I stated that the Security Council had now sent a strong message that the world supported a Sudan without war and that all had a role to play. However, the main responsibility for peace lay primarily with Sudanese leaders. I emphasized that a peace agreement would not only bring an end to the long-lasting conflict between North and South that had cost many lives and had inflicted tremendous human suffering, but could also provide a political platform for addressing the underlying causes of the continuing conflicts in Sudan, including Darfur. While the Norwegian Government fully supported Security Council resolution 1574, I said it was our belief that the first step towards a political solution in Darfur lay in the completion of the peace negotiations facilitated by IGAD. "We are only waiting for the parties to take the very last steps of peace."

In the Security Council resolution, devoted largely to what would soon be called the Comprehensive Peace Agreement, the parties were instructed to abide by a negotiating deadline of December 31st. The resolution thus contributed to the final push to finish the negotiations. Apart from his impressive work in 2002 and his engagement on Abyei, this was one of Danforth's most significant contributions to the negotiations of the CPA. With the new deadline, it was time to move quickly to complete the negotiations. My two friends got together briefly, discussed the way forward, and provided some instructions to their respective delegations. The technical negotiations continued after they returned.

Garang: Real Trouble at Home

From Nairobi Dr. John went to New Site and understood that the tensions in the SPLM/A had been building up to a point where it had become very serious for him and for the Movement. I was surprised about the timing, since the very final stage of negotiations had been reached. I would soon learn about the gravity of the personal drama that was unfolding between Garang and Salva Kiir. Towards the end of October the tensions had developed into a political crisis. According to Salva this was triggered by a lack of communication and by rumour mongering by "hardliners" trying to split the Movement. Some had also visited him and encouraged a confrontation. When he and the Chairman finally spoke on the telephone, the crisis had reached the point where Salva feared arrest. The Chairman suggested that they meet at Malwal Kon, but Salva insisted on neutral ground.[33] They agreed on Rumbek, and Garang called the SPLM/A leadership to meet there on 28–30 November.

Before the meeting, Riak Machar, Malik Agar and others came to see Salva. According to his own account, he was under great pressure from several quarters to confront the Chairman.[34] Some hardliners wanted to exploit him and his frustration for their own purposes, wanting Garang removed and Salva to take over the movement. Others did not want him to take action at all, and they put pressure on him not to rock the boat. When Salva arrived in Rumbek for the meeting, he therefore decided to remain in his house until the meeting was to take place, and not to be available to anyone.

Dr. John arrived late, on November 27th, and was received by crowds at the airport. Salva had to go and greet him, as was customary. He asked Deng Alor, whom both leaders trusted, to drive him. To avoid misapprehension Salva had only two soldiers with him in the car, and he was unarmed. At the Chairman's house there were guards outside whom Salva had known for years. Salva entered the compound and sat under a tree, not wanting to enter the house, lest speculation arise that he had been bought off. Salva told Dr. John that he had come only to greet him, and that he wished to discuss the issues the next day.

Salva Kiir's complaints related both to Dr. John's leadership style and his method of decision-making, which he regarded as authoritarian. Dr. John intervened and took decisions, he claimed, when others, such as his next in command, had already been mandated. Salva wanted change. Both the Leadership Council and prominent SPLA commanders were there. The meeting lasted three days. Accounts vary as to what happened in the leadership meeting.[35] The Chairman, Salva, and several other members of the leadership spoke, also others were critical. Reconciliation was achieved, however. By all accounts the discussions ended with Salva and Dr. John embracing each other, and Salva's promising his allegiance to the Chairman, committing himself to fully support him in the finalization of the peace agreement. A military band started playing, and everyone in the room embraced each other in relief. The movement had survived one of its toughest tests. Salva had withstood the pressure. When telling the story of these dramatic days, Salva Kiir underscores that it was never his intention to try to take over – he would rather have died at the hands of his friends.[36] In a written communication to his Commanders and the leaders of the SPLM/A later, Dr. John referred to the meeting and its conclusions and expressed full confidence in Salva.

When Salva Kiir later learned that Dr. John had not received any of his messages during the difficult weeks of October–November 2004, he of course immediately suspected treachery. According to Salva, Dr. John's bodyguards later admitted withholding the messages.[37] All of this is hard to verify. Garang was concerned too about another meeting taking place at the same time, in Nairobi, where Southerners long opposed to him had convened to discuss strategy,[38] an unlikely coincidence. Several of those at the Nairobi meeting had been allied to Khartoum at various times, and there was speculation that elements in the government had a hand in trying to undermine the Movement.

Recounting this period in discussions recently, Salva Kiir did not reveal where the pressure came from or who the "hardliners" were. From other sources, however, it is clear that Bona Malwal, Justin Yak and Dominic Dim were among those putting pressure on him.[39] They had all crossed swords with Garang, and wanted Salva to bid for the leadership of the SPLM/A. Before the meeting, Col Ding called a contact at the BBC's Africa desk,[40] and informed him that Bona Malwal was likely to call within the next thirty-six hours or so.[41] He would report a coup from within the SPLM/A and the ouster of Chairman John Garang. Col told the BBC that if and when such a call came through, they should get in touch with Dr. John immediately for verification.

And reportedly, Bona Malwal called and said that a coup had occurred in the SPLM/A. The contact duly checked with the SPLM/A Chairman and his people, only to disprove the story.

When it was all over, I talked to Dr. John on the phone, and he told me about the problems he had faced. He said that the situation had been really difficult, but that things had been sorted out and he was confident that the SPLM/A would move forward as a united movement. Ali Osman also called me and said he had been informed of a crisis in the SPLM/A. He referred to the rumours, and wanted my assessment of the internal situation in the Movement. It was clear that the government was well informed about what was going on. Taha said he was worried, and asked whether the situation was under control, and whether Garang was all right. I replied that all the information we had pointed to a situation under control, and that there was no reason to worry. Through other sources I later learnt that Taha also had called Dr. John in Rumbek during this period, to the latter's surprise.[42]

Both Ali Osman Taha and John Garang had faced challenges at home during this period. Although Ali Osman was not confronted in such an explicit way, the difficulties he had encountered earlier were far from over. We heard that there were subtle attempts at undermining his leadership from several quarters.[43]

Inching Forward

In the second week of December the two leaders were back in Nairobi for the final round of negotiations. Compared to the hoopla that had surrounded the earlier talks, the situation was completely different. From the international community hardly anyone attended. The envoys of the IGAD countries were less frequent visitors, and for the Troika the Norwegians and Americans remained the most engaged.

Five days into the round, on December 16th, I talked with Taha and Garang on the telephone. Dr. John reported intense negotiations, with two-three meetings a day between the two principals and good progress in the talks. At the same time, four technical committees were working full time. At this juncture, they had resolved the question of the transfer of oil revenues and organization of the Central Bank; only a few details remained on wealth sharing. On power sharing the discussions were focused on the timing of elections in the interim period. Garang told me that the respective positions had been reversed, with the government now wanting to delay elections for as long as possible, and not wanting presidential elections at all. The SPLM/A wanted elections four years into the interim period. To Dr. John I stressed: "We cannot support any monopoly of power by the two negotiating parties after the peace agreement"; elections should be held at all levels. In addition, this process was also intended as important peace dividends for the Sudanese people, contributing to political transformation.

The change of heart on the government side was interesting. Since they were uncertain about their relations with the opposition, they would rather delay elections. This was also why they insisted on the partnership with the SPLM/A. Garang said he wanted to give the National Congress Party the necessary reassurances in this regard. There were now separate talks on setting the parameters for a political partnership, with Pagan Amun representing the Movement and the government represented by Nafie Ali Nafie. Taha agreed that the issue of elections would be easier to resolve with progress on the political partnership. There was also another possible factor, the timetable for integration of the "other armed groups". The government seemed to be holding back on this, too, possibly until they had a satisfactory answer on partnership.

Abyei was again, or still, a problem. The parties were very far apart about defining its borders. They agreed, therefore, that this should largely be in the hands of the Commission, with its mandate for a decision that would be "final and binding". The Commission should start its work three months into the pre-interim period. Other border issues related to the definition of the Nuba Mountains, the border between it and Western Kordofan, and – perhaps amazingly at this point – the name of the area. Garang was sure that the government's positions had to do with oil. In the border area between Kordofan and Darfur there was even a new militia being formed. He predicted that the situation could become difficult.

Taha and Garang now agreed to deal with the ceasefire issues at the very end. The SPLM Chairman wanted to be home for Christmas, and stated that they would finish by December 23rd. Taha agreed. They were wrong again. They agreed on the composition and mandate of the Constitutional Review Commission, which would be tasked with drafting a new constitution. They sorted out details of the transition arrangements, with the deployment of Joint National Transition Teams composed of key people from both parties for the pre-interim period. These would be co-chaired; from the SPLM, Leadership Council members were selected. These teams would be charged with facilitating the transition, starting on 15 March 2005.

As the talks continued, the format was the same as it had been, with the two principals tackling the most contentious questions and assigning teams to thrash out the details in legal language after they had reached agreement. Security issues remained the major hurdle once again, and the process was slow on two major points of disagreement, the funding of the SPLA and the level of forces after demobilization. As so often before in the negotiations, the two leaders underestimated the difficulties. Charlie Snyder got Colin Powell to call and press both parties, reiterating the firm deadline set by the Security Council.

Dealing with Potential Spoilers

While the final talks went on, we were mindful of potential spoilers. While the agreement would be called the Sudan Comprehensive Peace Agreement (CPA), it was clear that the word "comprehensive" reflected the *issues* covered in the agreement, not its regional or political *representation*. Some opposition groups rightly pointed this out. What was not communicated clearly and strongly enough was that the government and the SPLM/A had committed to a sequential approach: the agreement would provide the basis for an inclusive political process with the other parties, and a model for dealing with the challenges in the West and the East. Indeed, unless these processes were started very soon, the peace agreement could be undermined. I continued discussing the issues with Dr. John and Ali Osman, and pressed them to start thinking about how they could forge ahead during the pre-interim period and beyond.

The most urgent issue was the Darfur crisis. On 21 December a fourth round of the AU talks would begin, but without much hope of progress. The format remained cumbersome, with a very formal negotiation process and a huge number of observers. I was under no illusion that the talks would lead anywhere soon, and was very concerned about jeopardising the CPA. At this stage I had discussions with Ali Osman about ways to speed up the negotiations. In my view, a Naivasha-like arrangement could be considered. This would keep the AU as the formal negotiating structure, but the parties themselves, possibly with the assistance of Dr. John and Ali Osman, could try to sort out some of the critical issues in advance. We would see in Oslo in 2005 that both main rebel groups in Darfur expressed interest in such a format – at least then, and at least orally.

The other challenge was relations with other parties in Sudan. The National Democratic Alliance needed to be brought into the equation. In July Dr. John had participated in the NDA meeting in Asmara. The various member parties had agreed to mandate its Chairman, the leader of the Democratic Unionist Party, to form a delegation to negotiate with the government. The two main rebel groups in Darfur were members of the delegation. Negotiations were held in Cairo. These were complicated, partly because many of the issues discussed overlapped those under discussion at Naivasha and Abuja. The intention therefore was to open a separate process once the CPA was signed.

Ali Osman Taha favoured an All Party Conference in Sudan during the pre-interim period (the first six months). The SPLM was open to this as long as it was fully involved in the process. These ideas had our full support. The Troika had, after all, pressed for a broader process much earlier in the negotiations.

Another aspect of Sudanese politics consisted of the Southern splinter groups. Although a lot of the groundwork had already taken place before the start of the Naivasha process, a few such groups remained disaffected. While the negotiations were going on, an SPLM team under James Kok worked full time on this, approaching the factions with offers of support and leadership positions if they decided to join. Riak Machar and his group rejoined the SPLM/A early in 2002; Lam Akol's SPLA-United in October 2003; and the Equatorian Defence Force, a faction around Torit, came aboard in December 2003. That last group had served as a channel for Khartoum's support of the Lord's Resistance Army, so it was very important to get it integrated into the SPLM/A.

But still other militias remained, including the Mandari of Clement Wani, Paulino Matip's force in Upper Nile, a Murle militia headed by Ismail Kony, and a few smaller factions, such as one from Wau under Tom al-Nur. The SPLM/A knew that such armed groups could be exploited in Khartoum to provoke destabilising incidents, undermine implementation of the peace agreement, and control key areas. Dr. John wanted a stronger and more anchored process, and talked to us about using the Moi Foundation as the basis for continued dialogue with other Southern groups. This process went ahead, with support from Norway and other donors, but it proved in the end to be less effective than we had hoped.

The Final Deal on Security

As we approached Christmas, a lot had been resolved. Only the ceasefire and security issues remained. Two of the most important related to the East and "other armed groups". On the latter, the SPLM insisted that the militia were obliged to join either the Sudanese army or the SPLA. After strenuous nego-tiations, the government accepted this. In the end, it was also agreed that a Joint Integrated Unit would be established in the East, in Kassala, following withdrawal of the SPLA. The parties were still stuck on the size of their armies, the degree of demobilization required, and funding of the SPLA. The talks were very heated, and dragged on and on.

The demobilization of forces on both sides was a numbers game; neither party was truthful about current forces or the level of troops needed after a peace agreement. Charlie Snyder and I coordinated our messages to both leaders. There were limited possibilities for us to influence the discussion on actual numbers, however, given the lack of honest information. It was impos-sible to know what a "sensible" demobilization level would be as long as the real number of forces was unknown. We just conveyed our concerns and appealed for sense. In the end the solution arrived at allowed troop numbers far too high on both sides.

Colin Powell engaged with calls to Dr. John and the government side. Dr. John argued that an army funded separately would be a first step towards secession. While the government agreed that the Joint Integrated Units would be funded from the national defence budget, it was out of the question to finance also the SPLA. It did not help that Garang did not reveal its true size.

No one in the government or among the Northern political forces would see any sense in funding the SPLA. At this juncture, Ali Osman Taha had begun receiving figures of how budgets would have to be cut to accommodate the wealth-sharing arrangements in the agreement. For people in the North to cut more in order to pay the SPLA was out of the question.

Between Christmas Eve and New Years Eve this was the only remaining issue before the Implementation Protocol could be signed. I kept in constant touch on the phone despite being bedridden with a serious back injury. For this reason I could not fly to Nairobi to help. The Indian Ocean tsunami had hit at the same time, and I had also to attend to that. I asked Dr. John to use his encrypted telephone so we could discuss the security issues freely. We talked repeatedly. Even the deadline of the Security Council would not make him budge.

We were getting closer to the deadline and I worried that the two negotiators would become a laughing stock. Having missed virtually every deadline from day one of the negotiations, and having almost caused the international community to give up on them, they could not now walk away on New Year's Eve without an agreement. I was adamant. The Security Council's deadline had to be upheld. I started to call people close to Dr. John. The Americans might be able to influence him, but despite trying repeatedly I could not reach Charlie Snyder on the phone these critical days. The SPLM/A-friends Roger Winter and Brian da Silva were not available either, and had not followed the negotiations lately. At this juncture, the days before New Years Eve, there seemed to be complete silence from the American side. I was not sure whether they had any idea of the drama unfolding in Nairobi.

In the end, I managed to reach a close friend of Dr. John and ally of the SPLM/A in the US. I asked him to help find a solution for funding the SPLA. As this friend began work, we learned that President Thabo Mbeki of South Africa could be on the way. He was visiting Khartoum briefly, and there was talk that he might travel to Nairobi to witness the signing ceremony of the Implementation protocol on the 31st. Taha called President Bashir and said that he should come to the signing of the agreement, and bring the South African President with him. This would be an obvious way of showing that the agreement had the backing of the President and the ruling party.[44] Bringing along a foreign dignitary would enhance the occasion.

Hearing about the problems in the negotiations, they delayed their departure, then told the parties they would be in Nairobi in a few hours to attend the ceremony. This had the desired effect. In the end a clause was inserted in the agreement giving the SPLA the right to import military equipment and receive financial support from outside the country, subject only to notification – not approval – of Khartoum. I had been on the phone with both sides all week, and was now able to offer my congratulations. In the interim, Taha had called President Bashir and they flew in. As the two presidents drove up from Nairobi to Naivasha, the Protocol on the Implementation Modalities was cleaned up and made ready for signature. The Protocol was signed that night, several hours later than planned but still within the deadline of the Security Council. Twenty-one years of civil war was over.

I did not understand why Dr. John was so adamant on the issue of SPLA funding. Even if Khartoum had conceded the point, good-faith implementation in this area would have been very unlikely. Much later I learned about his strategy. He had always known that Khartoum would oppose the SPLA's acquisition of arms from abroad if he tabled such a proposal during the security negotiations. Instead he decided to insist on central government funding of the SPLA, an even more unacceptable demand. When stalemate on the issue threatened the whole agreement he would make a major "concession", for the sake of peace – the clause allowing imports of weapons that he had wanted all along. Earlier on, as the IGAD-negotiations started, several donors had in fact offered the SPLM/A training in negotiation tactics and strategies, an offer that bemused Dr. John: "What would we need that for?" he asked. He proved that he could manage without "capacity building".

The rationale behind the clause was not a wish to start re-arming the SPLA after the peace agreement was signed. Garang was looking towards 2011 and beyond, taking out an insurance policy for the South should the situation deteriorate or the referendum opt for secession. This little-known clause has been valuable for the SPLA ever since. When the Government of Southern Sudan has been accused of violating the peace agreement by importing arms,[45] critics have been surprised to find it was well within its rights to do so.

Signing the Comprehensive Peace Agreement

The Comprehensive Peace Agreement was to be signed in Nairobi on 9 January 2005. I was concerned that high-level participation and coverage would suffer because of attention to the tsunami. To some extent this happened. And of course the shadow of Darfur was a major concern to all of us. Still, the event attracted ten heads of state and government from all countries in the IGAD region and beyond, many ministers of foreign affairs and international development, dignitaries from the United Nations, and leaders of regional organizations including IGAD, the African Union, the Arab League and the European Union. From the Troika, Secretary of State Colin Powell represented the US; Hilary Benn the UK; and I both Norway and the IGAD Partners' Forum, the latter with my Italian co-chair, the deputy minister of foreign affairs, Senator Alfredo Mantica.

The ceremony took place at the Nairobi City Stadium. Thousands of people gathered to witness this historic occasion. Southern Sudanese refugees had come in numbers from the camps close to the border. Other Southerners had travelled from afar, many having walked for days and hitched rides on trucks. From Khartoum, members of the religious communities, civil society and the political elite were present. Both President Bashir and First Vice President Taha took part, and most of the Cabinet were there. Dr. John was joined by the entire SPLM/A leadership. As so often in Africa, everything was delayed. No ceremony of this nature can start until all the dignitaries are present. This time President Museveni of Uganda was the latecomer.

After a delay of several hours the Kenyans gave the green light. It was an impressive event. A number of leaders spoke and conveyed their commitment to the peace accord and its implementation. Colin Powell and I did the same. It is particularly noteworthy that the Egyptian foreign minister, Ahmed Abu'l-Gheit, expressed his country's support, as did Amr Moussa for the Arab League. From the parties, Dr. John and Ali Osman Taha were the main speakers, committing themselves to implement the CPA and calling upon their fellow Sudanese and the international community to support the process. Dr. John spoke passionately, and for a very long time, about the history of Sudan, the reasons for the war, and why it was time to make peace. He saw the CPA as realization of the New Sudan:

> This peace agreement therefore signals the beginning of Sudan's second republic of the new Sudan. From here on Sudan for the first time will be a country voluntarily united in justice, honour and dignity for all its citizens regardless of their race, regardless of their religion, regardless of their gender or else if the country fails to rise to this challenge of moving away from the old Sudan to the new Sudan of free and equal citizens, then the union shall be dissolved amicably and peacefully through the right of self determination at the end of the six years of the interim period.

The crowds cheered. I had wondered whether President Bashir or the First Vice President would sign the CPA. While the President showed his endorsement by being there and addressing the audience, it was Ali Osman who signed.

First Vice-President Ali Osman Taha was equally enthusiastic:

> Having covered milestones, mines and mountains, we shall successfully deliberate on the post-peace challenges as well. My country has suffered from the scourge of war for so long, and we are determined, through the Government of National Unity, to bring about a real change on the ground so as to realize our reconstruction goals, development and unity. The people of Sudan are ready to walk back to the peaceful state where they came from. A prosperous Sudan, at peace with itself and its neighbours, is good for the region, for the continent and for the world at large.

Speaking on behalf of Norway and the IGAD Partners' Forum, I declared:

> You, the leaders of Sudan, have brought a challenging process to a successful end. Ahead of you is another, even more challenging one . . .
> The signing of an agreement is only a first step. Implementation will be

the test of true commitment. The agreement must be followed to the letter. Step by step, decision by decision, action by action. Signatures alone do not deliver peace. Action does, when the agreement is translated into reality. Implementation is what counts, not ink on paper.

We trust that you, the leaders, will bring about the new Sudan you have so often talked about . . . We count on you for the rapid reconstruction of areas devastated by war, and for accountability and transparency throughout the process. We count on you to bring about reconciliation in local communities . . . ensure peace and stability, and put an end to all fighting, by all actors. We count on you to find a swift and sustainable solution to the problems in Darfur. As we count on you to deliver, so you can count on us.

President Kibaki, President Museveni, Foreign Minister Ahmed Abu'l-Gheit, Secretary of State Powell, Hilary Benn and I, among others, signed the CPA as witnesses.

Now it was time to put the agreement into practice.

CHAPTER SEVEN

The First Taste of Peace

The signing ceremony on 9 January 2005 was a momentous event. It was the intention of the parties, General Sumbeiywo, and the IGAD countries that the witness signatures would betoken the international community's full support for the CPA and its implementation. Broad ownership and international guarantees would be critical to its success. Sudan's history of broken agreements had indeed permeated the negotiation of the CPA and been reflected in its provisions.

Many Sudanese welcomed the agreement. A woman from Dongola said: "'At first we were really worried [about the SPLM], but all praise be to Allah, we now have peace. We are really happy now and we don't need to have any animosity towards anyone.'"[1] Some wondered how an agreement between only two parties could be "comprehensive"? Yet this was not a North–South deal only, but an agreement intended to lead to a just peace for all the marginalized peoples in the country and to make unity attractive for Southerners.

After the signing I went to Dr. John's house in Nairobi with my bottle of champagne as we had agreed, accompanied by a couple from my team. Many were claiming his time, and his wife arrived first to tell us he was on the way. It was a moving evening. I had never before heard Rebecca talk about her life with Dr. John in such a way, from the day she joined the struggle in the bush in 1983, cooking, cleaning, and being a nurse, mother and sister to the first crowd of SPLA fighters. This morning she had had to pinch herself. A dream was coming true. She had looked in the mirror and said to herself and her husband: "From now on I am a new person."[2] After an hour or so Dr. John arrived, and for the first time I could congratulate him on a mission accomplished, and we raised our glasses to toast the Comprehensive Peace Agreement for Sudan. There was a lot of laughter, many stories, and even more predictions of what was to come. The most difficult job started now, putting the CPA into practice, making the transformation of Sudan a reality.

During my stay in Nairobi, I had brief meetings with both Dr. John and Ali Osman, focusing on the immediate steps ahead and on Darfur. A process to bring peace to Darfur and the East was essential. The pre-interim period would commence on January 10th, the next day. The parties had six months to create broad ownership of the agreement, and to ensure that all necessary preparations were made for the interim period. Six months was not much, as the parties would soon realize.

Not all fighting had ceased, but the ceasefire, building on the cessation of hostilities agreement, made an immediate impact on the lives of people all over

Southern Sudan, Southern Kordofan (the Nuba Mountains) and Southern Blue Nile. It would take time before normality could return to places such as Abyei. "'We feel like it is not like the previous peace agreement'", said a Nuer chief from Ayod. "'For instance, Addis Ababa was signed by the Sudan government and a few individuals and some people didn't know what it was about.'" A man from Kurmuk said: "'We are optimistic because the agreement is being set by the international community, the USA and UN.'"[3]

Expanding Peace to Darfur and the East

But conflict continued in two parts of the country, Darfur and the East. The pre-interim period was the window of opportunity. If Darfur and the East could be sorted out in time for the inauguration of the Government of National Unity on July 9th, the new regime would be based on a true, comprehensive peace. We had a strategy to make that happen. This had been discussed with both Dr. John and Ali Osman in the autumn. They were both committed to work for a solution, the more so now that the First Vice President had assumed the Darfur portfolio in the government. Progress on Darfur, if possible a breakthrough, before the Donors' Conference in Oslo on 10–11 April would mobilize more resources for reconstruction. These efforts were sabotaged, however, as we shall see.

Urgent action was needed. Soon after returning to Oslo on January 15th I called Dr. John. He had met representatives of the Sudan Liberation Movement in Nairobi, but its leaders were in Tripoli at the time, taking part in another initiative poorly coordinated with the overall peace effort. "Ghadaffi is in full swing, as usual," was how Garang put it. He expressed willingness to meet the rebel leaders soon, but wanted to discuss with Ali Osman what the government was willing to put on the table. He could then go to the rebel groups, listen to their side, and form an idea of what the way forward might be. The SPLM/A had already established a committee on Darfur composed of Abd al-Aziz Adam, Yasir Arman and Beyor Adjang. The Chairman said that he would take personal responsibility for the process.

Dr. John mentioned a risk that the CPA might be read to imply that the government could move military units from the South to Darfur. We needed to be aware of this. But at the moment he was just as worried about the East. The Beja Congress and the Rashaida Free Lions were unlikely to sign the Cairo Communiqué related to the National Democratic Alliance negotiations, and there was a danger of more unrest. The statement to which he referred was due to be presented to a meeting of the NDA on February 5th.

There was certainly a risk that the events in the East or West could undermine the whole agreement. There was no time to lose. The Donors' Conference was just around the corner. Since the Abuja talks were not making progress, I suggested to Garang that his relations with President Isaias Afeworki of Eritrea could now be put to good use, for the Eritreans had a host country's leverage with rebel groups in the East and the West and could encourage them to negotiate seriously. This could also have implications for the transfer of military equipment to the rebel groups. Garang had spent two days in January with the Eritrean President, who had given the CPA his full support. Dr. John agreed to travel to Asmara.

The following day, I talked to the First Vice President, and expressed our pleasure that he had assumed the government's Darfur portfolio. Taha confirmed that the military offensive planned in Darfur would no longer take place, and that he would have meetings the following day with the President, Minister of Defence, and military leadership to discuss the security situation in Darfur and how to ensure that the ceasefire was respected. I referred to my discussion with Garang the day before and to his willingness to engage. Such initiatives, I said, were pointless if military offensives were launched. Ali Osman agreed fully, and said that this was the reason for his decision.

I reminded the Vice President of the fast track we had wanted for Darfur and briefed him about my discussion with Dr. John, including the SPLM/A Chairman's plan to visit Asmara. He needed more information from Taha, however, to be able to help. The Vice President took note of this and said that after his return from Tripoli, where he was going in connection with the Libyan peace effort, he would contact us. I urged Taha to talk to Dr. John very soon; the encrypted phones we had promised them would be delivered in a day or two. Like us, Taha was concerned that the two rebel groups in the East might not sign the Cairo protocol. He wondered whether something could be done between the initialling of the agreement on February 5th and the signing ceremony set for the following week.

Ali Osman was clearly concerned about the role of Eritrea. It seemed that Hasan al-Turabi could be on his way to Asmara for a meeting: what role would the SPLM have in such deliberations? I assured him that Garang would try to influence the various rebel groups in a positive way and do his best to get the Eritreans on board. This illustrated, however, the need for the two leaders to coordinate their efforts and to talk frequently. The First Vice President also urged me to try to influence Eritrea to take a more constructive role in relation to the negotiations and the process. I told him that our State Secretary Vidar Helgesen was an old friend of Afeworki, and could be useful.

On the Darfur side, other events also had an impact on the situation. Soon after this discussion, on January 25th, the report of the International Commission of Inquiry on Darfur was published. This was a devastating compilation of documentary evidence of the crimes and atrocities committed. A sealed list of fifty-one individuals was submitted for criminal investigation. Ten were high-ranking members of the central government, 17 were local offi- cials, 14 *janjawid*, 3 officers of foreign armies, and 7 were rebels. A report by the Sudanese government, released earlier in January, had been poorly received. For this reason, the UN Security Council soon referred the cases to the International Criminal Court. This had a dramatic impact in Khartoum, where such an outcome had been unexpected.

On February 8th, both Dr. John and Ali Osman went before the Security Council in New York in connection with the CPA and the full mandating of the peacekeeping force in Sudan. Both leaders spoke at length on Darfur. Taha acknowledged the severity of the crisis, and presented a comprehensive framework for its solution, covering political aspects, security, and justice. Garang outlined measures needed to end the conflict. Before coming to the Security Council he had consulted the presidents of Kenya and Eritrea, the prime minister of Ethiopia, the Egyptian minister of security, and all the Darfur groups. He was confident that the provisions of the CPA could be applied to the conflicts in Darfur and eastern Sudan. He also emphasized that insinuations about the CPA's diminishing the chances for peace in Darfur were "flawed, counter-productive and morally inept, as they punished the peoples of both southern Sudan and Darfur".[4] He referred to his previous offer of ten thousand SPLA troops alongside the government's and AU's forces to ensure protection for the Darfurians.

Peace Building in Sudan

Peace building was as critical as peace making. The international community had watched other peace initiatives come and go. As we contemplated the situation in Sudan, we were fully aware that more than half of all peace agreements fall apart and the parties relapse into war. Sudan itself had provided an example of this with the Addis Ababa Agreement. Early on, several countries that supported the Sudan peace process and had been engaged in peace building issues commissioned research on lessons to be learned from previous efforts.[5] This was a valuable exercise. We tried to apply those lessons within the Troika and the IGAD Partners' Forum. I personally engaged in this. All too familiar with the risks of failure, I knew we needed to support Sudanese efforts along parallel tracks. In peace building processes these are often seen as essential pillars, related first to the political process itself, broadening and deepening the ownership of the peace agreement; second to the provision of security, ensuring that critical processes of protection and demobilization happen; and third to peace dividends, reconstruction and development of war-affected areas. People needed to feel the results of peace in their daily lives. These three critical pillars of peace building also applied to Sudan. I knew that the Sudanese needed to succeed along all three tracks if sustainable peace was to be achieved.

A woman in Ikotos grasped this very well: Peace is "'good because gunfire is brought to an end; however, it is not very clear that the signing of the peace agreement is a total and permanent agreement, which stops every suffering caused by the war.'" And an older Agar Dinka war widow in Rumbek put it this way: "'This peace of ours is like a sick man in hospital. You don't want to say for sure that he is going to be coming home, because as long as he is in hospital and sick, he still might die.'"[6] They had grasped that peace is not just the silence of guns: it must be built day by day, through a process that stops the suffering and heals the patient, and gets him home fully functioning.

In the pre-interim period, therefore, it was critical to ensure that there was no delay in relation to any of these processes. While the political processes were in the hands of the parties, the security arrangements and peace dividends were areas where the parties to a large extent were dependent on the commitment of the international community. I advocated timely and generous support, and appealed to key stakeholders and donors that this opportunity must not be missed. Unfortunately there were delays across the board. Both the parties and the international community were dilatory, and this led to serious slippage in the timelines of the CPA throughout the pre-interim and interim periods.

On the political side, the parties focused on a more inclusive process, through consultations with the other parties in the National Democratic Alliance in Cairo. Their endorsement of the CPA could lead to formation of an all-party Constitutional Review Commission, which in turn would lay the foundation for an inclusive Government of National Unity. The Cairo negotiations were hampered by the CPA's power sharing arrangements, which ensured the two parties' hold on power until elections during the interim period. Meanwhile they appointed a committee of seven representatives from each side to negotiate an Interim Constitution. The draft was based on the existing constitution of 1998 and the CPA. Fink Haysom, the constitutional lawyer from South Africa, moderated these negotiations. By mid-February the government had nominated sixty people for the Commission, but none from the major opposition parties in exile. Sadiq al-Mahdi wanted an All Party Conference to "ratify" the CPA, a risky proposition that might stall the Agreement indefinitely.

The government had also nominated members to the Joint Transition Teams to be deployed in Khartoum and the major cities. But although Garang and Taha had agreed on January 17th that those teams would start work soon, nomination of the SPLM members was still pending in mid-February. The teams were due to meet in Nairobi on March 8th, and the arrival in Khartoum of the Joint National Transition Team was set for March 15th. Because of SPLM delays they arrived only on March 31st, halfway through the pre-interim period. This two-month delay caused much frustration for the government,[7] and cost both sides a lot of time needed to prepare for the interim period. Many tasks were specified in the Implementation matrixes, and the deadlines were very tight. The SPLM/A never gave us a good explanation for the delayed nominations.

There were delays too in making changes within the SPLM/A, from movement to political party. In due course, and after completion of the Interim Constitution, a strong government delegation went to Rumbek for discussions on the way forward and the political partnership.[8] As the Joint National Transition Team arrived in Khartoum, it was already clear that the accumulated work would be too much for it. The parties privately acknowledged that the time lines they had set were unrealistic. The delays implied, regrettably, a loss of momentum in following up on the CPA. But appointment of the Government of National Unity and the arrival of the Chairman of the SPLM/A and key ministers in Khartoum were expected to get things moving.

I was deeply concerned about potential spoilers who could undermine the agreement from the Southern side. This had been consistently on my agenda with Dr. John every time we met, both during the negotiations and since. Ensuring an inclusive process for all Southerners, and the respective militias, was critical for a sustainable peace. The Moi Foundation provided a useful framework for moving the process forward, supported by several donors, including Norway, and a conference was planned for February 28th. A joint Action Plan for integrating the militias was also being discussed. This was very positive. Lessons learned from other post-conflict situations showed the need to include religious leaders, community organizations and women's groups. Neither of the parties had significant experience in this regard. We therefore helped the Sudan Council of Churches, through Norwegian Church Aid. Together with other donors, we ensured that women's groups were brought into the process. The Dutch had supported consultative conferences early on; we supported conferences in the North and the South of women's groups, and a joint meeting of both before the Donors' Conference. These political processes were essential for the peace building process to succeed.

Also in the North, there were potential spoilers, and for some the democratic transformation imbedded in the CPA was the key to their buy in. For many of the Sudanese in the North, the most important peace dividends were expected to be the visible signs and freedoms following an opening up of the political space. Among civil society leaders, academia and media, expectations were very high.

We were cognizant that aid and donor assistance are not a panacea in peace building, but peace dividends are. Concrete and tangible results for the population are among the most important factors that can help stabilize a fragile peace, a view supported by major studies in peace building.[9] This is particularly decisive in the earliest phase after the signing of a peace agreement. Just the fact that fighting is stopped has a major impact, leading to security and freedom of movement, the most fundamental peace dividends. This has an immediate impact on people's lives. A Nuer woman from the oil region, now displaced in Rumbek, put it this way: "'Peace is good. I built a house a year ago, and it has not been burned down like it was every year before.'"

Basic livelihood support, including seeds and tools, and basic services, including schools and health clinics, can be among the most important concrete peace dividends. If children and mothers continue to die, if starvation is just as prevalent as during war, if there are no educational opportunities for the children, what then is the difference? In Southern Sudan communication and roads were also seen as critical, and a prerequisite for reviving the local economy.

Expectations were high. "'If there is peace, there will be big schools, a hospital, water,'" a Gawaar Nuer man said. A Nuer Chief from Mading expected no less: "'If peace comes, hunger and health care will be solved.'"[10] For such peace dividends to be paid, aid had to be provided in a timely and effective manner. And as I said on a number of occasions, in Southern Sudan we were not talking about reconstruction after war, we were talking about construction: they were starting more or less from scratch. Basic social services were close to non-existent, and the roads, when there were any, were tracks. In the whole of Southern Sudan, a region the size of France and Germany combined, there was but one stretch of paved road, in Juba, and it was full of potholes. There had been no census since 1955, so we did not know how many people there were. Estimates varied widely, and were touted or denounced according to their political effect. The situation was similar in the Three Areas. The SPLM/A, shortly to be the Government of Southern Sudan, faced immense challenges.

Preparations for a collective donor effort had been under way for a long time. Before the high-level negotiations we had started the so-called "Planning for Peace" process. In the Partners' Forum I had pushed for this process, which was intended to serve two purposes. We wanted to be ready in the early post-conflict period, so as to avoid the mistakes in other countries of an "aid-gap" of six-to-ten months. Secondly, we were sure that a preparatory process on the donors' side would be useful in relation to the negotiations, by showing the parties incentives for reaching an agreement.[11] This process included donor meetings with broad participation, in the Netherlands in April 2003 and in Oslo in September 2004. We also pushed for an early start to needs assessment, through the Joint Assessment Mission (in UN terminology, Post Conflict Needs Assessment), to ensure no delays in erecting a framework within which the donors would provide support. The process started in September 2004. In March 2005 we helped to organize another donors' meeting, of the Partners' Forum, to prepare for the Donors' Conference.

Discussion of funding mechanisms became heated. None of the donors trusted the financial systems, in Khartoum or the South, sufficiently to be willing to transfer resources directly. The normal method in post-conflict settings was to establish a pooled funding mechanism administered by a third party. This was also the logical way to avoid a "donor circus", in particular in the South, where capacity to manage a multitude of bilateral donors and their thousands of individual projects were very limited. This is why the parties agreed to establish a Multi Donor Trust Fund to finance reconstruction. The question arose in the autumn of 2004 as to what agency would administer the Fund. The UN was a known entity to both the government and SPLM/A: both parties were sceptical. The Southerners had dealt with the UN for many years on the humanitarian side, and their relations were not without friction. On the government side, the concerns were more political in character. The two leaders were tempted to choose the World Bank, and they asked my opinion. I told them that the trust funds administered by the World Bank worked well when they were up and running, but that they were slow to start, and it would take at least a year before any money was disbursed and possibly longer for visible development results. UN-administered funds were speedier, and primarily allocated money to programs implemented by the UN and partners in support of government.

At the same time, the donors had already established the Capacity Building Trust Fund, hosted by UNICEF and administered by an international firm of accountants. Given UNICEF's longstanding experience with Operation Lifeline Sudan, we thought it would be the best partner to administer the Fund. The CBTF was relatively small, was meant to assist with resources during the transition, would take care of the SPLM's administrative costs and its transformation into a government, and would build capacity and take care of immediate recurrent costs. The Fund could also pay for quick impact projects in the pre-interim and interim periods, as necessary. This was, therefore, an arrangement that could be used as an interim financing mechanism until the Multi Donor Trust Fund started disbursing. Listening to the pros and cons of World Bank-administered funds, Garang was not at all worried about time. Nor was he particularly concerned that the Government of Southern Sudan would have very limited implementing capacity. I was somewhat surprised by this, knowing the importance that is attached to early peace dividends. The government and the SPLM/A decided to go to the World Bank.

I argued that NGOs and UN agencies had to be major beneficiaries of the Multi Donor Trust Fund and help to implement programs "on contract" from the government. As the World Bank's capacity for implementation was limited, I hoped we in this way would be able to see quicker disbursements and implementation of programs. Given the limited capacity, such arrangements were, in my view, necessary. After lengthy discussions with the UN and the World Bank, the UN was willing to try this arrangement, and the Bank gave very firm assurances that the model would work well. I discussed this model with both parties during my visit to Sudan in February.

The World Bank's Country Director for Sudan at the time, Isaac Diwan, promised at the September 2004 meeting in Oslo that the Multi Donor Trust Fund for Sudan would be up and running, with disbursements, after eight or nine months, a world record for the World Bank. Similar promises were made to both the SPLM/A and the government. On the basis of these assurances, I urged like-minded donors to put as much money as possible into the MDTF, and as little as necessary into bilateral programs. This would prevent draining the capacity of a government still largely non-existent. As it was critical to avoid a gap in the initial phase, I also pushed for scaling up assistance to the Capacity Building Trust Fund and using that fund effectively to ensure peace dividends through quick-impact projects during the first phase. The CBTF proved to be a very effective fund. Having learned the lessons of previous post-conflict environments, and in the interest of avoiding the usual problems of the donor "circus", we planned a Joint Donors' Office in Juba. This would maximize coordination and apply technical capacity to assess MDTF programmes upstream, as well as ensuring that the process was speedy enough and that resources were disbursed quickly.

Not much of this really happened. Although some results could be seen, people in Southern Sudan and in the war-affected areas of the Nuba Mountains and Southern Blue Nile had to wait for a very long time before they saw real, tangible dividends of peace.

Mission to Khartoum, Darfur and Rumbek

But at the time of my visit to Sudan in mid-February 2005 I did not of course know that our efforts would not produce the desired result. I first went to Khartoum for discussions with Ali Osman Taha, a number of ministers and the UN and AU representatives. After returning from a two-day visit to Darfur, I met both Ali Osman and President Bashir. The visit was a preparatory one for the Donors' Conference that now was scheduled for 10–11 April, and we spent some time on these issues as well as on the Joint Assessment Mission. Implementation of the CPA, inclusion of the political opposition, and the crises in Darfur and the East were higher on the agenda, and Darfur was my first priority. The Donors' Conference could not take place if Darfur was still ablaze. In my meeting with the First Vice President, he proposed that the Troika support the Darfur negotiations under the auspices of the AU as we had done with the IGAD talks. Garang needed to be part of such an arrangement. Taha wanted my engagement in the same way that I had been involved in the Naivasha negotiations. In my meeting with the Special Representative of the African Union for Darfur, Baba Gana Kingibe, I conveyed the thinking of the First Vice President and his desire to see the Troika engaged. Kingibe responded positively to this idea. But I knew that there were others calling the shots on the political side in the AU in Addis. Nevertheless, I hoped Ali Osman would be able to move the process in this direction.

The urgency of such a process was made very clear to me during my visit to Darfur, including the camps at Kalma and Geneina. When visiting the camps, I insisted on having private conversations with some of the displaced. In Kalma we managed to find a place where I could meet a group of women alone, without camp management, local leaders or security. Through some discreet manoeuvres, I was free to talk in the shade of a hut. I knew the taboos related to talking about rape, and I had anyway been warned that the women would likely have little to say to a stranger like me. Besides, they had to remain anonymous, since security agents would likely go after them and ask questions after our conversation. If they were sources of compromising information, they would face repercussions. I nodded and made sure I had the help of a credible woman who had their confidence and could translate. I made sure I sat on a log on the ground. It was better that I looked up and listened to them, than the opposite. As always, I started by asking questions about their families and children, building confidence. We talked about their lives, before we slowly ventured into uncharted waters.

I asked them to explain what they had gone through before they came to the camp, what they were most concerned about now, and the risks they were under. It was a very moving conversation. Asked whether they felt safe, they all said no. Some had been assaulted when their villages had been attacked and they had fled, but they were far from safe here. Girls and women ran a risk whenever they ventured outside the camp. Local police did not protect them, and gangs of men would approach, ready to attack. One told how she had been assaulted while collecting firewood outside the camp, and another relayed her daughter's experiences. They said that rapes happened all the time.

I had read the reports. The last one was from Doctors Without Borders, documenting a disturbingly high level of rape cases. But hearing about it directly, also from victims, was very different. I was furious. We knew that the authorities were either part of the problem or pretended that sexual violence did not take place. Now the inability of the international community to protect the girls and women made me equally upset. As I was leaving the camp, a woman came up to me with a piece of paper. She said she had heard that I was an important person and that I would meet the leaders of the government in Khartoum. She clung to my arm, and wanted me to deliver her message. The paper contained a desperate plea for protection. I decided to give it to Ali Osman, and to discuss the situation with him alone in Khartoum.

Just before my trip to Darfur, Baba Gana Kingibe had told me that Taha's travel to the Western region in early February had been an "eye opener". It was allegedly his first since the crisis unfolded. Kingibe said that from Taha's reactions during the trip it seemed clear to him that he could not have been fully informed about the atrocities committed in Darfur. It was difficult to tell. And it was now my turn to test this. When we met at Taha's house late in the evening I told him about the discussions I had had with the women and relayed their experiences. I could see that he found my stories hard to believe. He questioned the credibility of the report I cited. I said that the usual reaction of the government was to say that all reports from the NGOs were fabrications and smears. This and other reports were based on evidence, and I had myself enquired how the data had been collected, the procedure was very solid.

And what of the stories I had been told myself? He agreed that such practices were unheard of. They were against the Koran, and had to stop. I then produced the note from the woman who had desperately clung to my arm. I said this was a note for him personally, calling for him to take action. He should keep it on his desk as a reminder of what was going on in his own country, and of his responsibility to put an end to this horrific violence. We discussed a series of measures that could be taken. I was fairly certain that Ali Osman had been shaken by what he had heard. It seemed to me that he either had been kept in the dark about the details, or he had preferred not to know. Now it was his responsibility to put an end to it. My impression was that he sincerely wanted to. The question was how forcefully he would act and how strong the forces were that preferred the status quo.

In my view, Taha's speech to the Security Council and our discussions provided a basis for a way forward for Darfur. I suggested development of an Action Plan to detail what would be done, how and when. This should include steps to ensure that the ceasefire agreement and humanitarian protocol were fully implemented. The plan needed to outline steps to establish a credible and inclusive political process. On the enforcement side, impunity now had to end, with speedy and effective prosecution of perpetrators. Local reconciliation also had to take place, but this could not replace a political process. In this respect the Arab militias had to be included, one way or another.

From Khartoum I proceeded to the South, and first to Rumbek, where I met Salva Kiir and the SPLM/A leadership for long discussions, including on the transition and the deployment of the teams to the North, slow processes on the donors' side and the lack of support for the returning refugees. A meeting with the UN team there was disturbing. Having told the UN Sudan team in Nairobi over a year ago that they needed to start contingency planning for a return to Southern Sudan, I found that almost nothing had been done. The best people I had encountered previously working on Sudan had been sent to Darfur. The staff at Rumbek were not the ones who had managed the operation in Nairobi, but were at a lower level and had less experience. I was not impressed. They had not established a proper office, even though Rumbek had long been a hub for international organizations. The UN Work Plan was under way, which was good. But not much was happening on the ground. The UN had established a Sustainable Returns Team, and had started support operations for returnees, but the process was far too slow. An additional major concern was the "taxation" of returnees by both the government and the SPLM/A. This was very far from the "peace dividends" we had had in mind.

The problem was that people were already coming back, but systems were not yet in place to receive them. I vividly recall the makeshift camp that had popped up on the outskirts of Rumbek. I went there and sat with returnees to hear their stories. One woman had come from Khartoum. When she heard on the radio that peace had come to Southern Sudan, she could not believe her ears. She double-checked with people she knew, then took the courageous decision to go back home immediately. She told me of the hazardous journey she had undertaken with her three children, first by bus, then hitching rides on trucks, and finally on foot. They had managed to survive by sticking together with like-minded people, and using their remaining cash for food and water on the way. Their meagre belongings had been stolen or bartered away. They had been threatened by government soldiers, militiamen, and SPLA fighters, who extorted money to let them pass. They arrived with nothing but the clothes on their backs. But they had all survived, so she was happy. And she was not alone.

Now there was no support for them and the hundreds of people with them.

I looked for food and utensils, the assistance normally provided by UN agencies and NGOs in crises like these. There was nothing. I blamed the agencies. But they said that this was an interim camp, and that assistance was better made available where the people would finally settle. They had plans for this. Of even more concern to me was their claim of no funding for this operation. Although the plans were ready, it appeared that the donors had been unwilling to put money on the table before the peace agreement was signed; once that had been done, they seemed to be waiting for the Joint Assessment Mission and Donors' Conference. Donors apparently thought that the emergency phase in Southern Sudan was over. This was far from the truth. I was very worried, and promised to do what I could to help with fund raising.[12] But I also expressed clear expectations that the UN agencies needed to get ready, both to assist the returnees and to be part of the major post-conflict effort in the South and the Three Areas, by moving their offices and operational headquarters from Nairobi to the South.

Dr. John: More Challenges

I proceeded to New Site, in Eastern Equatoria, near the borders of Uganda, Kenya and Sudan, in Toposa country. The SPLM/A had built New Site as a conference centre and possible headquarters. It was peaceful, and the Chairman was there with a handful of people, a couple of assistants and only a few security guards in sight. This gave me more time alone with him, which we needed. We sat outside, under a tree. I referred to the difficulties that returnees were encountering, and said that he had to instruct commanders to stop taxing people who were returning home. He said he had been unaware of this, and promised to follow up. The SPLM/A too was frustrated with the lack of help for refugees now returning in big numbers. I encouraged him to sound the alarm publicly and call for additional resources, and promised to help from my end.

I briefed the Chairman on the Joint Assessment Mission, supported by the UN and the World Bank, and preparations for the Donors' Conference. I also explained the model for assistance that we were considering, of NGOs and UN agencies, contracted by the government, to help implement programs paid for by the Multi Donor Trust Fund. As neither the government nor the World Bank had this capacity, such an arrangement could facilitate continuation of UN and NGO programs in the South, with no gaps, at the same time ensuring government leadership and ownership. Dr. John thought this was a good idea, and was pleased that the UN agencies were open to this.

I briefed the Chairman on my discussions in Khartoum, and relayed the government's concerns about the delays on the SPLM/A-side in relation to pre-interim arrangements. Dr. John acknowledged delays owing to his trips to New York and Asmara, and that a number of issues needed agreement in the SPLM/A Leadership Council, a meeting they would now convene. The movement was ready to send "Advance Teams" to Khartoum and the major cities, and only the resource issue had prevented them from moving on this.[13]

These matters aside, we needed to discuss some sensitive issues. One of the most important was urgent establishment of measures against corruption in the South. I pointed to other oil-producing countries, where oil had become a curse rather than a blessing. We knew already of deals with oil companies behind Dr. John's back; I shared the documentary evidence with him, which we had obtained through our own sources, and said that this emphasized the need to act quickly. The Chairman appreciated the information and agreed that it was important to establish robust systems related to contracts and financial transfers. I proposed a series of measures, based on best practice, to prevent serious corruption problems. The SPLM/A leadership had discussed resorting to Norwegian expertise in the oil sector in this regard.

Even more urgent was the issue of security. Challenges had arisen in relation to the peacekeeping force and its composition. These involved monitoring of the ceasefire, protection of civilians, and the process of disarmament, demobilization and reintegration of forces on both sides. That last issue had been one of the hottest during the talks, and would prove to be among the most intractable processes of the post-conflict period. There was no way this process could go forward without a strong, UN-mandated, peacekeeping presence. That, in turn, required a Status of Forces Agreement between the UN and each party to the conflict. This had been delayed by a serious disagreement between the SPLM/A and UN, who had initially dealt only with Khartoum.

Now the UN had belatedly to sort out the issues with the Southerners. While the Movement wanted a UN-mandated force, and the structure had ended up as a traditional one, they were concerned about its composition. They wanted no Muslim or Arab countries' troops. The issue was becoming urgent, as a Forces Agreement was needed in order for the Security Council to pass a resolution on its deployment. But the UN did not have the luxury to pick and choose among its members. Few countries were anyway willing to send troops on peacekeeping missions, and Sudan was not a particularly attractive place. Almost no European countries deployed through UN peacekeeping operations anymore, at least in Africa. SRSG Jan Pronk was unable to get anywhere with the Chairman of the SPLM/A. I was asked to help.

Security is the most important pillar of any peace-building operation. In this case, peacekeepers were essential, not only for monitoring the ceasefire and conducting the process of disarmament, demobilization and reintegration, but also for the protection of civilians. Unfortunately, however, the successful operation of the Joint Military Commission in the Nuba Mountains would have to close down later in the year as a consequence of the UN's decisions. The Chairman and I went through the list of troop-contributing countries that I had received from the UN. Although I understood the SPLM/A's concerns about several of them, we narrowed down the list of "problem" countries. In the end, not long after my discussions at New Site, the UN and the SPLM/A managed to work it all out, and a Status of Forces Agreement was signed, opening the way for the Security Council resolution mandating the deployment of the UN peacekeeping operation.

A third sensitive issue we needed to discuss was integration of Southern militias into the SPLA. Dr. John reported progress in the dialogue with several groups; the Joint Action Plan under discussion with the government was very promising.

Dr. John went into detail about his talks in Asmara with Isaias Afeworki and the rebel groups. He had also discussed the situations in Darfur and the East with President Obasanjo and AU President Konare. I shared Ali Osman Taha's assessment of the Naivasha model, with Troika engagement and "pre-cooking" arrangements and that he was happy to work with him. Garang agreed and was ready to engage. He was also worried about the fact that the Beja Congress and "Free Lions" were reluctant to sign the agreement in Cairo. According to his information, Mohamed Osman al-Mirghani had asked them not to, because he wanted to represent Eastern Sudan, the wellspring of his family's and party's (the Democratic Unionists') support, in the discussions. The process in Cairo might drag on, and there could be separate negotiations between the government of Sudan and the Beja and Rashaida.

There was a "window" that should be used before the Donors' Conference. Not yet a member of the Government of National Unity, the Chairman could act as an interlocutor during this period. Garang agreed. With the Joint Transition Teams in Khartoum, another basis for active cooperation on critical issues presented itself. But without progress, it would be difficult to organize a successful Donors' Conference at all. Recently, the military situation in Darfur had calmed down, but the challenges of civilian protection and humanitarian access remained as difficult as ever. There was no progress on the political side: the rebel groups were unwilling to negotiate, at least within the framework of the African Union, so no new talks were convened before the Oslo Donors' Conference in April.

That conference was a great success, despite these challenges. It was opened by the Secretary General of the UN, Kofi Annan, with participation at the ministerial level or above by a large number of countries. Despite the shadow of Darfur, the conference raised more than had been requested, $4.6b.[14] Learning from previous donor conferences, when pledges had been made but failed to materialize, we tried to set up a more robust framework for tracking pledges. Our ambition was to set up a monitoring mechanism that would regularly report on the delivery of aid. This proved to be very difficult, as several donors preferred not to be transparent about their pledges.

The resources were desperately needed. There had never been much investment in Southern Sudan, whether in infrastructure, education and health services, or public administration. Virtually nothing had happened during colonial days, and little was done later. The SPLM/A had governed so-called "liberated areas" in the South, but while the war went on and without financial resources little could be accomplished. Outside assistance was mainly humanitarian. The SPLM/A started virtually from zero in every way. Hardly any post-conflict government had been faced with challenges at this level.

New Darfur-Efforts: Pre-cooking for Abuja?

My main concern continued to be Darfur. An informal meeting of interested parties had taken place in New York on March 30th at the invitation of Jan Egeland, the UN Emergency Coordinator and Andrew Natsios, the USAID Administrator. Before the Donors' Conference, and knowing that Darfur would not be high on that agenda, I had invited leaders of the rebel groups to Oslo on 12–13 April, for a follow-up meeting of the New York group.[15] This was an opportunity to push for stronger international support and to preclude others, such as the San Igidio initiative and the various Libyan moves for tribal reconciliation, from diverting attention. Only three months remained before the interim period was due to start. This "window" had to be used for progress on Darfur.

I had also discussed a Naivasha-style arrangement in relation to the AU-talks with Yemane Gebraib, President Afeworki's right hand man and a key interlocutor with the rebel groups. The Eritreans were hosts to the National Democratic Alliance and most of the Darfur rebel groups, and were allegedly supporting the rebels in the East. The Eritreans could therefore influence the positions of almost the entire Sudanese opposition. In this context, I questioned whether the Eritrean policy of regime change in Khartoum was useful. Significant changes were taking place after the signing of the CPA and, after all, the SPLM would be part of the government in a few months. Gebraib said that the Eritreans were now reflecting on this, and in that connection he had an invitation. President Afeworki wanted me to come to Asmara as soon as possible to discuss the issues. I promised to do so.

The Darfur meeting in Oslo convened after most of the delegates to the Donors' Conference had left. Pagan Amum, Nhial Deng Nhial and Luka Biong Deng of the SPLM/A had met the rebel leaders and encouraged them to take this initiative seriously. The key leaders of both the Sudan Liberation Movement/Army and the Justice and Equality Movement were there, with only one exception, Minni Minawi of the SLM/A, who sent his deputy. Abd al-Wahid Mohamed al-Nur and Khalil Ibrahim came with their senior members. Our main aim was to win the rebel groups' participation in the Abuja talks and to support those talks more effectively, primarily through a Troika-Plus arrangement. We did not table proposals for "pre-cooking" arrangements, but there was agreement that a much more active approach was necessary. The AU representative at the talks agreed to this.

After the meeting I briefed both the government and the SPLM/A. I met Said al-Khatib, who remained one of the National Congress Party's key people, and told him that I would have separate discussions on my own with the rebel leaders. As he was remaining behind, I would alert him of any possibility of rebel interest in discussing with him the idea of Troika involvement and of Garang and Taha's assisting the talks behind the scenes. The idea was clear. The model had worked in relation to the IGAD talks; a variation could be applied to the Abuja negotiations on Darfur.

The next day (13 April) I met the three rebel leaders alone, with only one staff member on each side. The meeting lasted for more than four hours. For the most part, I listened. They gave me their assessment of the background of the crisis in Darfur and the current situation, how they perceived the negotiations, the government, the African Union and the international community. It was worth every minute. There was a major crisis of distrust between the rebels and virtually every outsider that had been engaged in the talks. The African Union was in the worst position. The rebels had no confidence in the organization, and cited examples to justify this position. The situation had become even worse than I had predicted in July 2004. We discussed strategies for breaking the current stalemate. The rebel groups all wanted an All-Party Conference for Darfur and the East. However, with the AU having anchored its responsibility for the negotiations in numerous Security Council resolutions, I argued that it was impossible to change the negotiating framework. Far better to adopt the approach of the Naivasha negotiations, working with what you have and with a much stronger role for the international community behind the scenes.

I presented the idea of stronger Troika engagement, and said that both Ali Osman Taha and John Garang were committed. The rebel leaders were receptive. After a long discussion they agreed to return to the table, but would only go to Abuja and the AU if they saw a much stronger engagement from international actors. I asked whether they would discuss such a process now with a representative of the Sudanese government, Said al-Khatib. They responded that they needed to consult the rest of their leadership.

Two weeks later I went to Asmara to meet President Isaias Afeworki and various Sudanese rebel leaders. So far, Eritrean strategy of regime change in Khartoum had discouraged any effort to make peace between the Sudanese government and any of the opposition groups. That might still be their agenda; my visit could certainly be part of that strategy. Eritrean advocacy of an All-Party National Conference was seen as a way of uniting the opposition groups against the government – and against the Comprehensive Peace Agreement. I was not sure that the Eritreans were reconsidering their position.

I went to see the President soon after my arrival in Asmara on 26 April. Stories abounded about this African "loner". Isaias Afeworki had led the Eritrean People's Liberation Front, the EPLF, in its war of independence against Ethiopia, and ruled Eritrea ever since. So idiosyncratic was his rule that, at the time of my visit, there was even speculation among international observers that Afeworki was beginning to "lose" his way. Thus both then and later I was surprised to find an interlocutor who was focused and sharp. One could dislike his policies and his approach, and he certainly was not a person who would bend when his priorities were set, but he was still an interesting discussion partner. The Eritrean President had never been fond of the UN and AU, and was now particularly critical of the AU's Darfur negotiations. In our meeting he pressed the case for an All-Party conference to deal with both Darfur and Eastern Sudan.

I agreed with the President that Abuja had not been a success, and told him that I had from the very beginning tried to avoid such a complex and formal negotiating framework for Darfur. I shared the ideas we had worked on ten months ago for a fast-track approach using Garang and Taha. But now that the AU had become the negotiation forum, there was no way the African leaders would accept any other. We could retain the framework, however, and see what could be done behind or through it. I hinted at a Naivasha-like process, with pre-cooking arrangements wherein the two leaders would play the most important role, supported by the Troika. I relayed the outcome of the meeting in Oslo, and that Garang and Taha were ready to play a role, supported by Troika Plus, including the EU, the UN and the Netherlands. After a lengthy discussion Isaias accepted this approach, so long as the AU was only an "umbrella" for the negotiations and the US and Norway played a key role. The President then expressed willingness to "push" the Darfur rebel groups to negotiate.

Closer to home, an Eastern Front had now been established, composed of the Beja Congress and the Rashaida "Free Lions". Afewerki still wanted a joint negotiation of both the Darfur and Eastern conflicts, for example in a compre-hensive National Conference. There was no way the Eastern Front would go back to the Cairo talks anyway, because they had lost all confidence in the National Democratic Alliance's Chairman, Mohamed al-Mirghani. I was unenthusiastic about negotiating both issues in one framework. We on the Norwegian side had been considering a workshop to prepare for negotiations in Asmara, something the Eritreans were quite willing to facilitate. This could in turn lead to a negotiating process for the east. There now seemed to be two options: either to negotiate both conflicts in parallel in Abuja; or to follow a separate track for the east, for example in Asmara, but with the same players involved informally behind the scenes, ensuring coherence.

Appeasement of Khartoum

The main reason for the President's invitation to me was not, as I had thought, Darfur or the East. After we had discussed those conflicts for almost two hours, he asked to my surprise whether I could arrange for him (and attend myself) a meeting with Ali Osman Taha and John Garang. The agenda would be a speedy end to the remaining conflicts in Sudan following the signing of the CPA. I asked whether President Bashir would not be the correct inter-locutor for him, a suggestion he dismissed. He wanted to meet Taha, and the meeting had to be kept secret. Although he would gladly invite the First Vice President to Asmara, he appreciated the difficulty and said he was ready to meet anywhere, at any time. I promised to do my best to facilitate. Clearly the Eritreans had reconsidered their whole strategy.

Later I met leaders of the National Democratic Alliance. Their main problem with the CPA, they said, was the power-sharing arrangements, that awarded the current ruling party a 52 percent majority in the central government. In my view, the parties needed to consider this in relation to the interim constitution: without some arrangement it would be difficult to settle the remaining conflicts. At the same time, of course, I knew that the National Congress Party and SPLM had been determined to maintain their preponderance. I would, however, take up the issue with Taha when next we met.

I left Asmara in good spirits. The signals of a shift in Eritrean policy had the potential of leading to positive change in relation to Darfur and the East. The Eritreans had supported all the Sudanese opposition parties and movements, one way or the other, most notably the SPLM/A. The rapport between Garang and Afeworki remained good, while relations between Khartoum and Asmara were fraught with animosity. When I returned to Oslo, I called both Dr. John and Ali Osman to brief them about the discussions. Garang was very receptive to the idea of a Sudanese-Eritrean meeting. Taha was pleased with my report on the Oslo discussions on Darfur as well as my talk with the Eritrean President. He said that there now seemed to be a clear vision on the Eritrean side for resolving the conflicts in both Darfur and the East. What had been achieved in the discussions with the Eritrean President was very welcome, including the necessity to stick to the AU framework, combined with active international efforts; there was no point in irritating all the African leaders. I was gratified by Ali Osman's support of the Naivasha type "pre-cooking" model – "especially if you participate", as he put it, for that would "reassure the rebels".

Regarding President Afeworki's approach, consultations within the Sudanese government would obviously take place. But the Vice President said that he had nothing in principle against the proposed meeting, so long as its preparations took into account the role that other neighbouring countries were playing on Darfur, such as Libya and Chad. He was not enthusiastic about a meeting in Asmara: Abuja, before the next round, was preferable. And the agenda must be limited to Darfur and the East, and not touch on relations between Sudan and Eritrea. I undertook to relay this response to Afeworki and would keep the exchange strictly confidential, informing only the Americans at the political level. Ali Osman said he would consult his colleagues and call me back with a more formal response.

During the following week there was no word from Ali Osman. I knew that an opening to Eritrea might be controversial. And indeed, the next time we talked, Taha was cautious: he wanted more details on the agenda, and some idea of the expected outcome; what I had told him was too vague. I spoke to Yemane Gebraib, who produced a three-point agenda to (i) ensure implementation of the CPA, (ii) find a solution for Darfur, and (iii) identify a solution for the Eastern front. Bilateral relations could be discussed in this context; the expected outcome of which would be agreement on a "precooking-arrangement" to make all this happen. Eritrea would not negotiate on behalf of any group, but would facilitate a process that could lead to an agreement. Yemane stressed the seriousness of the approach: they were not playing games.

I conveyed this message to Ali Osman Taha on May 12th, and urged the government to take advantage of this opportunity. Ali Osman held back: the expected outcome remained unclear. Referring to the history of animosity between the two countries, he expressed concern that Eritrea would complicate things: there were enough parties to the process. I replied that Eritrea played a major role already – the question was how to make that role constructive. Taha suggested that if Afeworki wanted to signal cooperation he could take part in the Darfur summit of Sudan, Chad, Libya and the AU scheduled for the 16th in Tripoli. If he did so, an official meeting could take place with President Bashir, possibly breaking the ice. I knew that Afeworki had considered participation, and said that a positive signal now from Khartoum might be decisive. But from Ali Osman's response, I understood that Bashir had not been enthusiastic about a bilateral meeting. I pointed out to him, however, that the government had to make a strategic decision, and that this was an opportunity for fast tracking the talks on Darfur and the East that the government should not let slip. Ali Osman promised a response later in the day.

At this point there was considerable disarray on several fronts. A significant split had occurred between the two rebel groups: The Justice and Equality Movement was much the weaker on the ground, and the Sudan Liberation Movement/Army demanded recognition of its pre-eminence before agreeing to a common platform for the negotiations. But the SLM/A itself was increasingly divided between its political leadership and commanders in the field. Attempts were under way to hold a conference to settle those differences, and Norway had taken the initiative to hold a workshop in Asmara to prepare the rebel groups for negotiations. The AU talks were due to re-start in late May. But now Jan Pronk criticized the Norwegian initiative, and called for donor countries to refrain from any activities uncoordinated with all partners. The AU, UN and Pronk personally also opposed any activities based in Asmara, and warned against such arrangements.

Before we were able to get a formal response from Khartoum and proceed with plans for a meeting between the Sudanese government and the Eritreans, the Libyans took action. Isaias Afeworki came to the Tripoli summit, and the Libyans corralled the two presidents, of Sudan and Eritrea, into a conference room. Although the possibility of a meeting had been mentioned from the Eritrean side, neither president was prepared for this encounter. The meeting was a disaster, with each accusing the other of meddling. This was very unfortunate. Relations were now worse than before. I agreed with Ali Osman that the Eritrean initiative had to be regarded as dead, at least for now. Opportunities for speeding up the process on Darfur and the East were now diminishing by the day.

The African Union and Darfur

Later I was told that within the African Union there had also been displeasure with the Darfur meeting in Oslo in April. Although the AU representative, Baba Gana Kingibe, had several times expressed support and had actually been in Oslo, the situation was different at AU headquarters in Addis Ababa. At a meeting on May 27th AU leaders, particularly the Commissioner for Peace and Security, Ambassador Djinnit, were very negative. They worried that the international community would "take over" the Abuja negotiations, and opposed anything "pre-cooked" by others. In a meeting at which Troika-Plus and other countries' representatives were present, Djinnit stated explicitly that references to such processes and to the approach taken in the IGAD talks were unwelcome.

The message from our Embassy in Addis was that we needed to reassure the AU that it had our full support in the Darfur negotiations. This proved difficult to achieve. I had tried several times to reach Alpha Oumar Konare, the former president of Mali and current AU President, to express our support, explain the rationale for our interest, and offer help. The informal and personable man I had met several times in Bamako, was now more difficult to reach and, once reached, rather distant and ceremonious. When I tried to explore the possibility of "massaging" things a bit, Konare was friendly but noncommittal. Without at least the acquiescence of the AU it would be very difficult to move the process forward.

Another opportunity arose through the appointment of a new chief negotiator for the AU. I knew Salim Ahmed Salim already, and was hopeful that he would be more open to support from the Troika-Plus. A week before the next round of negotiations was scheduled to start I went to Dar es Salaam to see him. To my surprise, he had not yet been briefed in any detail by the AU team. I sat in Salim's house for hours, going over the background of the Darfur conflict, the status of the negotiations, the lessons of Naivasha and the IGAD talks, and the role of Eritrea and other countries. Of those, a complicating factor was the role of Chad and Libya. It was clear that Libya saw Darfur as part of its "backyard", and was using various rebel groups to destabilize Chad and spread its influence in Sudan; Chad had its own agenda. Salim was aware of these factors. I mentioned Robert Zoellick's recent appointment as Deputy Secretary of State in the US, and the keen interest he had already shown in Sudan. It was clear that we could benefit from his engagement in the Troika in relation to Darfur. Salim was open to this kind of cooperation. He was not planning to stay in the job for long, and wanted Darfur dealt with quickly.

I told Salim Salim about the challenges of the AU negotiating effort. Sam Ibok had not gone to Asmara to meet the rebel groups, despite promising a number of times to do so. Lack of consultation about the timing and agenda of the next round of talks was another problem: through our sources we had learned that none of the rebel groups had even been consulted about the resumption and timing of the talks; the Justice and Equality Movement had received a letter of invitation only on June 1st, while the Sudan Liberation Movement/Army had not yet received one at all. These were the sorts of things the rebel groups had repeatedly complained about and that had led to their inability to prepare properly for the talks. The SLM/A had now let us know that they could not come to the talks before June 15th. As for the workshop in Asmara, the SLM/A had asked Norway to conduct it, but now there would not be time to do so before the next round of talks; the SLM/A wanted to hold the workshop in parallel with the negotiations in Abuja. Salim promised to try to facilitate this, and in general to do his best to improve relations between the rebel groups and the AU. He also offered to call from Abuja to brief me on these and other issues. I was pleased with this outcome, and hoped that we could move forward despite the resistance in Addis.

I followed up the meeting with a series of calls, briefing key interlocutors and trying to prepare the ground for a constructive approach to the negotiations before they convened in Abuja. These included Yemane Gebraib, whom I called three days later and urged to press the rebel groups to appear in Abuja on the prescribed date, June 10th, despite the lack of consultation. He agreed, and confirmed that Eritrea would participate. He also acknowledged that it was not in anyone's interest to undermine the new mediator or start anything that could be apprehended as competitive. Dr. John also confirmed his willingness to engage. The agreement with the National Democratic Alliance had now been completed, and both Taha and he would be going to Cairo for the signing ceremony on June 18th. He would also visit London and Tripoli. This was promising. But for me Darfur was the most pressing issue. I reached Abd al-Wahid al-Nur the next day, and conveyed Salim's wish to meet both rebel groups before the negotiations began in Abuja. Despite his annoyance at the AU's "paternalistic" approach and insulting behaviour, he confirmed that the SLM/A would come to Abuja for June 10th.

I exchanged information with the Americans, and we agreed that things now seemed set for the next round of Abuja negotiations. The question remained whether there was any chance for discussion of the issues ahead of the talks. Ali Osman and Dr. John were extremely busy with the opposition parties, the Constitution, discussions on the East, implementation of the CPA and preparations for the inauguration. The constitutional process was scheduled for ratification by the Sudanese parliament and the SPLM/A Leadership Council in June. But there was now a tiny "window" between June 10th and July 9th, when the new Presidency would be inaugurated. This provided the opportunity for any opposition groups to join the new equation and come into the Government of National Unity. With the AU Summit scheduled for Tripoli on 3–4 July, the window became even smaller. If results could be obtained in the Darfur negotiations very quickly, there was still a remote possibility that the rebel groups' representatives could be part of the new government, or that a precursor could be introduced if adequate progress had been made (pending final agreement). I knew that a quick deal might be unsustainable, but I was inclined to push for it now: it would be much more difficult to change even an interim Constitution once it has passed through Parliament and the inaugeration had taken place.

Another factor was the role of Ali Osman Taha. Rumour had it that he would lead the government delegation, which would include members of the Naivasha team. In the event, however, neither he nor they appeared. Dr. Majzoub al-Khalifa Ahmed, seeing himself as a competitor of Taha, came to Abuja and took control of the talks.[16] It may have been thought too early to send the Vice President, given the state of the talks. The fact that al-Khalifa was chief negotiator did indicate, however, that the government was less serious than we had hoped. At the same time, the SPLM/A Chairman was again travelling abroad. In other words no supporting role had been prepared for the two leaders or the Troika, but such was anyway probably premature before the new chief negotiator had established himself in Abuja.

I was not sure how the talks would go. I assumed that Salim Salim would call me at some point. I made sure that our observers conveyed our availability, but there was no attempt to follow up. I interpreted this as a signal that the African Union preferred to move forward on its own without active international assistance behind the scenes. I was not going to ask. The signals we had received from Addis the last two months could not be misinterpreted. Salim may have received a clear message from Addis and his AU colleagues to keep these Troika people at arm's length.

Arrival in Khartoum

As we monitored the Abuja negotiations in June from afar, the clock was ticking towards final approval of the interim constitution and the inauguration ceremony scheduled for July 9th. There was great concern over security. Although the government wanted to ensure that the incoming First Vice President was safe in the hands of its National Security apparatus, the Movement was worried that some elements in the capital might have a different agenda. We talked to the SPLM and the Americans about what measures they should take. We assumed that the Americans could take care of transport arrangements from the South to Khartoum, and possibly help with close protection in the capital, should that be deemed necessary. At the very least, training of SPLA cadres in close protection of the Chairman was imperative. After a lot of back and forth, it became clear that the Americans were unable to organize transport quickly enough. Norway then offered to help, and hired the plane of the Nuba Mountains Joint Monitoring Mission.

The atmosphere was electric. This would be the first time that Garang himself and other members of the SPLM/A leadership would set foot in Khartoum in more than two decades. When we were told that the plane was approaching, the crowd moved towards the tarmac. A red carpet had been laid out for the "rebel leader" soon to be First Vice President. The SPLM/A delegation in Khartoum, headed by Yasir Arman, organized a receiving line. I would be among the first to greet Dr. John, standing in the first line with members of the SPLM leadership, high-level representatives of the government, and other Sudanese dignitaries. It was an unbelievable moment.

The door of the plane opened. In the blazing heat, the tarmac almost at the point of melting, he descended from the plane. He did not kiss the ground, but I knew he was moved. Khartoum was full of banners, honking cars, cheering crowds and people in celebration. The SPLM/A had prepared well. All over the town there were huge banners with pictures of Dr. John and Ali Osman, featuring various iterations of the "New Sudan" and what this meant for the people and the country.

The next day, the dignitaries gathered at the Republican Palace to witness the inauguration of President Bashir, incoming First Vice President Garang, and Vice President Ali Osman Taha, on the basis of the newly approved interim constitution. Kofi Annan, the Secretary General of the UN was present, as were a number of heads of state and government from the region and beyond. Seeing Ali Osman step aside in favour of Dr. John made a strong impression on me and, I believe, on everyone present. For once there were no long speeches, but in their statements they underscored a strong commitment to uphold the new constitution and implement the Comprehensive Peace Agreement.

After the inauguration, the whole town exploded in joy. No one knew how many were gathered, but if felt as though millions of people had come into the city, crowding the streets, cheering, dancing in the heat, waving flags in celebration. There were not only Southerners, but also people from every ethnic group and corner of the country. In the evening Garang and Taha were scheduled to talk to the crowds at the Green Square. Hundreds of thousands gathered. Dr. John shouted out that they were now free. But the people could not hear over the din. There were so many people on the move that the whole sound system was crushed. So Dr. John and Ali Osman just stood there, waving to the cheering crowds. Afterwards, the party continued in the streets.

After his inauguration as First Vice President, and the fantastic reception of all the people in Khartoum, Garang really believed that his vision, a New Sudan, could come true. That night he told his closest advisors: "After this, Sudan will never be the same again". Yasir Arman says that after this experience, "Dr. John was born again".[17] Others confirm the impact on him.[18]

The next day I had a series of meetings with Kofi Annan, Jan Pronk, the AU's Kingibe, Foreign Minister Mustafa Ismail and President Bashir – who jokingly referred to me as "the mother of the bride" – in which I concentrated on the peace process for Darfur and on Eritrea's role. I also had meetings with both Dr. John and Ali Osman. The most important issues stemming from the CPA were to get the Government of National Unity appointed, to finalize the interim constitution for Southern Sudan, and to establish the new Government of Southern Sudan. Delays during the pre-interim period had caused problems in relation to the time lines of the CPA.

This was unfortunate, and I urged the two leaders to speed up the pace of implementation. I would later speak privately with Dr. John about some of the sensitive issues in the "South–South" process.

Although we had not heard from Salim Salim, I had not given up hope that the two Sudanese vice presidents could make a difference in relation to Darfur and the East, and urged them to pursue our strategy ahead of the next negotiation round in Abuja, most likely in September. Interestingly, Jan Pronk now wanted to pursue the idea of a workshop in Asmara, and to use that for discussions between the SPLM and the Justice and Equality Movement, with international involvement. I agreed and noted that the Sudan Liberation Movement/Army had initiated this idea and must be included; it was interesting how ideas could shift from being unacceptable to being pursued in just eight weeks.

A few weeks before Garang's inauguration Ashraf Ghani, former finance minister of Afghanistan, a good friend and world-renowned expert on fragile states, had reported to Dr. John. I had engaged his help and, with a colleague, Clare Lockhart, he had done fieldwork in the South and met a range of Southern leaders. They had developed a set of recommendations for how the Southern Sudanese could approach the establishment of their government, develop the ability to capitalize on their own resources, and do so with transparency, accountability and increasing capacity. He had very useful proposals on setting up a functioning President's Office, what to do and not to do, and what to watch out for. Dr. John sat with Ashraf for more than four hours, going through his findings and recommendations. Now it was time to see how his advice could be implemented. I sat with Dr. John going through the recommendations. We discussed a strategy on how to take these processes forward, and who could help to set up the President's offices in Khartoum and in Juba. Garang was willing to include experienced foreign experts in his own office. We agreed that I would send him names and CVs. If a team could be assembled that could help Garang to work effectively from the start, everything else would be so much easier.

The third evening after the inauguration, Garang, his wife and a couple of his closest colleagues visited Taha at his new house. By that time Taha had vacated his official residence to make room for the SPLM/A Chairman and his family, but Dr. John had not wanted this, and had asked for another house instead. Getting their families together was another step in strengthening the personal bonds between the two; it was a strong signal for both of them.[19]

A week of meetings continued. According to Pagan Amum, Dr. John tabled several proposals, prepared by his own team, covering economic issues, national reconciliation and CPA implementation.[20] At this stage, Bashir seemed quite comfortable with his new colleagues in the Presidency, but we also heard that the same crowds that had so delighted him had frightened some of the National Congress Party's core leaders. They had seen nothing similar for themselves, and they had certainly not expected such massive expressions of support. They understood that they now had a national political leader in their midst.

But in the middle of the new government's first week in office, the Abyei Boundary Commission presented its report. This was the first test of their partnership. Bashir rejected it outright, and Ali Osman Taha also made critical statements, despite the provision in the CPA that its findings would be binding. Dr. John declared his acceptance of the report; the commission had acted within its mandate and its report was final and binding. This was a first indication of the difficulties ahead.

Salva is "Appointed"

On 15 July Dr. John announced a number of decisions relating to the SPLM/A. He knew he had to reconfigure the leadership and prepare for the changes that government implied. He therefore dissolved the SPLM/A Leadership Council, intending to appoint the new leadership later. The Chairman appointed various SPLM/A leaders to Southern state governorships, mostly on a caretaker basis. Riak Machar was sent to Western Equatoria. He retired all members of the Political Bureau from the Army, and appointed Oyay Deng as Army Chief of Staff. Pagan Amum and Abd al-Aziz were given responsibility for the party. Salva Kiir was made Vice President of the Government of Southern Sudan, even before the constitution had been crafted, and stayed on also as deputy chair of the SPLM/A. Garang consulted no one before announcing all these decisions, nor was anyone even informed of them in advance.[21]

Dr. John remained in the North for a total of eighteen days before returning to Rumbek on July 27th. There he had convened a meeting of the leadership, scheduled both to endorse his decisions and plan for the critical actions that now needed to be taken. The Council addressed issues related to the start of the interim period, the South–South processes, and internal changes in the Movement as it made the transition from guerrilla movement to political party. They decided on who should lead the transition clusters in different sectors and took steps to get the constitutional process off the ground.

Salva Kiir was unhappy with the decision to dissolve the leadership, and criticized the Chairman. After the decision was announced, Riak Machar asked what would take place if anything happened to Dr. John now. Dr. John had reportedly replied, "We have a deputy and a Vice President, so there is nothing to worry about." After the meeting, there was a public rally on Freedom Square in Rumbek. A picture was taken with everyone on stage holding hands with their arms upraised. Dr. John made a speech that Salva later recalled as painful.[22] Garang said: "We have lost all our brothers from the start of the movement. What is left are the two 'Abeer'." Abeer is a Dinka expression for orphans. Then he said: "I want you, my people, to take care of Salva Kiir. Because he is the one who has remained with me always, loyally, and I entrust you to him."[23] Others heard him say even more plainly that: Should anything happen to himself, Salva Kiir is the one who should take over as SPLM/A leader.[24] People were puzzled by this, and not least the timing of the message.

An important meeting to follow up the Donors' Conference was taking place in Paris between July 29th and August 3rd. Dr. John asked Salva to go. In an email from July 28, Dr. John is communicating to a friend in the US from Khartoum, saying that he was going to the South. He did not know where he would be the next three days, but they would be able to connect. He was expecting an American delegation.[25] He then proceeded to New Site. One of his closest advisors says that there had been some plans for him to visit the Ugandan President.[26] It was still a complete surprise to most that he went to Kampala at this particular time, and without his usual team supporting him. When Dr. John said he would inform President Bashir of his travel plans, his wife protested:[27] she feared for his safety. But Dr. John insisted that, as First Vice President of the country, he could not just travel to a neighbouring country without informing his colleagues. It was a short visit, and he was scheduled to return the next day, in time to meet the delegation.

At this juncture I was on vacation in Sweden. My cell rang, and I got the terrible message that John Garang's aircraft was overdue. The available information was inadequate, so I called Andrew Natsios, who had already heard the reports, and asked whether American satellite technology could be used to locate the aircraft. If it had made an emergency landing or crashed, getting in help as soon as possible was essential. Andrew said that they had looked at this option, but it was technically difficult. I also got in touch with Khartoum and was informed that all was well and that the plane apparently had been found, but it was all tentative. Later I called Theodros ("Ted") Dagne in Washington DC, to check again. He conveyed that this was not correct. Before I could do much else my cell rang. It was now nearly midnight. Ted was on the line once more and told me that the aircraft had been found, not very far from New Site. No one had survived the crash. I broke down and cried. I knew that this disaster was not only about the death of a friend and leader but was likely to have significant consequences for the future of Sudan.

Dr. John Garang de Mabior died on 30 July 2005, twenty-one days after his inauguration as First Vice President of Sudan, and twenty-one years after the outbreak of civil war. After this terrible news, I had to get in touch with my friends in Sudan. The next day, I called Rebecca, Garang's wife – who was amazingly composed and courageous. I then phoned Ali Osman Taha, who seemed numb with shock. We both knew this would have huge implications for the peace process in Sudan. I was hoping to see him at the funeral, but he told me he was likely to remain in Khartoum and that President Bashir would go to Juba that day.

Twenty-one days after the crowds in Khartoum had welcomed the Southern leader, they now exploded in anger and fury at the news of his death. They were certain that Dr. John had been assassinated. Mobs burned markets and houses in Khartoum, Juba and other towns throughout the country. Many lost their lives. The riots lasted for days, and finally stopped only after repeated calls for calm from Southern leaders. The SPLM/A leadership took other critical steps to calm the South.

Immediately after Dr. John's death was confirmed, the leadership gathered at New Site and chose Salva Mayardit Kiir as SPLM/A Chairman and future President of South Sudan. Dr. John's words a few nights earlier at Freedom Square in Rumbek struck many as premonitory. Salva immediately reinstated the dissolved SPLM/A Leadership Council, an act that would later have some unintended political consequences.[28] Plans went ahead for the funeral. Rebecca and the family wanted Dr. John to be laid to rest as close to home as possible, in Bor, but the decision was finally made for burial in Juba, the de facto capital of the South. The coffin carrying Dr. John's body was sent to New Site, Bor, Yei and Wau, and finally Juba, where a grave was prepared.

Dr. John Returns to Juba

Along the Nile, with mango trees, lush gardens and neat houses, Juba was once a beautiful little town, frequently visited by foreigners in colonial times. Since then it had deteriorated completely. Nothing of its old pride remained. During the war it had been a garrison town under government control, and was now utterly run down, on the verge of collapse from neglect. The little stretch of tarmac was full of potholes, and the other streets were but dirt tracks. I had been there several times in the past; Juba was like a dusty ghost town, with empty buildings and virtually no one in the streets.

On August 6th the place suddenly came to life. The SPLA had entered the town only two days before, after 21 years of struggle in the bush. Thousands of people were gathering. Banners were everywhere, but the atmosphere was thick with anxiety, tension and grief. For the first time since the war had started, Juba was about to receive the Chairman of the Sudan People's Liberation Movement and Army. In Dinka tradition people do not shed tears or wail over the death of a war hero or chief, so awesome silence prevailed. Thousands were just standing there, staring beyond the horizon, their eyes dark with grief. Despair was written over their faces. Not only had their leader died. The dreams of so many of them, elated by the peace agreement, were shattered.

A number of dignitaries came too, to pay their respects. No one in Juba had ever seen so many planes fly in on one day. For this reason alone, the funeral would be delayed for several hours; the airport was unable to handle the traffic. President Bashir and other heads of state, heads of government, ministers, special envoys and ambassadors arrived. I was sorry that Ali Osman Taha, Dr. John's partner in peace, was not there. He had remained in Khartoum in the same way that Salva had stayed behind at Rumbek when Dr. John left for the inauguration. The rows of soldiers lining the main street, one from the SPLA and the next from the government, made a great impact. I watched the solemn, yet peaceful faces of the soldiers. Just a few weeks ago they had been at war. It was not only impressive. It was deeply moving. It was as if Dr. John's death had brought about a transformation that none of us would have expected. We were all guided to a large area next to the Anglican cathedral, which could not accommodate us all. Hundreds of chairs had been set up under awnings outside, allowing both the dignitaries and thousands of grieving people to participate.

The funeral rites were led by the archbishop of Juba, Joseph Marona. Dr. John's coffin was placed on a dais erected outside the church. There the celebrant said:

> Moses is not with us anymore, our leader who led us out from Egypt, and across the river to the Promised Land. He didn't get the opportunity to join us there. It is Joshua who now has to take on the difficult task of leading our people in this new era, and through the difficulties that are lying ahead.[29]

The prelate called on all Southerners to support Joshua, their new leader Salva Kiir, in his important mission. To many people, Archbishop Marona provided at least some meaning to what had happened. Salva Kiir, Garang's widow, and the two eldest of Dr. John's children gave powerful eulogies. President Bashir also spoke, in praise of Garang as a peacemaker. After the funeral we all proceeded to the gravesite, where the arrangements were in the hands of the two armies. Powerfully symbolic of the New Sudan, a team of young soldiers drawn from both armies carried Dr. John's coffin, wrapped in the SPLA and Sudanese flags, to the grave.

After most of the dignitaries had flown away, a few of us remained behind. The loss was immense, not only for those that were closest to Dr. John and for the SPLM/A. The loss was greatest for Sudan as a whole. Akol Maror, an elderly gentleman from the Apuk section of the Dinka, expressed the feelings of the Southerners:

> The death of Garang Mabior is a sign that God may be angry with us, the black people of Sudan, and that our ancestors are really not on our side at this time. Garang was our only hope. There is always this thin rope that will pull us across the river from loony (slavery), Arab domination and massacres against us. Garang was the one holding the end of that rope on the other side of the river.[30]

Epilogue
Achievements and Challenges

The Sudan Comprehensive Peace Agreement might have died with the man who negotiated it. That this did not happen, and that both sides showed discipline in the first critical weeks after John Garang's death, was a significant achievement in itself. But many questions remained. Would Salva Kiir be able to keep the SPLM/A and the South united? How long would it take for the Movement to regain its momentum? Would the government in Khartoum honour the CPA, or try to evade the parts it had never really liked? Would a transformation of Sudan still be possible? Friends of Sudan were all very worried.

After the funeral in Juba, I used the opportunity to spend some time with Salva alone, in the house where he was staying. It was more important than ever to reassure him of our support, and encourage him to continue Garang's mission of creating a New Sudan through the CPA. Salva certainly felt the weight of the burden that had suddenly been put on his shoulders. Although he was reputed to prefer independence over unity,[1] he pledged to follow in Garang's footsteps, pursue his vision of a New Sudan, and work diligently to implement the CPA. He had moved swiftly to promote unity in the South; and told me of his outreach to several militia leaders. On my side, I briefed him on some of the recent discussions I had had with Dr. John;[2] I was sorry that Ali Osman Taha was not there to talk over the situation with him directly, and to agree on what should be done to keep the process on track. He had called to propose a tripartite meeting of himself, Salva and me immediately after the funeral, but had had to remain behind. Following the riots in Khartoum, hundreds of Southerners had been arrested. Raids and harassment were continuing. The atmosphere had suddenly turned hostile. Was all of this some kind of panic that would soon subside, or a sign of general deterioration? It was hard to tell. It would not be long before we got indications of where things were headed.

Ambassador Vraalsen, still our Special Envoy for Sudan, visited both Khartoum and Juba immediately after Garang's funeral. He met almost all the key people on both sides. Despite repeated efforts, however, he was unable to see Ali Osman Taha. This was the first sign of what I had feared when news of Garang's death broke. There was no doubt that Dr. John's death would have a significant impact on Taha's standing in the government and party. We had already heard from many sources that he had largely withdrawn from the stage. People close to him told me later that he had been personally shaken by

Dr. John's death. Rumours were rife, of course. The Vice President had taken a big political risk, which could have taken him to new heights; with his powerful partner gone, his position had been significantly weakened. We were now told that the view among many within the National Congress Party and government circles was that Taha had given too much away in the negotiations, and that others now were ready to "repair the damage".[3] Previous support for the negotiation positions was conveniently forgotten; and those who wanted to scuttle the CPA through delaying tactics or less subtle means would most certainly try.

From Vraalsen's visit we got some signals. They were not promising. Cooperation between the two parties was poor. There was serious disagreement over the composition of the Government of National Unity and the allocation of ministerial posts, most heatedly over the Energy portfolio, with all that that implied about oil revenue. Deadlines the parties had set themselves were repeatedly pushed back. Government officials were frustrated with the SPLM's slow and sometimes confused decision-making processes. Representatives of the Movement complained that implementation of the CPA was turning into an extension of the Naivasha talks. There were problems in setting up the Assessment and Evaluation Commission and the Joint Defence Board. In the latter case, the Minister of Defence had apparently kept the leadership of the SPLA waiting for a week before Salva Kiir intervened to arrange a meeting. There was also disagreement over information sharing, the calculation and transfer of oil revenues to the South, and the lack of transparency regarding Darfur.

Out of Office

I followed these developments with concern during the Norwegian election campaign. On September 12th my party suffered a severe defeat and our coalition lost power. We would remain in office until October 17th, when a new coalition would take over. My life as a Minister, juggling an over $3 billion aid budget with global needs and responsibilities relating to Sudan, would soon be over. When I got in touch with my Sudanese friends after the elections they had still not agreed on the composition of the government, and in particular on the Ministry of Energy and Mining. The SPLM insisted that the National Congress Party could not control both the finance and oil portfolios, and viewed the compensatory offer of the Petroleum Commission chairmanship as almost insulting.

Talks on Darfur were scheduled to start at about this time, with preparatory meetings from September 16th and the negotiating round commencing a week later. The team leaders Salim Salim had selected were all from the region, and no attempt was made to involve the Troika. It seemed clear that the African Union now wanted to assert its independence and deal with the negotiations alone. With the death of John Garang, the challenges Ali Osman Taha was facing at home, and my own imminent departure from office, my strategy on Darfur now seemed completely futile. The Americans, however, fully supported by the UK and Norway, were engaged in trying to unite the rebel factions within the Sudan Liberation Movement/Army through a separate reconciliation conference. Since Minni Minawi was unlikely to send anyone to Abuja, this was even more important. The SPLM/A team in Khartoum, referring to the meetings prepared for Garang before his death, remained serious about engagement in the peace effort. They complained, however, that their colleagues in government were not taking them into their confidence over Darfur, and they feared that developments there would have a deleterious effect on implementation of the CPA.

The SPLM's leadership was now divided between Khartoum and Juba, or commuting between the two, trying to ensure that there was adequate participation and follow up in the processes in both places. In mid-September the Interim Constitution for the Government of Southern Sudan was ready to be presented to the provisional Parliamentary Assembly. This had also taken much longer than planned, and had held back establishment of the Government of Southern Sudan, in turn delaying several important processes. I called Salva Kiir on September 20th, three weeks after our last conversation, and discussed the need to follow up with speed and rigour. I also enquired about the talks in Khartoum over establishment of the Government of National Unity. The latter was long overdue, and we had started to discuss with the Americans whether to assert some pressure from international stakeholders. I was going to Washington, DC for the Annual Meetings of the World Bank and IMF and would see Bob Zoellick on 24–25 September. Among the issues on our agenda was the CPA and possible action, if need be, with regard to the non-establishment of the Government of National Unity.

Such action proved unnecessary. Salva said that decisions were imminent. Sure enough, the next day, September 21st, President Bashir announced the new Cabinet. After several weeks of "tug of war" between the parties, a ministerial list was finally presented. This was revealing: of twenty-nine posts, sixteen went to the National Congress Party. And they not only held a majority in the government, they also controlled the most important ministries – Finance, Energy and Mining, Interior, Defence and Justice.

This line-up meant that the institutions most critical to the economy (and the oil sector), National Security (and Military Intelligence) and the application of *Sharia* law, were all in the hands of the National Congress Party. The SPLM, on the other hand, got eight ministerial posts, including Foreign Affairs, Foreign Trade, Investment, Education, Health, Humanitarian Affairs, and the Ministry of Cabinet Affairs. Other Southerners got the four remaining portfolios. The SPLM would have ministers of state or junior ministers in virtually all the Ministries they did not control, but most observers concluded that the SPLM had got a pretty bad deal; the real positions of state power – critical also for implementation of the CPA – remained outside their control. On the positive side the marginalized areas of the Nuba Mountains, Southern

Blue Nile and Darfur were better represented than before. The Northern opposition parties, however, had decided not to participate in the Government of National Unity.

For me the most important factor in the implementation of the CPA was not the positions, but the people who occupied them, both in the Government of National Unity and in the new Government of Southern Sudan. The biggest concern was that very few people from the Naivasha talks on the National Congress side had been given ministerial positions. It also seemed that the balance of power between Bashir and Taha had shifted, with critics of the CPA gaining the upper hand. One of them was the hardliner Nafie Ali Nafie, now named Assistant to the President, an honorific misrepresenting his real power. Many observers discerned his emergence as the new "strongman" of the regime and even possibly the main architect of the new Cabinet. But this was all speculation.

People I had assumed would be obvious choices for Cabinet posts had been left out. They had been ministers of state or held high-level positions during the Naivasha talks, and it would have been natural that those who had negotiated the CPA – on both sides – would have roles in implementing it. But with the exception of Idris Mohamed Abd al-Kader, the chief negotiator, they were nowhere to be seen, either in the Cabinet or even as ministers of state. Only Mutrif Siddiq remained as Under Secretary in the Ministry of Foreign Affairs. At the same time, twelve Special Advisers in the President's Office had been appointed, among them Mustafa Osman Ismail and Ghazi Salahuddin. Such appointments had usually been time-honoured Sudanese devices for rewarding cronies or silencing critics. Now, however, they seemed to constitute an "inner cabinet" or in some cases perhaps counterweights to SPLM/A ministers. Even more striking, Southerners strongly opposed to Dr. John Garang were included among the Advisers: Bona Malwal and the militia leader Riak Gai Kok. Within the SPLM this was disconcerting. Many of the Advisers, both Northerners and Southerners, had either openly criticized the CPA or damned it with faint praise.

The fact that few of the SPLM/A ministers in the Government of National Unity had any background in the CPA negotiations also worried me. Deng Alor, the new Minister for Cabinet Affairs, was virtually the only one with extensive experience at Naivasha; I assumed that other key figures were being held back for the Government of Southern Sudan. Implementation of the CPA would be difficult enough, without its being assigned to people uninformed of the rationale behind the commitments, the background for the concessions, or the ways in which the negotiators had intended the provisions to be carried out. Unless President Bashir himself showed very strong leadership, the peace agreement seemed to have few powerful defenders in the national government. To show genuine Northern interest in creating a just, united Sudan, and preventing the SPLM from "retreating" to the South (particularly after Garang's death), more real sharing of power in Khartoum would have been undertaken. The opportunity seemed to have been lost, at least for now.

There are several possible reasons for these developments. The leadership of the National Congress Party may have concluded that the South – after John Garang's death – would go its own way in any case. If this was a foregone conclusion, there was no point in making concessions ahead of a referendum. If this was not the thinking behind the scenes, weakening the SPLM, buying time, holding back concessions for later might make sense; the "cards" could well be needed later. In one of my darker moments I thought that the Government of National Unity looked like the "Government of National Split". I hoped I was wrong. Optimism prevailed: there were six years to go before the referendum in the South was due to take place. There was time. A lot could happen during the interim period.

In early October I went on a farewell visit to Sudan as Minister of International Development.[4] I met the President and officials in Khartoum and Juba. I saw Ali Osman at his house, as so often before. But it was a different man I met. He had always been quiet, choosing his words with care, never raising his voice. But now he was also subdued. The internal political dynamics in Khartoum were now a major concern and, for Ali Osman, clearly a matter of political survival.

From Moses to Joshua – Life in "The Promised Land"

The next five years would provide the true test of Salva Kiir's leadership and authority. The challenges were immense. "The promised land", the New Sudan, needed to be created from scratch. In order to build peace, however, progress in the area of security was imperative. The ceasefire largely held, at least until midway through the interim period. This was a major achievement. There were no significant incidents, although in the monitoring body there were heated discussions on violations from time to time. The United Nations Mission in Sudan (UNMIS) had now taken over responsibility. While that operation went pretty well, the structure of the force was highly centralized, and it was deployed insufficiently where protection was most needed. The process of disarmament, demobilization and reintegration of combatants was also significantly delayed. That process in any former war zone reflects contemporaneous political developments; neither of the two parties was keen to follow through. Their primary concern was to retain their armies. For the SPLM the Army meant insurance of the referendum and its two options. That defence would account for 40 percent of the Southern government's budget signified its priorities. For the National Congress Party an army at full strength was seen as essential, not only immediately in Darfur, but also to retain capacity in the event the conflict in the South resumed. Both sides imported more arms. There was anyway a lack of funds to finance the downsizing process; this was an area in which donors seemed less prepared to invest. UNMIS had serious problems in moving the process forward.

A serious violation of the ceasefire occurred in May 2008, midway through the interim period. I was in Sudan on a UNICEF mission, and accidentally landed in the middle of it all. I had just returned to Khartoum from Juba when we heard of an incident that had escalated into shooting between a local SPLA unit and police and Sudanese Armed Forces near Abyei town. Within a couple of days the fighting had spread and the whole town was burnt to the ground, leaving only the mosques standing. More than 50,000 people fled the area. UNMIS had been present at Abyei, but had taken no action to protect civilians. UNICEF and partners in the UN and beyond immediately prepared a humanitarian operation.

I worried that the situation could escalate. Abyei had been one of the thorniest issues in the Naivasha negotiations, and no progress had been made since. Despite the ruling of the Abyei Boundary Commission, and subsequent negotiations within the government, if there was one place in Sudan where things could get out of hand, it was Abyei. I checked with the Secretary General's representative for Sudan, Ashraf Qazi, as to whether I might contact Salva Kiir to see what could be done to calm the situation. As he was awaiting a meeting with President Bashir, he said he had no problem with my getting involved.

As I was entering Ali Osman's house that evening the Norwegian ambassador, Fridtjov Thorkildsen, called me from Juba. He said that things were heating up at the SPLM Convention there, with a lot of strong rhetoric about what had happened, in particular from Edward Lino of Abyei. Thorkildsen expected retaliation the next day. I informed Taha and urged him to call Salva soonest. Each side at Abyei had tanks and heavy weapons, and a pitched battle could escalate quickly into something much worse. Taha listened to my account; he would check first with his own people, and call Salva immediately thereafter. I was pretty sure that Taha would be able to take action. I called Juba and said that the Vice President was likely to call about Abyei. But before that happened the tanks started moving into Abyei town. At around noon the next day, the SPLA opened fire; a full tank battle ensued. It was only after several hours, and after Taha and Salva had been able to talk, that the shelling stopped, apparently on their orders.

What had happened was horrible. At the same time, the political leaders had been able to resolve the situation quickly, despite strained relations. The incident led to new meetings both of the Assessment and Evaluation Commission, which undertook a mission to Abyei, and subsequently of the ceasefire monitoring body, which included representatives from both parties. UNMIS management of the Abyei situation was also criticized in the Security Council. After lengthy negotiations, a roadmap was agreed upon and the Abyei problem was handed over to the Permanent Court of Arbitration in The Hague. The Court's ruling in 2009 was not fully satisfactory to either side, but both accepted it.

As serious as direct violations of the ceasefire between the parties could be, there was always a risk of violence from militias, whether proxies or acting on their own in communal violence. With the exception of the clashes in

Malakal in November 2006, militia attacks were rather rare during the early part of the interim period. They became much more frequent later. This was also a reflection of the problems the parties encountered on the political front.

Security is always a reflection of political dynamics. Not unexpectedly, the political process in Sudan proved to be a major challenge. The partnership between the National Congress Party and the SPLM continued to be uneasy. Most of the deadlines in the CPA were violated, and delays in the implementation process were serious. In some cases, the root problem was a lack of capacity, in other cases an apparent lack of commitment. There was continuous tension in the transfer of oil revenues and the transparency of data on oil production; transfers were late, and towards the end of the interim period at times paid in local currency, in contravention of the CPA. The Assessment and Evaluation Commission, the Petroleum Commission and the Joint Defence Board never functioned as intended, and decisions specifically related to the referendum were put on hold. These included border demarcation and the Referendum Act.

Now on the political sidelines, I was extremely worried that insufficient pressure was being put on the two parties. Paying less attention to the CPA, and with the international community's eyes turned elsewhere, they could easily slide back into a cycle of tension and conflict. And indeed, there were continuous difficulties in a number of areas. On 12 October 2007 dissatisfaction with the CPA process led to the SPLM's suspending its participation in the Government of National Unity. At the same time, tensions ran so high that both parties deployed additional troops to the border areas. The SPLA moved 15,000 troops to the Bentiu area and the Sudanese Armed Forces allegedly deployed 8,000 soldiers in addition to the division already there.[5] American intelligence showed even higher numbers.[6] No incidents occurred. The SPLM/A rejoined the Government only after a series of negotiations had ended in credible commitments to implement the key CPA provisions.

Peace building was dependent not only on this partnership, but also on the political process in the regions of past and current conflict. The period immediately after Dr. John's death had also shown how critical a strong, coherent leadership was for the South. Whereas events at Rumbek in November 2004 had cast long shadows over relations within the Movement during the first year or so of the interim period, the leadership found a new *modus operandi* and emerged more united. Salva Kiir made significant progress in conciliating militia and opposition leaders in the South. He moved the process forward with speed, ensuring the inclusion of many former militia leaders in his government and the Army. This resulted in the Juba Agreement on 8 January 2006, a major achievement, by which the South Sudan Defence Force was integrated into the SPLM/A. Paulino Matip, the powerful Nuer militia leader, was made Deputy Commander in Chief of the SPLA. The political process proved quite successful. In July 2006 the SPLM/A initiated negotiations with the Lord's Resistance Army.

But the political process that would have the most significant impact on the peace building process in Sudan was that of Darfur. In April–May 2006 a major effort was made to get a final agreement there. And it was for this fifth round of negotiations that Ali Osman Taha finally went to Abuja, leading the government delegation. Before that, he had not participated there, nor had he been in charge of the process from Khartoum.[7] But this first involvement in the Darfur negotiations would prove also to be his last.

What had happened behind the scenes in Khartoum around this issue was unclear to me. It was obvious that there was no use of informal channels to help move the process forward, as had been the case in Naivasha. At this juncture, the Troika had almost ceased to exist, and it was only during this same negotiation round in Abuja that Robert Zoellick and Hilary Benn engaged directly, on site, together with President Obasanjo. The Darfur Peace Agreement was signed by only one of the rebel factions, Minni Minawi's, an anomaly that later proved fruitless and counterproductive. After this the Darfur process was served by new Special Envoys and Chief Negotiators, both from the AU and the UN, and with the same multitude of actors observing. I had no illusions that the process would lead anywhere. Darfur had needed a completely different approach. The opportunity of 2005 had been lost. Later, it would be primarily in the area of reunifying the Darfur rebel groups that the SPLM/A played a role.

Direct talks between the government and the Eastern Front commenced in the middle of 2006, and a peace agreement was signed in October. The talks took place in Asmara, with Mustafa Osman Ismail as the chief negotiator, and supported by the Eritreans, whose relations with Khartoum had improved significantly. For me, this was evidence that my initial advice on engagement with Eritrea and improving relations between Asmara and Khartoum had been correct. It was also a sign that the timetables we originally had discussed, calling for a peace process for the East to be completed within the CPA's pre-interim period, had not been unrealistic. The conflict in the East had gone on without notice from the international community; the peace agreement went unnoticed as well. Nor did the people of the East see a peace dividend, as both international donors and their own government largely ignored them. Darfur got all the attention.

In the Three Areas there were severe tensions. In the Nuba Mountains of Southern Kordofan and in Southern Blue Nile cooperation between the SPLM and National Congress proved very difficult. The parties distrusted each other, and getting the Protocols implemented was problematical. Only in 2009, with a change of governors in the Nuba Mountains, did relations improve, paradoxically with Ahmed Haroon – indicted by the International Criminal Court – as Governor and the SPLM's Abd al-Aziz Adam as his Deputy. They managed to defuse tensions and establish working relations that impressed everyone. Likewise Malik Agar managed, through strong leadership as Governor, to ensure stability in Blue Nile.

The overall peace-building process, however, was in trouble, and relations between the coalition partners remained very shaky. Overall implementation of the CPA lagged. In late 2009 a number of laws, including referendum and national security statutes, were still pending. These were critical CPA provisions, and on 19 October 2009 the SPLM/A decided to withdraw from the national parliament in protest against the lack of progress. They went back only when the laws were enacted at the end of the year. By 2010 many requirements of the CPA could be ticked off as "done". But many had been delayed and very hard won, and the changes that were supposed to come as a result did not materialize. The key to change at the centre, as intended in the many provisions of the CPA, was not legislation, but control of the levers of power.

Not unrelated to this rather sluggish, grudging process was the decision of the traditional Northern parties to remain outside the political process. Since elections were also delayed, they had good reason. The political transformation was not really happening, another of the peace dividends that did not materialize – despite the expectations of many Northern Sudanese. The delay in the elections was the result of the two partners' apparent lack of commitment to carry the process through on time, further slowed down by technical challenges. The indictment at The Hague of President Bashir may also have contributed to the delay. When elections were finally held, in April 2010, the Northern parties ultimately boycotted them. The SPLM withdrew its presidential candidate too. In the end, therefore, the elections were not the tool for inclusion of all political forces that the Troika initially had foreseen.

Broken Promises

For war-affected Sudanese, peace was what counted most – and tangible peace dividends. They wanted to see change in their daily lives; not only the absence of war, but also the benefits of peace with security, freedom of movement, and economic development. They wanted health clinics, schools, roads, secure livelihoods. Interviews conducted among thousands of Sudanese people clarify their expectations. A woman in Yambio put it this way: "We have just heard [about peace]. It has not been put into practice and action, because our problems still persist, such as education, health. There is no money."[8] A Funj man in Jarot said: "Everybody has an interest to come back. The only thing making people not come back is lack of school facilities, hospitals and many others."[9]

Peace building literature suggests that such changes, in particular in the first six-eighteen months after a conflict, are among the most important factors for sustaining peace. The absence of concrete and tangible benefits can create instability in an already fragile situation. At the same time, aid has to arrive in the right way and be sustained over the long term for sustainable peace to be achieved.[10] In this case, many of the donors failed to deliver on their pledges at the Sudan Donors' Conference. And for those who did, a good deal of the resources did not go to the war-affected population in the South and the Three Areas but were diverted to Darfur. Of the resources that did go to the South and the Three Areas, delivery was very slow, and with limited results during the critical first eighteen months. The famous "gap" in early post-conflict situations had occurred again, despite the knowledge we had acquired from the past, and despite the donor consultations that had taken place so early and regularly. It was all very disappointing.

There were glaring gaps in funding, provision of capacity, and deployment of human resources. There were gaps on the donor side as well as among implementing agencies. The donors somehow got the impression that the emergency was over, so they curtailed humanitarian funding that had previously gone to agencies in South Sudan under the umbrella of Operation Lifeline Sudan. Much of the funding went to Darfur, which was seen as the larger humanitarian crisis. The consequence was that many basic services the population had received in the past, whether food, health services or education, were cut back: in other words, in some cases services actually declined with the advent of peace.[11] As the development agencies were slow in coming in, and the resources in many instances came too late, the "gap" occurred. For people in the Nuba Mountains and Southern Blue Nile, nothing changed: they were marginalized before the peace agreement, and to a large extent afterwards. In Southern Kordofan a Nuba man gave voice to his dissatisfaction: "'The peace is now three years, and there is supposed to be tangible things. The government should have expressed its presence, but for us here there is no government.'"[12]

Half a year after my visit to the returnees' camp outside Rumbek, supplies were still not coming in. People were returning to nothing. This was reconfirmed when I went back in October. After the end of the rainy season the same month, many more Southerners would come. But the UN still lacked funding for its programme. The returnees had to manage largely on their own. On the donor side, it was clear that the Capacity Building Trust Fund, intended primarily to fund the transition to a Southern administration, in addition to quick impact programs, worked well. But donors did not use the fund to its full potential, filling the "gap" when the Multi Donor Trust Fund proved to be slower than planned. The funds were allocated to the MDTF, as the World Bank wished. Bilateral donors running their own programmes were slow in deploying qualified staff to Juba, often operating with contractors or inexperienced people. And virtually nothing happened in the Three Areas. Interestingly, the donors to the Multi Donor Trust Fund paid on time, according to their commitment, and on a multi-year basis. It was all the more frustrating that these funds remained on the MDTF account or other accounts, largely unspent, for more than two years before much happened. As two-thirds of the funds in each MDTF-funded project were from the governments' own resources, their own money was also being held up by Bank procedures. The Bank did not live up to its promises and commitments to the Sudanese or to the donors. The supposedly "speediest" MDTF in World Bank history proved to be the world's slowest.

The Joint Donors' Office never functioned as intended. The team was largely excluded from the upstream process by the Bank, which seemed to prefer to go it alone, and the Office was incapable of ensuring that resources were disbursed in a speedy fashion. The UN and World Bank, on their side, could not work out their problems with fiduciary transfers before two years had passed. Instead of taking responsibility for the situation and fixing it, Bank officials tended to blame others, first the UN (which returned the favour) and then the Government of Southern Sudan, but still insisted on replenishing the fund, promising that things would improve. They did not. Despite disbursement statistics that showed some progress, more than five years into the life of the MDTF only one third of the resources had been spent.[13] As "disbursement" in Bank jargon often implies transfers from one account to another, the real accounting rests with implemented programmes and achieved outcomes on the ground. And on that basis, only very limited dividends were seen.[14]

Many Southerners viewed the Bank as the worst performer of all the international aid actors. The World Bank, as a bank, relies on others – governments, effective implementing agencies or contractors – to make the money move. With a nascent government having almost no capacity, this is extremely difficult. The Bank knew that this would be the case. When the Bank also insisted on its own procedures in relation to all implementing agencies, the result was stasis. Even on the contracting side, progress was very slow. Alarmed after another visit to Juba, I personally contacted the Bank's top leadership in 2006 and called for immediate action and followed up with donors. But the Bank did not deploy the necessary capacity on the ground to administer the MDTF, address these challenges, and speed up implementation.[15] Only very late in the day did the Bank leadership acknowledge the problems and do something. Donors ended up reducing the amount of resources they put into the MDTF, and in 2010 some started reallocating elsewhere.

The people of Southern Sudan and other stakeholders had no notion of these complications. They saw only that what they had been promised did not come. One can hardly separate aid from its context. Whether it comes or not, and how it comes, has consequences, and in some cases significant political impact. The MDTF that was intended for the war-affected areas in the North was, if possible, even slower than that of the South. The combined absence of donors and government assistance had a potentially worse impact on the population also in the Three Areas, as expressed by a young Nuba man from Heban: the CPA was "'bad because it does not provide anything good to Nuba Mountains, compared to North or South Sudan'".[16] Knowing how important the credibility of leaders is in fragile post-conflict situations, I blamed myself for having put the Southern Sudanese and the people of war-affected areas in this situation. I was pretty sure that more resources would have been going to other channels and agencies, giving better results more quickly, if not for my strong advocacy of pooling funds through the MDTF. The education programme run by UNICEF, funded without a penny from the MDTF, was a case in point.[17] It had increased the number of children in school more than three times in three years, whether in a tent, under a tree or in a proper school.

The numbers were still too small and more should be done, but results were achieved.

I also saw the failure of the Joint Donors' Office as my own responsibility. I tried to repair the damage through privately talking to donors, to the World Bank at the highest level and to the Government of Southern Sudan during repeated visits later, but nothing seemed to help. Too much prestige had been invested in a partly dysfunctional model for the necessary changes to be made. The lessons learned from previous peace-building processes had resulted in even tougher lessons learned this time. I would never forget them. But for Sudan, the damage was done. As an Agar woman said: "People say there is peace, but there are still two sides of the river."[18] The "promised land" was nowhere to be seen.

The transition of the SPLM/A from guerrilla movement to political party and Government of Southern Sudan was never going to be easy. And many of us knew all too well the challenges they would face. The Movement had been running its own affairs in the so-called liberated areas with some success. Running a government was a different story, however, and managing significant oil revenues was yet another. As is the case in most oil-producing countries, there were already problems with governance, financial management and corruption in Sudan. Now, the Government of Southern Sudan was battling the same. It was almost impossible to overcome the constraints of weak capacity, manage the multiple challenges of establishing a functional Government of Southern Sudan, and keep up with CPA implementation. Salva Kiir also encountered major problems with his team. He dismissed his first Minister of Finance and a number of his officials on corruption charges after only a year. Issues of economic mismanagement and corruption would haunt his government thereafter. Significant oil revenue had been transferred to the South; ordinary people wondered were all the money had gone. They blamed the North for not transferring the funds they were entitled to, and some questioned their own leaders.

The President of Southern Sudan was acutely aware of all this. He disciplined several ministers, and tried with international help to establish a more robust financial management system. At the same time, progress had been made in building a functioning Southern capital comparable to several others in the region, and in establishing an administration in Juba and the states. From the donors' side, both bilateral and multilateral, things had picked up by the late interim period, UN agencies included. But it was the international NGOs that ended up bearing the brunt of social-service delivery to the Southern Sudanese, providing the population with basic health care and education, and building basic infrastructure in the rural areas. They often did this with limited resources from international donors. It was impressive. But it was also a concern, because it continued the pattern established during the civil war.

In 2009 many of the NGOs in Darfur and other Northern states were expelled by the government. The order applied also to the marginalized areas of Southern Kordofan/Nuba Mountains and Southern Blue Nile. The little assistance these areas had received so far was at risk. Only a few of the NGOs were permitted to stay or to come back later.

For the Three Areas this exacerbated an already bleak situation, even more difficult, if possible, than in Southern Sudan. Very few aid agencies operated in the Three Areas, and they arrived very late in the interim period. The security situation was also difficult, both in Abyei and in Southern Kordofan (the Nuba Mountains). Opinion studies conducted in Southern Kordofan in late 2008 showed that the vast majority of people believed that the situation in the state was deteriorating. Some people even suggested that things had been better before the CPA.[19] For Southern Blue Nile, the situation was less bleak, with most people opining that things were moving in the right direction. But a lot of confusion prevailed in both areas, with many people expecting an exercise of self-determination.[20] A Nuba woman put it this way: "'If there is no referendum that allows the people of Southern Kordofan to choose where they want to be, we'll go back to war.'"[21] Numerous similar statements were recorded.

At this time a few cracks began to appear on the "South–South" side. In October 2007 Lam Akol, the former guerrilla leader of Western Upper Nile who had been made Foreign Minister, left office. Many had seen in his performance a reflection of National Congress positions, not those of the SPLM/A. Moreover some of the militia leaders had been retained on the government side from the very beginning, and been placed in Joint Integrated Units, which violated at least the spirit of the CPA. Among those integrated on the Southern side, some ex-militia leaders decided to run as independent candidates in the elections, while retaining their affiliation with the SPLM/A. Increasing violence was an obvious sign that things were not moving in the right direction.

During 2009 and 2010, the situation deteriorated in Upper Nile, Jonglei state and Equatoria, where there were attacks by militia and an increase in communal violence. Tensions between communities were exploited. In the far South this was also related to the persistent incubus of the Lord's Resistance Army, with a significant number of people being displaced. UNMIS was unable to protect civilians in the hardest affected areas. The SPLA had very limited capacity to deal with peacetime operations where civilians were involved. By 2010 some 400,000 people were displaced, largely as a consequence of militia attacks, a number comparable to that of wartime and with serious humanitarian consequences. The food crisis in 2009/2010 made things worse. But again, getting attention and resources to respond to the crisis was very difficult.

The CPA and Scenarios for Sudan's Future

While to some extent Darfur had been held hostage by the Naivasha talks, the opposite was the case from late 2004 onwards. With all the focus of the international community on Darfur, CPA implementation was clearly held hostage to developments in Darfur. It became yesterday's news, and it seemed that all those who had signed the CPA as witnesses had forgotten that Sudan was bigger than its Western region, and that peace in Darfur was inextricably linked to peace in the rest of the country. Whether this resulted in part from a deliberate successful strategy among forces less supportive of the CPA is difficult to tell.

Whatever the case may be, the international community almost "dropped the ball" during the interim period. They did not take the necessary comprehensive approach to the country and its conflicts and peace processes. High level leadership in monitoring implementation of the CPA and holding the parties to account was missing, and there was not much pressure for key decisions that could make unity more attractive for the South. There was engagement at lower levels, but no drive from the top. This void has had serious consequences for Sudan as a whole. Without a "driver" coordinating the efforts of the international community, and thus without a comprehensive approach to Sudan, peace building in the country was likely to fail.

The Comprehensive Peace Agreement was not only a partnership of the SPLM and National Congress Party. It would not have been completed without the intense and unflagging efforts of key partners in the international community. Without that support, and that of the Troika (particularly the US and Norway), in waging peace, the CPA would not have become a reality. But the international community also had major responsibilities for what would happen in the ensuing interim period. International partners for the most part failed to honour their commitments to the CPA. It was only towards the end of the interim period that the UN, the AU and others woke up and started to realize what was happening. But it was far too late. In opinion studies conducted throughout the interim period,[22] covering thousands of people, there has been one consistent message from Southern Sudanese: they do not trust the North and they want to secede.

In the period immediately after the signing of the CPA, there were concerns expressed about Garang's engagement with the North and his stated vision for a united (New) Sudan. As one 2004 report based on opinion studies in Southern Sudan put it, "Because there is so little confidence that a united Sudan is viable, due to perceived hostility and dishonesty of 'the Arabs' in Khartoum, there is virtually no support for Garang's discourse related to a united Sudan."[23] The same message was delivered in later opinion studies, with few participants able to imagine any scenario in which they would vote for unity in a referendum. In other words, it would take a significant effort by all political forces in the country and internationally, and the delivery of tangible and sizeable peace dividends, to be able to turn such opinions around. But this did not happen. Already in 2007 a common joke in Southern Sudan went like this: Two men are talking to each other, looking at the girls passing by. One says to the other: "Have you seen that girl named Unity? I have not seen her in a long time. She was supposed to be so attractive." And the other responds, "Her? Oh no – she departed a long time ago."

But implementation of the CPA was still essential for maintaining peace in Sudan. The US and their new Special Envoy[24] and Norway knew this, and the Troika was revitalized. Intense shuttle diplomacy started in 2009. The international institutions became more engaged, with the former president of South Africa, Thabo Mbeki, engaging actively on behalf of the AU,[25] and Haile Menkerios as the new Special Representative of the Secretary General of the UN in 2010. Issues relating to the referendum were most critical, including the preparatory process related to the referendum commission, trying to ensure demarcation of the border and negotiation of a number of post-referendum issues.

A referendum is scheduled for 9 January 2011. In accordance with the CPA, Southern Sudanese are entitled to opt for unity or independence. During the interim period, unity has not been made more attractive. In the last opinion studies, reported on in September 2009, the views of people in Southern Sudan and the Three Areas are overwhelmingly clear: the vast majority would vote for independence.[26] Their views on government performance, development, security and implementation of the CPA revealed that attitudes had actually darkened since 2007. A Nuer chief in Malakal put it this way: "'You will never confuse me to vote for unity. Separation is all we need.'" A Kakwa chief from Yei was equally clear: "'We will be divided; even children know that. All these years they have been developing Khartoum without the South.'"[27] These are anecdotal quotations, of course, but according to the regular opinion studies conducted between 2004 and 2009, they do represent broad opinion among Southern Sudanese.

The SPLM and the Government of Southern Sudan expect the referendum to be held on time. Should this not be the case, it would in itself be a violation of the Comprehensive Peace Agreement and is therefore fraught with risks. The Secretary General of the SPLM/A, Pagan Amum says, "Any attempts to delay the referendum shall threaten the enduring peace."[28] If a delay happens without a credible process, outbreaks of violence are very likely. It is the referendum that is at the very core of the CPA for the SPLM/A. That was the main reason for their signature on 9 January 2005. If Southerners are denied a referendum outright, this would be an act that would trigger a return to war between the North and the South. Khartoum is well aware of this. It is my understanding that neither party wants such a scenario to happen, nor does anyone want to pursue a strategy of reigniting Africa's longest civil war. With the current sentiments in the South and the Three Areas, however, any delays and episodes of violence can spin entirely out of control, including for the SPLM/A.

As regards the possible outcome of a referendum, an overwhelming public opinion in Sudan expects a clear majority among Southerners for secession. The same goes for international observers and experts following Sudan. For the SPLM/A the expectation would be that such a referendum would be followed by a declaration of independence after a transition period of six months, as the agreement foresees. If the referendum goes smoothly, if post-referendum and separation issues are negotiated in a flexible manner, and there is an orderly transition, the chances are good for neighbourly relations. This includes agreement on dual citizenship and arrangements such as freedom of movement of goods and people, as already granted to Egypt.[29] But even more importantly, this implies that critical issues need to be resolved. These include demarcation of the border between the North and the South; agreement on oil-production, revenues and the use of the pipeline to Port Sudan; and border management. The separate referendum in Abyei (and the expected transition there) will also have to be well managed, as would the popular consultation processes in the other two special Areas. If negotiations on these issues are successful, then close cooperation on a number of post-referendum issues, important to both parties, is fairly likely. With the current state of affairs, this scenario, based on a smooth transition, close cooperation and friendly relations between neighbours, would be an optimal scenario from the perspective of peace and stability for all Sudanese and for the region as a whole. However, even in this scenario episodes of violence are not unlikely.

At the same time, many impediments can be introduced to make things difficult, as the heated negotiations on the Referendum Act and on voter eligibility showed in late 2009. The delays in the establishment of the Referendum Commission were also of concern. Procrastination in the border demarcation has been another challenging factor. Political forces may attempt to make the conduct of the referendum itself, and the implementation of its result, as difficult and costly for the Southerners as possible. A second possible scenario is therefore that the referendum takes place, but where logistical, technical and other hurdles serve as a basis for disputes relating to the conduct – and the results – of a referendum. This would imply delays in the implementation of the results of the referendum. In such a scenario agreement on key post-referendum issues would be left for later, with great pressure and heightened tensions between the National Congress Party and the SPLM/A, factors that can further derail the process.

It is important to be aware that violence is likely in all scenarios, with a delay of a referendum, and whatever the results of a referendum. If the outcome is unity it will be read by Southerners as a flawed result, with outbreaks of violence. This is likely to lead to a unilateral declaration of independence for Southern Sudan, which in turn will lead to more violence that can easily take a life of its own, including between the two parties. Such a scenario can also be deliberately triggered if political forces find this opportune. If the outcome is secession, Southerners may be victimized, with episodes of revenge in the North against Southern Sudanese in a way experienced after the death of Dr. John Garang and the riots that followed. There is also speculation that expulsion of all the Southerners in the North can happen in such a scenario. In both cases violence would initially be localized, but the critical factor will be how this situation is managed, both by the leaders on both sides and by the international community. Should the latter scenario become real-istic, the transition will be very difficult to manage. Such a process would likely lead to more violence, possibly involving proxy militias and tensions in the Three Areas. There are enough tricky issues on the list above, and enough hot spots in the country, to make this a high-risk scenario.

Even with such scenarios in mind, I have always thought that the Sudanese parties would "muddle through", usually after all deadlines has passed and they have peered over the edge of the abyss, but in time to pull back and get things on track again. I still believe so. However, such a situation could easily spin out of control, and is fraught with complex challenges that need to be managed with political maturity and strong international support. If there is weak and incoherent international leadership and support, and hesitation in managing the conflict, the risk is of a domino effect. A major incident such as the violent episode and later destruction of Abyei town could be the first domino. It was handled then because it was in the interest of both parties to retain the peace. In a situation involving even more significant interests, and if relations have deteriorated further, such incidents might be more difficult to handle. The Abyei area is already among the most militarized areas in the whole country, with significant troop presence from both sides.

A referendum that leads to the secession of Southern Sudan could easily trigger unrest elsewhere in the country. Also the situation in the North is fragile and needs to be managed very carefully. Illustrations of this are recent statements by Khalil Ibrahim, the leader of JEM, now requesting self-deter-mination for Darfur. This is also linked to the question of change at the centre. Jok Madut Jok puts it this way: "Many Sudanese living in areas peripheral to the centers of power have often stated clearly that Sudan has never existed as a unified state, except in name. From the vantage point of marginalized groups, the nation has never secured from them any legitimacy."[30] Allowing the situation in the South or one or another of the Three Areas to slide out of control is therefore all the more risky. Also in the North there is an under-standing of the factors that are at play. A known academic, Dr. Abdurrahman Ahmed Osman of Universal African University, close to the ruling party, said the following at a conference with reference to the "so-called marginalized regions" recently:[31]

> The south will go, Darfur needs a little push and will go, the Nuba Mountain will go, the Southern Blue Nile will go, the East will go away from Sudan; the region stretching out from the south of Egypt to the two rivers of the Nile, i.e. "Hamdi's Triangle" has enough land and enough resources to accommodate its people.

John Garang outlined this danger in 2005 for the Security Council:

> . . . the logical consequence of that position is that the situation in the south, the Nuba Mountains, the Blue Nile and Abyei . . . [would] drift

back towards war, thereby combining with the present desperate situation in Darfur and the situation brewing in eastern Sudan. That would lead to a scenario of a failed State in the Sudan – the very scenario we wanted to avoid in the first place by signing the Comprehensive Peace Agreement.[32]

It is my hope that maturity on both sides, and among leaders in the Three Areas and other marginalized areas, as well as strong and competent engagement and leadership by the international community, will prevent such a worst case scenario from becoming a reality.

A prominent Northern Sudanese recently thanked me for the Comprehensive Peace Agreement: "You saved my country from falling apart", he said. I looked at him in surprise, knowing that the referendum was just a few months away. His view was that the policies in effect before the CPA negotiations would ultimately have led to a full fragmentation of Sudan. "The process was well under way," he said. Even an orderly partition of the country and an independent Southern Sudan he regarded as much better than the alternative: continuing conflict with and in the South, unrest and violence in the East, chaos in Darfur, and the likelihood of violence in Abyei, the Nuba Mountains, Southern Blue Nile and possibly elsewhere. He did not mention – but I would add – the risk of significant involvement also of neighbouring countries.

Time will tell whether he was right, whether the Comprehensive Peace Agreement did save the Sudan from full fragmentation. There is one important lesson to learn from the negotiations that ended Africa's longest civil war, however, and that is the need for engagement – continuous, coherent and forceful – from the international community. The same leadership is needed now. Waging peace in Sudan is more important than ever. In fact, it is now that the job really begins.

Notes

INTRODUCTION **Africa's Longest Civil War**

1 Interviews with Deng Alor, 16 April 2010; Salva Kiir Mayardit, 15 April 2010; and Pagan Amum, 12–13 June 2010.
2 This section is based on personal knowledge and on interviews with members of the SPLM/A Naivasha delegation, SPLM/A leaders, relatives of John Garang, and others who knew him well.
3 Interview with Abel Alier, 19 April 2010.
4 Interview with Ali Osman Taha, 21 April 2010.
5 Interview with Salva Kiir, 15 April 2010.
6 Interview with Rebecca Nyandeng de Mabior, 16 April 2010.
7 This was in late 2002, when the SPLM/A insisted on negotiating the Three Areas as part of the overall IGAD peace process.
8 Interviews with Salva Kiir, 15 April 2010; Rebecca Nyandeng de Mabior and Mabior Garang de Mabior, 16 April 2010; and Mansour Khaled, 15 April 2010.
9 Abel Alier: *Southern Sudan: Too many agreements dishonoured*, 2nd ed., Exeter 2003.
10 Interview with Yasir Arman, 18 April 2010.
11 Francis Mading Deng, ed., *New Sudan in the Making?* Trenton, 2009, 476.
12 Group interview, Sudanese govt. delegation to CPA negotiations, Khartoum, 19 April 2010.
13 Interview, 21 April 2010.
14 This section on Ali Osman Taha is based on personal knowledge and interviews with friends, colleagues, political opponents, and participants in the Naivasha negotiations.
15 Interviews with Col Ding, 17 April 2010; Ambassador Mathiang Malual Mabur, 22 April 2010; and Abel Alier, 19 April 2010.
16 Interview with Mansour Khalid, 15 April 2010.
17 Interviews with Abel Alier, 19 April 2010, and Ali Osman Taha, 21 April 2010.
18 Interview with Col Ding, 17 April 2010.
19 Interview with Ali Osman Taha, 21 April 2010.
20 *Ibid.*
21 Justice Africa, *Prospects for Peace in Sudan: Briefing*, June, July, August 2001, and interview with Dr. Ghazi Salahuddin, 18 April 2010.
22 Justice Africa, *Prospects*, July 2001, 3 and August 2001, 3.
23 Justice Africa, *Prospects for Peace in Sudan: Briefing*, July 2001.
24 Group interview, Sudanese govt. delegation to CPA negotiations, Khartoum, 19 April 2010, Interview with Charles Snyder, 30 May 2010.
25 http://fpc.state.gov/documents/organization/155571.pdf.
26 Group interview, Sudanese govt. delegation to CPA negotiations, Khartoum, 19 April 2010.

27 Interview with Yasir Arman, quoting Lual Diing, a prominent SPLM/A-leader, Khartoum, 18 April 2010.
28 Interview with Ghazi Salahuddin, 18 April 2010.
29 The sanctions were related to Security Council resolution 1054 (1996) of 26 April 1996 and were lifted in the SC meeting 4384, as reflected in: http://daccess-dd ny.un.org/doc/UNDOC/PRO/N01/556/78/PDF/.
30 Group interview, Sudanese govt. delegation to CPA negotiations, Khartoum, 19 April 2010.
31 Private information.
32 Interviews with Ali Osman Taha, 21 April 2010; Ghazi Salahuddin, 18 April 2010; and Charles Snyder, 30 May 2010.
33 Interview with Ghazi Salahuddin, 18 April 2010.
34 *Africa Confidential*, 22 February 2002, 2.
35 IMF Country Report 02/245, November 2002, 9.
36 "Uganda-Sudan: Joint statement marks much improved relations", *IRIN News*, 20 March 2002 (http://www.irinnews.org/report.aspx?reportid=30797 accessed 4 April 2010).
37 Group interview, members of Sudanese govt. delegation to CPA negotiations, 19 April 2010.
38 *Ibid.*
39 Interviews with Abel Alier, 19 April 2010; and Col Ding, 17 April 2010.
40 Interview with Abel Alier, 19 April 2010.
41 International Crisis Group, *Capturing the Moment: Sudan's Peace Process in the Balance*, April 2002, 3.
42 Agence France-Presse, 16 March 2002.
43 Reuters, 22 March 2002.

CHAPTER ONE   The Troika

1 The Inter-Governmental Agency on Drought and Desertification (IGADD) in the 1990s became the Intergovernmental Authority on Development (IGAD), encompassing Ethiopia, Eritrea, Somalia, Djibouti, Sudan, Uganda and Kenya.
2 Interview with Charles Snyder, 30 May 2010.
3 Assistant Secretary of State for Africa Susan Rice, Gayle Smith of the National Security Council and John Prendergast at the State Department were key players on Sudan in the Clinton Administration during this period, a team I worked closely with during the years 1998–2000.
4 According to private sources, this happened primarily through a number of phone calls.
5 Interview with Charles Snyder, 30 May 2010.
6 International Crisis Group, *Capturing the Moment: Sudan's Peace Process in the Balance*, April 2002, 14.
7 Clare Short, E-mail communication, 8 May 2010.
8 Telephone interview with Col Ding, 20 April 2010.
9 *Ibid.*
10 Address by the Prime Minister of Great Britain to the Nigerian Parliament, Urhobo Historical Society, 080202, Nigeria, http://www.waado.org/NigerDelta/FedGovt/ForeignAffairs/TonyBlair.html.
11 The SPLA did not have any police units to speak of, and hence the uniforms were new and needed to be provided.

12 See Douglas H. Johnson, "Why Abyei Matters: The Breaking Point of Sudan's Comprehensive Peace Agreement?", *African Affairs* 426, 2008, 1–19.

13 Julie Flint and Alex De Waal, *Darfur: A New History of a Long War*, London, 2008, 47–55.

14 *Ibid., 51–5.*

15 *Ibid., 86*

16 Alex de Waal, cited in Julie Flint, "Oil fuels flames of war in Sudan: Civilians pay price as Khartoum mobilises for showdown with newly united rebels", *The Guardian*, 7 March 2002.

CHAPTER TWO   **The Watershed Agreement on Self-Determination**

1 Ambassador Sahnoun had extensive historical knowledge of the Sudan, as he had been active in the negotiations of the Addis Ababa Agreement in 1972. The UN increased its presence in the talks as the UNMIS-preparations got under way.

2 Telephone interview with General Sumbeiywo, 17 May 2010.

3 Waithaka Waihenya, *The Mediator: Gen. Lazaro Sumbeiywo and the Southern Sudan peace process*, Nairobi 2006, 85.

4 Interview with Deng Alor, 24 September 2009.

5 Group interview, Sudanese govt. delegation to CPA negotiations, 19 April 2010.

6 Interview with Nicholas "Fink" Haysom, 1 June 2010.

7 Interview with Pagan Amum, 12–13 June 2010.

8 *Ibid*; Interview with Deng Alor, 24 September 2009 and group interview with members of SPLM/A delegation to CPA negotiations, 16 April 2010.

9 Interviews with Deng Alor, 24 September 2009; and Pagan Amum, 12–13 June 2010.

10 Interviews with Nicholas "Fink" Haysom, 1, 28 June 2010; telephone interview with General Sumbeiywo, 17 May 2010.

11 Group interview with members of Sudanese govt. delegation to CPA negotiations, 19 April 2010.

12 Waihenya, *The Mediator*, 87.

13 Interview with Fink Haysom, 28 June 2010.

14 Group interview with members of Sudanese govt. delegation to CPA negotiations, 19 April 2010.

15 *Ibid.*

16 Interview with Charles Snyder, 30 May 2010.

17 *Ibid.* and interview with Andrew Natsios, 11 July 2010.

18 Interview with Fink Haysom, 1 June 2010.

19 *Ibid.* and telephone interview with General Sumbeiywo,17 May 2010.

20 Telephone interview with General Sumbeiywo, 17 May 2010.

21 Interview with Deng Alor, 24 September 2009, Group interview with members of SPLM/A delegation to CPA negotiations, 16 April 2010.

22 Interview with Deng Alor, 29 September 2009.

23 Group interview with members of Sudanese govt. delegation to CPA negotiations, 19 April 2010.

24 *Ibid.*; Interview with Ali Osman Taha, 21 April 2010.

25 Interview with Fink Haysom, 1, 28 June 2010.

26 Telephone interview with General Sumbeiywo, 17 May 2010; interviews with Fink Haysom, 1, 28 June 2010.

27 Telephone interview with General Sumbeiywo, 17 May 2010; interview Deng Alor, 24 September 2009; group interviews with Sudanese govt. delegation to CPA negotiations, 19 April 2010 and members of SPLM/A delegation to CPA negotiations, 16 April 2010.
28 Group interview with members of Sudanese govt. delegation to CPA negotiations, 19 April 2010.
29 *Ibid.*
30 Telephone interview with General Sumbeiywo, 17 May 2010; group interviews with Sudanese govt. delegation to CPA negotiations, 19 April 2010 and members of SPLM/A delegation to CPA negotiations, 16 April 2010.
31 Email-communication with Dr. Ghazi Salahuddin, 11 August 2010.
32 Group interview with members of Sudanese govt. delegation to CPA negotiations, 19 April 2010.
33 Interview with Fink Haysom, 28 June 2010.
34 Interview with Dr. Ghazi Salahuddin, 18 April 2010.
35 *Ibid.*
36 Interview with Deng Alor, 24 September 2009.
37 Interview with Dr. Ghazi Salahuddin, 18 April 2010.
38 United Nations, "Press Statement on Sudan by Security Council President", New York, 25 July 2002.
39 Group interview with members of SPLM/A delegation to CPA negotiations, 16 April 2010.
40 Telephone conversation with Dr. John Garang, 28 or 29 July 2002.
41 *Ibid.*
42 Justice Africa, *Prospects for Peace in Sudan: Briefing*, 27 December 2002.
43 Group interview with members of Sudanese govt. delegation to CPA negotiations, 19 April 2010; interview with Ali Osman Taha, 21 April 2010.
44 Interview with Fink Haysom, 1, 28 June 2010.
45 Group interview with members of Sudanese govt. delegation to CPA negotiations, 19 April 2010.

CHAPTER THREE   Peace-Making in Peril: Conflict and Confrontation

1 Waihenya, *The mediator*, 93–4.
2 Interviews with Fink Haysom, 1, 28 June 2010.
3 Interview with Pagan Amum, 12–13 June 2010.
4 Interviews with: Yasir Arman, 18 April 2010; Pagan Amum, 12–13 June 2010; and Fink Haysom1, 28 June 2010.
5 Interview with Pagan Amum, 12–13 June 2010.
6 Waihenya, *The Mediator*, 95.
7 SPLM/A News Agency, "NIF Forces Run In Disarray", 12 June 2002, http://www.sudan.net/news/press/postedr/149.shtml.
8 Group interview, members of SPLM/A delegation to CPA negotiations, 16 April 2010; members of Sudanese government delegation to the CPA negotiations, 19 April 2010; interview with Pagan Amum, 12–13 June 2010.
9 Interview with Pagan Amum, 12–13 June 2010; group interviews; members of SPLM/A delegation to CPA negotiations, 16 April 2010.
10 Waihenya, *The mediator*, 97. This was confirmed by Pagan Amum, 12–13 June 2010.

11 Waihenya, *The mediator*, 95–6; Telephone interview with General Sumbeiywo, 17 May 2010.
12 Justice Africa, *Prospects for Peace in Sudan: Briefing*, September 2002.
13 Interview, 18 April 2010. Also confirmed in interview with Pagan Amum, 12–13 June 2010.
14 Flint and De Waal, *Darfur*, 86–8; Interview with Yasir Arman, 20 April 2010.
15 Flint and de Waal, *Darfur*, 89.
16 Group interview with members of SPLM/A delegation to CPA negotiations, 16 April 2010; interview with Col Ding, 17 April 2010.
17 Private information.
18 Flint and de Waal, *Darfur*, 104.
19 Group interview with members of SPLM/A delegation to CPA negotiations, 16 April 2010; interview with Beyor Adjang, 16 April 2010.
20 *Ibid.*, 89–90.
21 Interview with Yasir Arman, 18 April 2010.
22 Private information.
23 Flint and de Waal, *Darfur*, 88–94.
24 Group interview with members of Sudanese govt. delegation to CPA negotiations, 19 April 2010.
25 Flint and de Waal, *Darfur*, 93.
26 *Ibid.*, 104.
27 Group interview with members of Sudanese govt. delegation to CPA negotiations, 19 April 2010.
28 Clare Short, *An Honourable Deception: New Labour, Iraq and the misuse of power*, New York 2004.
29 Interview with Ali Osman Taha, 21 April 2010.
30 This section is based on information from the Ministry of Foreign Affairs; interview with Col Ding, 17 April 2010; and telephone interviews with him, 20 April 2010, and interviews with Abel Alier, 19 April 2010, and Mathiang Malual Mabur, 23 April 2010.
31 Interview with Col Ding, 17 April 2010.
32 Interview with Mathiang Malual Mabur, 23 April 2010.
33 Group interview with members of Sudanese govt. delegation to CPA negotiations, 19 April 2010.
34 Clare Short, e-mail communication, 8 May 2010.
35 Interview with Pagan Amum, 12–13 June 2010; group interview, members of SPLM/A delegation to CPA negotiations, 16 April 2010.
36 Interviews with Col Ding, 17 April 2010; and Abel Alier, 19 April 2010.
37 Flint and de Waal, *Darfur*, 91.
38 Flint and de Waal, *Darfur*, 115.
39 *Ibid.*, 122.
40 *Ibid.*, 38.
41 Interviews with Fink Haysom, 1, 28 June 2010.
42 *Ibid.*
43 Waihenya, *The Mediator*, 90.
44 "Draft Framework for Resolution of Outstanding Issues Arising out of the Elaborations of the Machakos Protocol", Article 31.4 (presented at Nakuru, July 2003).
45 Group interview with members of SPLM/A delegation to CPA negotiations, 16 April 2010.

46 "Draft Framework", Article 8.
47 "Draft Framework", Article 3.
48 Interviews with Fink Haysom, 1, 28 June 2010.
49 Group interview with members of SPLM/A delegation to CPA negotiations, 16 April 2010.
50 Interview with Pagan Amum, 12–13 June 2010.
51 Interview with Fink Haysom, 28 June 2010.
52 Group interview with members of Sudanese govt. delegation to CPA negotiations, 19 April 2010.
53 Waihenya, *The Mediator*, 115.
54 Interview with Ghazi Salahuddin, 18 April 2010.
55 International Crisis Group, *Sudan: Towards an Incomplete Peace*, December 2003. Interviews with Ali Osman Taha, 21 April 2010; Ghazi Salahuddin, 18 April 2010; members of Sudanese govt. delegation to CPA negotiations, 19 April 2010; members of SPLM/A delegation to CPA negotiations, 16 April 2010.
56 Justice Africa, *Prospects for Peace in Sudan: Briefing*, September 2003.
57 *Africa Confidential* 44, 21, 24 October 2003 has an alternative analysis: "On 15 October [2003], Cairo's Foreign Minister, Ahmed Maher, told parliament that his government 'rejected the Machakos agreement' (the 2002 framework) and had 'refused to take part in these negotiations since their start because of the acceptance of southerners' right to self-determination.'"

CHAPTER FOUR **From Enemies to Partners in Peace**
1 Interviews with Col Ding, 17 April 2010; and Mathiang Malual Mabur, 23 April 2010. The prominent Southerners in Khartoum had also seen his desire to engage with the South as a positive and promising sign.
2 Interview with Pagan Amum, 12–13 June 2010.
3 Interview with Abel Alier, 19 April 2010.
4 Private information.
5 *Ibid.*
6 Interview with Abel Alier, 19 April 2010.
7 Private information.
8 Waihenya, *The Mediator*, 120; telephone interview with General Sumbeiywo, 17 May 2010.
9 Private information.
10 Interviews with Ali Osman Taha, 21 April 2010; and Ambassador Mathiang, 23 April 2010.
11 Private information.
12 Telephone interview with General Sumbeiywo, 17 May 2010. It is also likely that there was resistance from within the SPLM/A: see Waihenya, *The Mediator*, 123–4.
13 Interview with Pagan Amum, 12–13 June 2010; and telephone interview with General Sumbeiywo, 17 May 2010.
14 Interview with Col Ding, 17 April 2010.
15 Interviews with Salva Kiir Mayardit, 15 April 2010; Yasir Arman, 18 April 2010; and Pagan Amum, 12–13 June 2010.
16 Interview with Yasir Arman, 18 April 2010.

17 Interview with Pagan Amum, 12–13 June 2010.

18 Several members of the SPLM/A Leadership Council say that Pagan Amum opposed the meeting, but he insists that he advised in favour. One informant states that Deng Alor was opposed, but others support him in stating he favoured the meeting, as is consistent also with Norwegian communication with him at the time.

19 International Crisis Group, *Sudan: Towards an Incomplete Peace*, 3; interview with Pagan Amum, 12–13 June 2010.

20 Several sources confirm that Salva told the story of Lual Diing Wol who had been driving a car in Nairobi. At one point the car hit a police car. He then took his stick and his documents and left. If the driver had hit any other car, there would have been no problem, but with a police car, one cannot get away. Salva advised the Chairman to go to meet Taha, and not disappoint the Kenyans. (Interviews with Salva Kiir, 15 April 2010; Pagan Amum, 12–13 June 2010; and Yasir Arman, 18 April 2010.)

21 Interview with Pagan Amum, 12–13 June 2010.

22 Interviews with Salva Kiir Mayardit, 15 April 2010; Ali Osman Taha, 21 April 2010; Yasir Arman, 18 April 2010.

23 Interview with Col Ding, 17 April 2010 and telephone interview, 20 April 2010.

24 Telephone interview with General Sumbeiywo, 17 May 2010; group interview with members of Sudanese govt. delegation to CPA negotiations, 19 April 2010; interview with Col Ding, 17 April 2010; and telephone interview, 20 April 2010; interview with Ali Osman Taha, 21 April 2010. The delegation notably did not include Dr. Ghazi: Waihenya, *The Mediator*, 121.

25 Interview with Salva Kiir Mayardit, 15 April 2010.

26 *Ibid.*

27 Interview with Pagan Amum, 12–13 June 2010.

28 Interview with Ali Osman Taha, 21 April 2010.

29 Other informants state that Abel Alier met John Garang in Nairobi for several hours before proceeding to Naivasha. This seems anachronistic.

30 Interview with Ali Osman Taha, 21 April 2010.

31 *Ibid.*

32 *Ibid*; group interview with members of SPLM/A delegation to CPA negotiations, 16 April 2010.

33 Group interview with members of Sudanese govt. delegation to CPA negotiations, 19 April 2010; interviews with Ali Osman Taha, 21 April 2010; Yasir Arman, 18 April 2010.

34 Interviews with Yasir Arman, 18 April 2010; Pagan Amum, 12–13 June 2010, not confirmed by government sources.

35 Interview with Yasir Arman, 18 April 2010.

36 Interview with Ali Osman Taha, 21 April 2010.

37 *Ibid.*

38 Group interview with members of Sudanese govt. delegation to CPA negotiations, 19 April 2010.

39 Interview with Pagan Amum, 12–13 June 2010.

40 Interview with Ali Osman Taha, 21 April 2010. Also confirmed in interview with Pagan Amum, 12–13 June 2010.

41 Private information.

42 Interviews with Ghazi Salahuddin, 18 April 2010; and Ali Osman Taha, 21 April 2010.

43 Interviews with Abel Alier, 19 April 2010; and Ambassador Mathiang Malual Mabur, 22 April 2010.
44 Interviews with Col Ding, 17 April 2010; Abel Alier, 19 April 2010; Fink Haysom, 28 June 2010.
45 Interview with Fink Haysom, 28 June 2010.
46 Group interview with Government delegation, 19 April 2010; interview with Chol Ding, 17 April 2010.
47 Group interview with members of Sudanese govt. delegation to CPA negotiations, 19 April 2010; interview with Col Ding, 17 April 2010, and telephone interview, 20 April.
48 Interview (Khartoum, 21 April 2010).
49 The freeze proposal implied two standing armies in the South with their existing positions frozen and subject to an independently monitored ceasefire until the referendum.
50 Danforth and Ranneberger confirm in email communications of 10 August 2010 that Garang categorically rejected any such proposal.
51 Interview with Dr. Ghazi Salahuddin, 18 April 2010.
52 Interview with Abel Alier, 19 April 2010.
53 Interview with Ali Osman Taha, 21 April 2010.
54 Interview with Pagan Amum, 12–13 June 2010.
55 Interview with Ali Osman Taha, 21 April 2010.
56 Group interview with members of Sudanese govt. delegation to CPA negotiations, 19 April 2010.
57 Reuters, October 21, 2003
58 E.g. reports from Human Rights Watch, International Crisis Group and Sudan Small Arms Survey.
59 International Commission of Inquiry on Darfur, *Report to the United Nations Secretary-General, Pursuant to Security Council Resolution 1564 of 18 September 2004*, Geneva, 25 January 2005.
60 Interview with Yasir Arman, 18 April 2010; group interview with members of Sudanese govt. delegation to CPA negotiations, 19 April 2010.
61 Interview with Pagan Amum, 12–13 June 2010.
62 Interview with Dr. Ghazi Salahuddin, 18 April 2010.
63 Private information.
64 8 & 9 December 2003.
65 Interview with Charles Snyder, 30 May 2010.
66 "Popular consultations" was a term introduced both by Fink Haysom (the experience of East Timor) and myself. It was ambiguous enough to cover the views of both parties.
67 In the negotiations in Machakos in 2002 there was an understanding between the parties that ownership of the oil resources would not be agreed, but they would agree on how to share the revenue from the oil production.
68 Interview with Dr. Ghazi Salahuddin, 18 April 2010.
69 It was agreed between the parties to only focus on revenue sharing as early as 2002, in the Machakos negotiations.
70 Quote from "Sudanese President vows to annihilate Darfur rebels", AFP, 31 December 2003.

CHAPTER FIVE   **Inching Forward**

1 Interview with Abel Alier, 19 April 2010.
2 Abel Alier's paper was distributed to Taha, Garang, Sumbeiywo, and the observer delegations. (Interview with Mathiang Malual Mabur, 23 April 2010.)
3 Interview with Pagan Amum, 12–13 June 2010.
4 Members of the government delegation recently claimed that Taha left the talks in frustration over the delaying tactics of the SPLM/A (Group interview with government delegation, 19 April 2010). Other sources on the SPLM/A side say that Taha had conveyed to Dr. John in Naivasha that the problems in Darfur were increasing, and given these concerns he had to leave to help sort these issues out (Interview with Pagan Amum, 12–13 June 2010).
5 Private information.
6 Interview with Mathiang Malual Mabur, 23 April 2010.
7 International Commission of Inquiry on Darfur, *Report to the United Nations Secretary-General, Pursuant to Security Council Resolution 1564 of 18 September 2004*, 25 January 2005, 3.
8 *Ibid.*
9 Centre for Research on the Epidemiology of Disasters, *Darfur: Counting the Deaths*, Brussels 2005; J. Hagan and A. Polloni, "Death in Darfur", *Science* 313, 5793, September 2006, 1578–80.
10 Flint and De Waal, *Darfur*, 93.
11 Flint and De Waal, *Darfur, passim.*
12 Private information, April 2010.
13 Interview with Yasir Arman, 18 April 2010.
14 Flint and De Waal, *Darfur*, 98; confirmed in interview with Yasir Arman, 18 April 2010.
15 Interview with Theodros Dagne, 12 April 2010.
16 Interview with Mansour Khalid, 15 April 2010.
17 Taha's serious challenges on the home front during this period were underscored in an interview with Mathiang Malual Mabur, 23 April 2010.
18 Including in October 2003, January 2004, March 2004, May 2004, June 2005 (Nairobi). Similar visits to the negotiations took place in the fall of 2004 (Nairobi).
19 H. F. Johnson, 13–14 February 2004.
20 Group interview with members of Sudanese govt. delegation to CPA negotiations, 19 April 2010; interview with Ali Osman Taha, 21 April 2010.
21 Interview with Charles Snyder, 30 May 2010.
22 Interview with Ali Osman Taha, 21 April 2010.
23 Interview with Pagan Amum, 12–13 June 2010.
24 Group interview with members of Sudanese govt. delegation to CPA negotiations, 19 April 2010.
25 Email-communication with Roger Winter, 22 July 2010.
26 Telephone interviews with Charles Snyder, 28 May 2010; and Andrew Natsios, 10 July 2010.
27 Email-communication with Roger Winter, 22 July 2010.
28 Interview with Abel Alier, 19 April 2010.
29 Group interview with members of Sudanese govt. delegation to CPA negotiations, 19 April 2010; interviews with Ali Osman Taha, 21 April 2010; Mathiang Malual Mabur, 23 April 2010.

30 Interviews with Mathiang Malual Mabur, 23 April 2010; Private information.
31 Group interview with members of Sudanese govt. delegation to CPA negotiations, 19 April 2010.
32 Group interview with SPLM/A delegation, 16 April 2010.
33 My notes quote Ali Osman Taha saying: "Nobody back home will accept anything like this, nor that existing laws will be hampered or frozen. That is the bottom line."
34 Interview with Ali Osman Taha, 21 April 2010; group interview with members of Sudanese delegation to CPA negotiations, 19 April 2010.
35 Fink Haysom, who at Nakuru had considered this a red line for the government and not the SPLM/A, thought the fate of the Nakuru draft could have been different if this had been acknowledged (Interview with Fink Haysom, 28 June 2010.)
36 These negotiations all took place on 9–12 April 2004.
37 Interview with Mansour Khalid, 15 April 2010.
38 Agreement was reached by which the SPLM would have 28% of the seats in the national legislature, other parties getting 14%, and the National Congress Party would have 52%.
39 Group interview with members of Sudanese govt. delegation to CPA negotiations, 19 April 2010.
40 In a group interview with Sudanese govt. delegation to CPA negotiations (19 April 2010) it was said that Ali Osman Taha was comfortable with the term "New Sudan" and would gladly refer to it.
41 Interview with Rebecca Nyandeng de Mabior, 16 April 2010. Also mentioned in interview with Mansour Khalid, 15 April 2010.
42 Interview with Andrew Natsios, 11 July 2010, and email-communication with Charles Snyder 21 July 2010.

CHAPTER SIX   **Sealing the Deal**

 1 According to Fink Haysom (interview, 28 June 2010), he and Julian Hottinger, insisted that the parties negotiate an Implementation Protocol because other peace agreements they had assisted with had suffered from lack of clarity and time lines for implementation. They had Norwegian support.
 2 Group interview with members of Sudanese govt. delegation to CPA negotiations, 19 April 2010.
 3 *Ibid*; and interview with Ali Osman Taha, 21 April 2010.
 4 UN Integrated Regional Information Networks,'*Sudan: Darfur is World's Greatest Humanitarian Disaster, Says UN Official*', 22 March 2004 (see www.allAfrica.com).
 5 Interview with Ali Osman Taha, 21 April 2010.
 6 *Ibid*; Flint and De Waal, *Darfur*, 149.
 7 These observers were referring to Taha's facilitation of the release of Musa Hilal from prison – where he had been held on charges of bank robbery (*ibid*., 117–18)
 8 *Ibid*; and interview with Mathiang Malual Mabur, 23 April 2010.
 9 Private information.
10 *Ibid*.
11 *Ibid*.
12 Flint and De Waal, *Darfur*, 198.

13 Interview with Mutrif Siddiq, 18 April 2010.

14 Overseas Development Institute, Sara Pantuliano and Sorcha O'Callaghan, London, December 2006.

15 Abd al-Wahid, still chairman of the SLM/SLA repeatedly pleaded with me and other Norwegian officials to engage in Darfur negotiations again, and he called for Oslo as a venue several times between 2004 and 2007.

16 Minister of Finance Kaha, Minister for International Trade Kasha and Sudanese Ambassador El Hadj.

17 The SPLM/A Chairman had at this time credibility with the SLM/A, but limited leverage over Khalil Ibrahim, the JEM-leader. At this juncture, however, the military power of JEM on the ground was rather limited compared to the SLM/SLA.

18 Interview with Ali Osman Taha, 21 April 2010.

19 Telephone interview with Said al-Khatib, 11 July 2010.

20 Flint and De Waal, *Darfur*, 149.

21 Interview with Ali Osman Taha, 21 April 2010.

22 *Ibid.*

23 UN Integrated Regional Information Networks, "Annan briefs Security Council on 'grave' situation in Darfur, Sudan", 7 July 2004 (see also www.un.org).

24 SCR 1547 June 11 2004.

25 Voice of America, "Sudanese Rebel Leader Garang Backs US Depiction of Darfur Violence as Genocide – 2004–09–09".

26 Private information.

27 Justice Africa, *Prospects for Peace in Sudan: Briefing*, 4 September 2004.

28 Private information,.

29 Justice Africa, *Prospects for Peace in Sudan: Briefing*, 4 September 2004.

30 Confirmed in interview with Ali Osman Taha, 21 April 2010.

31 Confirmed in interview with Mathiang Malual Mabur, 23 April 2010.

32 Usually recruited from certain ethnic groups,

33 Interview with Salva Kiir Mayardit, 15 April 2010.

34 *Ibid.*

35 Interviews with Salva Kiir Mayardit, 15 April 2010; Pagan Amum, 12–13 June 2010; and Theodros Dagne, 12 April 2010.

36 Interview with Salva Kiir Mayardit, 15 April 2010.

37 *Ibid.*

38 Interview with Theodros Dagne, 12 April 2010.

39 Private information; interviews with Col Ding, 17 April 2010; and Rebecca Nyandeng de Mabior and Mabior Garang de Mabior, 16 April 2010.

40 Interview, 17 April 2010.

41 According to Col Ding, reportedly this had happened before, in connection with the split of the SPLM/A in 1991, when Riak Machar left the Movement and later created the SPLM/A–Nasir faction together with Lam Akol and Gordon Kong Chuol.

42 Private information.

43 *Ibid.*

44 Interview with Ali Osman Taha, 21 April 2010.

45 This was the case in relation to the shipment high-jacked by Somalia pirates in 2008.

CHAPTER SEVEN   The First Taste of Peace

1 National Democratic Institute for International Affairs, *Embracing the Promise of Peace: Citizen Views on Sudan's Future After the CPA*, Findings from Focus Groups, 16–28 June 2005, 12 October 2005, 45.
2 Interview with Rebecca Nyandeng de Mabior, 16 April 2010.
3 National Democratic Institute for International Affairs and New Sudan Centre for Statistics and Evaluation, *A Foundation for Peace: Citizens Thoughts on the Southern constitution*, Findings from Focus Groups, June 2005, 43.
4 United Nations Security Council, "Transcript of the 5120th meeting", New York, 8 February 2005.
5 This was commissioned by the "Utstein group" countries, resulting in Dan Smith, *Towards a Strategic Framework for Peacebuilding: Getting their Act together: Overview Report of the Joint Utstein Study of Peacebuilding*, Oslo 2002.
6 National Democratic Institute for International Affairs, with the assistance of New Sudan Center for Statistics & Evaluation, *On the Threshold of Peace: Perspectives from the People of New Sudan*, Findings from Focus Groups with Men and Women across Southern Sudan, December 2004, 15.
7 Group interview with members of Sudanese govt. delegation to CPA negotiations, 19 April 2010.
8 *Ibid.*
9 James K. Boyce, *Investing in Peace: Aid and Conditionality after Civil Wars*, London 2002; Smith, *Towards a Strategic Framework*; Roland Paris and Timothy D. Sisk, *The dilemmas of statebuilding: confronting the contradictions of postwar peace operations*, London 2009.
10 *On the Threshold of Peace*, 16.
11 This was part of a "carrots and sticks"approach common to most peace negotiations.
12 Following this visit an appeal immediately went out to donor governments calling for their support to the UN Work Plan, and asking donors not to wait for the Sudan Donors' Conference in April.
13 The resource issue had been immediately sorted out following my visit through payments from the CBTF. The Sudanese government provided significant resources to the SPLM in the pre-interim period, reportedly $ 60m for the transition-process (Group interview with government delegation, 19 April 2010).
14 Dr. John and I celebrated with dancing at the gala dinner at the Oslo City Hall. I could not convince Ali Osman to join me.
15 The AU, the UN, the EU, as well as the US, the UK, the Netherlands and Norway were represented at high official or ministerial level. Both AU's Baba Gana Kingibe and SRSG Jan Pronk were present.
16 Flint and De Waal, *Darfur*, 202.
17 Interview with Yasir Arman, 18 April 2010.
18 Interview with Pagan Amum, 12–13 June 2010.
19 Interview with Ali Osman Taha, 21 April 2010.
20 Interview with Pagan Amum, 12–13 June 2010.
21 Interviews with: Pagan Amum, 12–13 June 2010; and Salva Kiir Mayardit, 15 April 2010.
22 Interview with Salva Kiir Mayardit, 15 April 2010.
23 Interview with Rebecca Nyandeng de Mabior, 16 April 2010.

24 Interview with Salva Kiir Mayardit, 15 April 2010.
25 Email-communication John Garang–Theodros Dagne, 27/28 July 2005.
26 There was, according to Pagan Amum (interview 12–13 June 2010), a need to discuss support for SPLA transformation, containment of the Lord's Resistance Army, and the opening of the borders between Southern Sudan and Uganda to facilitate economic development.
27 Interview with Rebecca Nyandeng de Mabior and Mabior Garang de Mabior, 16 April 2010.
28 The composition of the Government of Southern Sudan would logically follow the rank in the SPLM/A Leadership Council.
29 The notion of John Garang as Moses was not new. A former child soldier in Rumbek said in 2004: "*We consider John Garang to be like Moses, who took his people away from Egypt.*" (NDI/SCSE-report Dec. 2004: *On the Threshold of Peace*), 18.
30 Quote from Jok Madut Jok in Francis Deng: ed., *New Sudan in the Making?* Trenton, 2009, 458.

EPILOGUE **Achievements and Challenges**

1 Francis Deng, "*New Sudan in the making*", 484.
2 Including preventing corruption and misuse of public funds, where I offered our assistance, also with Ashraf Ghani & team, Salva responded very positively and would follow up with the SPLM/A Leadership Council which was scheduled to meet the same day, on 7 August 2010.
3 Private information; Group interview with members of Sudanese govt. delegation to CPA negotiations, 19 April 2010.
4 In this context I also received the Award of the Two Niles, First Class, the highest order of the Republic, in appreciation for the role played in the peace negotiations in Kenya, crowned with the signing of the Comprehensive Peace Agreement between the government of Sudan and SPLM/A.
5 Telephone interview with SPLM/A sources, July 2010.
6 Telephone interview with former high level American official, July 2010.
7 Interviews with Ali Osman Taha, 21 April 2010; and Mathiang Malual Mabur, 23 April 2010.
8 *A Foundation for peace*, 14–15.
9 National Democratic Institute for International Affairs, *Lost in the Middle of Peace: An Exploration of citizen opinion on the implementation of the CPA in the Three Areas of Abyei, Southern Kordofan and Blue Nile*, February 2009, 23.
10 Smith, *Towards a Strategic Framework for Peacebuilding*; Dina Esposito and Batsheba Crocker: A Report on the CSIS Post Conflict Reconstruction Projects, 2004; 'To *Guarantee the Peace: An Action Strategy for a Post-Conflict Sudan*', Washington D.C.
11 Lise Grande: Joint NGO Briefing paper: "*Rescuing the Peace in Southern Sudan*", January 2010, 24.
12 *Losing Hope*, 23.
13 Barney Jopson, 'Fury at unspent funds for Sudan', *Financial Times*, 16 February 2010.
14 Several evaluations were conducted. They showed mixed performance. But the parameters of the assessments were focusing on the functionality and effectiveness of the MDTF, rather than its outcomes and results.

15 Documented in Lise Grande: Joint NGO Briefing paper: "*Rescuing the Peace in Southern Sudan*", January 2010, 22.
16 *Losing Hope*, 14.
17 Lise Grande, Oral Statement by UN Deputy RC/HC Southern Sudan, Donor meeting, The Hague, 8 March 2009, based on education statistics from the UNICEF Country Office, Sudan.
18 *A Foundation for peace*, 14.
19 *Losing Hope*, 6.
20 See *ibid.*, 37.
21 *Lost in the Middle of Peace*, 26.
22 Series of opinion studies based on Focus Group research, conducted by National Democratic Institute for International Affairs, 2004–2009.
23 *On the Threshold of Peace*, 10.
24 General Scott Gration was the last Special Envoy to be appointed by the Obama Administration, and he took on this role on 18 March 2009.
25 Mbeki was Chairman of the AU Panel for Darfur, and was later granted an expanded special mandate by the AU related to peace in Sudan as a whole.
26 National Democratic Institute for International Affairs, *Imagining the election: A look at what citizens know and expect of the 2010 vote*, Findings from Focus Groups with Men and Women across Southern Sudan and the Three Areas, September 2009, 65.
27 *Ibid.*
28 "Statement", 12 May 2010, http://splmtoday.com/splmvoices/.
29 The so-called "Four Freedoms Agreement" allows citizens of Egypt and Sudan to freely move across the border separating both states, and the rights to reside, work and own property in either country without a permit.
30 Quote from Jok Madut Jok in Francis Deng: ed., *New Sudan in the Making?* Trenton, 2009: 464
31 Report from the 2nd Annual conference on Darfur by KACE, the Al Khatim Adlan Center for Enlightenment and Human Development (KACE), with the title: "The Search for A Lasting Peace for Darfur", July 17 and 18 2010, 4.
32 Speech in the Security Council, 8 February 2005.

List of Interviewees

Most interviews were conducted in person either individually or in groups, and some by telephone. Information has also been contributed through correspondence. Some of the informants wished to be anonymous and are not included in the list.

Sudanese Interviewees
Abd al-Rahman al-Khalifa, Abel Alier, Al-Dirdiri Mohamed Ahmed, Ali Osman Mohamed Taha, Beyor Adjang, Col D. Ding, Deng Alor Kuol, El-Fatih Siddig, George Nyombe, Ghazi Salahuddin Attabani, Idris Muhamed Abd al-Kader, Kosti Manibe, Mabior Garang de Mabior, Malik Agar, Malual Mathiang Mabur, Mansour Khalid, Majak d'Agoot, Mutrif Siddiq, Pagan Amum, Rebecca Nyandeng de Mabior, Said al-Khateeb, Samson Kwaje, Salva Kiir Mayardit, Yahia Hussein Babikir, Yasir Said Arman.

Non-Sudanese Sources and Interviewees
Theodros "Ted" Dagne, John D. "Jack" Danforth, Vegard Ellefsen, Nicholas "Fink" Haysom, Kjell Hødnebø, Andrew Natsios, Michael "Mike" E. Ranneberger, Clare Short, Charles "Charlie" R. Snyder, Endre Stiansen, Lazarus Sumbeiywo, Roger Winter.

Group interview with the members of the negotiation delegation of the Government of Sudan
Mutrif Siddiq, Said al-Khateeb, Yahia Hussein Babikir, Idris Muhamed Abd al-Kader, Abd al-Rahman al-Khalifa, Al-Dirdiri Mohamed Ahmed, El-Fatih Siddig.

Group interview with members of the negotiation delegation of the SPLM/A
Deng Alor Kuol, Cirino Hiteng, Samson Kwaje, Kosti Manibe, Majak d' Agoot, George Nyombe.

Other Sources
When information is not referenced in footnotes according to any of the above informants, interview-sessions, or other sources, the sources are the following:
My own personal notes (period 1998–2005), reflected in 11 private note books and relevant email-correspondence.

The Royal Ministry of Foreign Affairs of Norway (archives 1998–2005), both in the form of reports, notes for the record and other relevant information I have been privileged to have access to.

Index